THE HAIG WHISKY GUIDE TO
COARSE FISHING
IN
BRITAIN

THE HAIG WHISKY GUIDE TO
COARSE FISHING
IN
BRITAIN

Edited by Colin Dyson

WILLOW BOOKS
COLLINS
8 Grafton Street, London W1

Willow Books
William Collins Sons & Co Ltd
London · Glasgow · Sydney · Auckland
Toronto · Johannesburg
First published in Great Britain 1985
© Antler Books Ltd 1985

Produced by Antler Books Ltd
11 Rathbone Place, London W1P 1DE

Designed by Norman Turpin
Drawings by John Lawrence
Diagrams by Rodney Paull
Index by Geraldine Christy

British Library Cataloguing in Publication Data

The Haig guide to coarse fishing in Britain
1. Fishing
I. Dyson, Colin
799.1'2   SH439

ISBN 0 00 218156 8

*Previous pages: Sunset on a monastery stewpond
in Sussex
Angling for grayling; an autumnal scene on a
tributary of the Test*

ANTLER BOOKS WOULD LIKE TO EXPRESS THEIR
APPRECIATION OF THE CONSIDERABLE HELP RECEIVED IN
THE PRODUCTION OF THIS BOOK FROM THE FOLLOWING:
Mike Amey, Jim Boyd, Rodney Coldron, Adrian Czarnecki, Cath
Dyson, Neville Fickling, Ray Forsberg, Dave Houghton, Tim Marks,
Graham Marsden, Mike Millman, Colin Mitchell, Arthur Oglesby,
Dave Plummer, Gerry Savage, Alan Smith, Jonathan Townsend, John
Wilson, Mike Wilson, Norman Worth and Chris and Clair Yates.

Typesetting and illustration origination by Fakenham Photosetting Ltd
Printed in Spain by Grijelmo SA, Bilbao

Contents

Foreword   *James Wolfe Murray*   7
The Contributors   8
Acknowledgements   9
Introduction   11

Fish

Pike   *Colin Dyson*   15
Carp   *Mike Wilson*   23
Roach   *John Wilson*   33
Perch   *Vic Bellars*   41
Bream   *Graham Marsden*   49
Tench   *Tim Marks*   56
Eel   *Brian Crawford*   64
Zander   *Neville Fickling*   69
Chub   *Dave Plummer*   76
Grayling   *Colin Dyson*   82
Rudd   *Colin Dyson*   87
Dace   *Dave Thomas*   91
Barbel   *Archie Braddock*   100

Areas: *Colin Dyson*

South-West Water Authority   108
Wessex Water Authority   115
Southern Water Authority   121
Thames Water Authority   128
Stillwaters *(Thames & Southern Water*
Authority Areas)   133
Anglian Water Authority   135
Severn–Trent Water Authority   141
Welsh Water Authority   146
North-West Water Authority   151
Yorkshire Water Authority   156
Northumbrian Water Authority   162
Scotland   166

Notable Catches   *Kevin Clifford*   171
Species Records   174
Some Useful Addresses   183
Index   189
Picture Credits   192

Foreword

The Haig Whisky Guide to Coarse Fishing in Britain is a natural sequel to two extremely successful illustrated fishing guides: *The Haig Guide to Salmon Fishing in Scotland*, published in 1981, and *The Haig Guide to Trout Fishing in Britain*, published in 1983.

I am well aware that coarse fishing, in terms of numbers of participants, is the most popular sport in the U.K.; and I cannot conceive of a better companion to the thousands of coarse fishermen – as they sit beside river, stream or lake – than a bottle, or indeed flask, of Haig Finest Old Scotch Whisky, especially on those many days when the rain falls relentlessly.

I hope that this *Haig Whisky Guide to Coarse Fishing in Britain* will give a great deal of pleasure not only to the large number of confirmed enthusiasts but, more importantly, to those who have not yet enjoyed the pleasures of the sport.

JAMES WOLFE MURRAY
Managing Director
John Haig & Co. Ltd.

Contributors

Colin Dyson is one of Britain's best-known angling journalists. He is editor of *Coarse Angler* magazine, the official journal of the National Federation of Anglers, and also runs a freelance news agency serving angling newspapers, the northern edition of the *Daily Mirror*, the *Sheffield Star*, several other provincial newspapers, and BBC Radio Sheffield. He has written a number of books for expert anglers, including *World Class Match Fishing* with former world champion Kevin Ashurst, and *Reservoir Trout Fishing* with Bob Church, which in angling terms is a best seller. One way or another he writes the equivalent of a book a week, but still finds fishing the best way to relax. He is an all-round angler with a fair match record and has caught good fish of most species. His one remaining angling ambition is to catch a 30 lb pike – his favourite species.

Vic Bellars started fishing seriously at the age of 4. He is an all-round angler who has caught most British fish to specimen size. He also enjoys game and sea fishing; during his service with the Royal Navy he was severely reprimanded for unseamanlike behaviour when he hauled a 52 lb conger abroad. He is president of the Pike Anglers Club of Great Britain and has two pike over 32 lb to his credit. Although he has a reputation as a specimen hunter, he now prefers quiet fishing for pleasure. He particularly enjoys designing hooks, tackle rigs, and gadgets – some of which actually work, he says.

Archie Braddock started fishing seriously at the age of 13, and a year later caught 53 pike in a winter, the best being 11 lb 2 oz. During his teens he fished local ponds and the Trent for tench, bream, eels, and pike, but was bitten by the carp bug when he was 20. About 1970 he transferred his attentions to the barbel, which has been his favourite species ever since, though he continues to fish for most others. His best barbel is one of 7 lb 8 oz from the Dove; his ambition is to catch a Trent double.

Kevin Clifford has been a regular contributor to the angling periodicals for many years. Among the clubs and associations to which he belongs are the Carp Society, British Carp Study Group, Pike Anglers' Club, Chub Study Group, and the National Association of Specialist Anglers. For a number of years he concentrated on carp fishing, but now thinks of himself as an all-rounder. His list of big fish includes bream to 12 lb 1 oz, carp to 30 lb 6 oz, roach to 21 lb 12 oz, rudd to 21 lb 9 oz, tench to 8 lb 13 oz, chub to 6 lb 12 oz, and pike to 21 lb 7 oz. With Len Arbery he is co-author of *Redmire Pool*, a history of Britain's most famous carp water.

Brian Crawford has specialised in eel angling for more than 20 years, and has been studying the species closely for about 15 years. From 1974 to 1981 he was chairman of the National Anguilla Club, and at the time of writing is its treasurer. Since 1983 he has been secretary of the NASA National Coarse Fish Record Committee and chairman of the National Association of Specimen Groups, besides holding many other honorary positions. He is a member of the Pike Anglers Club and is also interested in tench, chub, barbel, and catfish. He is the author of *Catch More Eels* and *Fishing for Big Eels*, also of numerous articles on eels and eel angling in the weekly and monthly angling press.

Neville Fickling, a fisheries inspector with Severn-Trent Water Authority, has had a particular interest in zander since 1968. In 1981 he received a Master of Philosophy degree for work on the fish's ecology. Pike remain his favourite, because of their wide availability, but he continues to fish for zander each season. His best zander, a 12 lb 13 oz fish from the Great Ouse Relief Channel, was the record in 1970 and his second that year to beat the previous record. His achievement of catching 13 zander of more than 10 lb put him in the top three anglers for this species.

Tim Marks is employed as a university researcher, specialising in the retail trade. He began fishing at the age of 7 whilst on holiday in Ireland and is now a keen all round angler. His first love is coarse fishing and he has been a member of The Tench-fishers organisation for the past 5 years (he is also a member of NASA and the ACA). As well as catching many tench to 6 lb 2 oz, his other captures include carp to 18 lb, eels to 5 lb 9 oz, pike to 28 lb 5 oz and a rudd to 3 lb 8 oz. Foreign trips have resulted in the capture of salmon in British Columbia and catfish in Bavaria and one of his angling ambitions is to catch a bonefish.

Tim is currently resident in Scotland so his tench fishing is limited to regular trips south of the border. The relative lack of tench in Scotland has prompted a recent switch to pike and salmon fishing.

Graham Marsden, a Cheshire man, started fishing along the Congleton/Macclesfield canal and on his local river Dane. In his early twenties he graduated to the Cheshire meres, where he had many notable catches of big bream. Since then he has become an all-round coarse angler. He wrote his first article on the sport in 1968, has contributed a regular column to the Crewe *Chronicle* for the past eight years, and before that did an angling programme on BBC Radio Stoke-on-Trent. He has also written three books and contributed to many others. His best bream was 11 lb 1 oz; he has caught scores over 9 lb and hundreds over 8 lb.

Dave Plummer, who took an early interest in specimen fish, caught a roach of 2 lb 3 oz when he was 11. He has been actively involved with NASA for 20 years, and has served on its committee. He is a senior member of PAC and a founder member of the Barbel Catchers Club. He has been writing on fishing since the late sixties, and contributes a weekly column to *Anglers Mail*. He favours the all-round approach, doing a little trout fishing and sea fishing, as well as taking most species of coarse fish. In one season he caught 11 double-figure barbel, the largest 13 lb 6 oz.

Dave Thomas is an innovative Leeds angler who came to prominence in the mid-1970s, winning matches on the river Trent with maggot against the traditional caster. It changed the approach on that river and many others. He won the Matchman of the Year title in 1977/8, in a competition based on match results all over the country, and was picked for the England world championship squad in 1978. He was reserve that year in Austria, going on to represent England in several international matches before becoming world champion on the Warwickshire Avon at Luddington in 1981. He had

the rare distinction of winning both the team and individual matches. He has always claimed that his skill derives from dace fishing on the Yorkshire rivers.

John Wilson, who has a fishing tackle business in Norwich, lives beside a Norfolk lake. He was born in London and caught his first roach in the river Lea. Later, during a period when he lived abroad for several years, he had the opportunity to enjoy big-game fishing in the West Indies. His first love is trotting for roach. From the Wensum he has caught hundreds of specimen roach to close on 3 lb.

Mike Wilson has been fishing for 26 years, mostly for carp, though he has caught specimen fish of nearly all British species. He has been involved in angling administration for the past 20 years, and at the time of writing is a member of NASA's executive committee. He was involved in the establishment of the Carp Society and assisted with the production of *Carp Fisher*. He has given many talks and slide shows about catching big fish, but has not yet fulfilled his ambition to catch a genuine 3 lb roach. At present he is researching the beginnings of specimen hunting.

Acknowledgements

It is impossible to write a book of this kind without assistance from others. One of the pleasures of doing it has been the contact with so many people united by a common bond – the love of a great sport. I have been helped enormously by club secretaries and tackle shop proprietors too numerous to mention. I mention other names with some trepidation; a mind numbed by a six-month geography lesson may overlook somebody, but I must take the risk and hope for forgiveness if I err.

Those who gave a lot of time include Alastair Keir, of the Scottish FCA; Jim Brown, from Kirkintilloch; Dave Houghton, for help with Wales; Norman Worth, for the Midlands; David Bird, in the South; Peter Weston, who researched the Thames; Colin Scull, in Wessex; John Weedon, in Lancashire; Pete Burrell, in Essex; Colin Mitchell, *Angler's Mail*, who always had a telephone number when I needed it.

My thanks to them all, and also to the authors of the species chapters, who have helped in many ways.

Colin Dyson.

Introduction

NOBODY REALLY knows how many anglers there are. The latest estimate, based on a survey by NOP, is that more than 3·5 million go fishing at least once a year. The figure divides into three basic classes – game, sea, and coarse – and then breaks down again into more different specialist interests than I can count, and I have earned my living writing about nothing else but angling for almost 20 years.

My own special interest is coarse fishing, the subject of this Haig Guide. It follows two excellent Haig Guides on salmon and trout fishing, and the all-rounders among the readership should buy and read them. They certainly renewed my interest in the other branches of my sport; they also made me realise the challenge I face in extending the series into a trilogy.

What exactly is coarse fishing? This is an inadequate and faintly derogatory term, to be sure, though none of the popular alternatives seem to fit any better. Pleasure fishing? Every form of angling is surely that. Sport fishing? The same applies. It literally means the pursuit of freshwater fish other than trout or salmon, and it is a game which grips the great majority among that 3·5 million.

It is difficult for anyone picking up a rod and reel for the first time to see where it might lead. A cynical friend of mine, now sadly departed, once summed it up in a cartoon. He had a bewildered youngster standing at the entrance to a maze, but a maze without too many blind alleys. Most of the avenues led to places called peace, tranquillity, boredom, joy, contentment, and frustration. Others led to bankruptcy, the divorce court, a mental home, and even prison.

We both knew anglers whose obsessions had taken them to most of those destinations – some-times several at the same time. My friend had, himself, been driven to the verge of a nervous breakdown, principally because he had devoted too much time and effort in one particular direction, and had then lost the one fish he had worked so hard to catch. Next day he went to a bridge and hurled his tackle into the depths of a river. When asked the obvious question he came out with a reply which is still imprinted on my mind more than 20 years later: 'Sell it? Give it away? How could I? Next day I would have been crawling on my knees, begging for it back!'

I was fortunate to have known him. He taught me never to take any form of angling too seriously. He also saved me when my hobby became my living. There are brilliant reporters who can write with apparent authority on any subject, no matter how complex, but I am a comparative dimwit. I need to know something of everything I write about; thus the door to any form of specialisation was firmly closed to me.

I have been through that maze my old friend drew, without taking too many wrong turnings. My blunder through the angling scene is, perhaps, not very typical, but recalling it will serve to illus-

Opposite: A typical varied selection of bait for tench and bream

trate how many different interests have gathered under that all-embracing heading of coarse fishing. Not a single member of my family fished, but I was driven to it as a boy by some primeval instinct. I had no relative to help me, no friend who knew or understood what drove me to the river bank. I do not recall too much encouragement from the fish, either.

I failed and lost interest, but that was rekindled some years later when I met a fellow journalist with claims to being an angling expert. He taught me a lot, but our newspaper failed to stand the strain of both of us continually taking the same day off. After one deeply satisfying trip we switched on the radio to hear that the paper had folded. A disaster for some, but it was the best thing which happened to me. Since I was passably good at the game I soon had several other jobs lined up, but I chose the one which paid the least. It took me to the Norfolk Broads...

If journalists are good at anything, it is putting feet in doors. I planted mine in quite a few, and they all belonged to anglers of exceptional ability. There was Ken Smith, a former national match fishing champion, and at the time easily the best competitive angler in Norfolk. There was Frank Wright, who had been Norfolk's star matchman, though when I met him he was making a name for himself catching big fish, especially pike.

There was Dennis Pye, a pike angler of world renown; Syd Baker, for many years the holder of the national perch record – but that's quite enough name dropping. There were many others, all pulling my soaring angling interest in so many directions I knew not which to take. I solved the problem by taking them all. In between trying to break the pike record and catching my first 2 lb roach, I contrived to learn how to win fishing matches, albeit at a very low level.

I also set myself weight targets for every other species known to inhabit Broadland. I exceeded most of them in those idyllic years, and convinced myself that I had made the great breakthrough into that magical 10 per cent who, it is said, catch 90 per cent of the fish. I was soon to learn I was mistaken.

It was not that I was good; it was the fishing. I have never since lost sight of the fact that being in the right place is half the battle; it is also half the point of this book. However, anglers who live in the wrong places and choose to stay there, can be every bit as good as those who take almost unbelievable catches from the major hotspots.

Never despair, therefore, if your journey through this book convinces you that you are not well-placed geographically. I now fall into that category myself. The late Colin Graham spent nearly two years tempting me away from my Broadland paradise, and won in the end. I joined him at his Sheffield freelance news agency, specialising in fishing, and for a long time wondered what on earth I had done.

Sheffield has no fish worth talking about, but it has anglers in great abundance – possibly more per acre than anywhere else in Britain. The reason is historical. Heavy industry breeds anglers like rabbits. The sport is a natural antidote to the daily grind of life in steelworks, coal mines, heavy engineering, and railways.

Mere absence of fish is scant deterrent. There is good fishing 40 to 200 miles away, and the men of Sheffield have been flocking to it since steam power produced the railways. Now they travel by anything with two, three or four wheels. I do not need to know what the roads will look like if we ever have a nuclear alert. I have witnessed the exodus from Sheffield on 16 June, the opening day of the coarse fishing season.

The first time I saw it I was staggered. I was going into Lincolnshire for a spot of tench fishing, but where on earth were that lot going? Over the years I have found out. They were going to fish big matches for a lot of money, or small matches where little more than pride was at stake.

Others were doing what I was in Norfolk. They were specimen hunters, a new term invented for those who sought to catch big fish. They belonged to little cells called specimen groups, most of which had less than a dozen members. The aim was to gain and pool knowledge in order to catch more and bigger fish.

Some groups crossed social barriers to a remarkable degree. There cannot be many sports which can unite, for example, surgeons, schoolteachers, engineers and miners in common interest and lasting friendship. Do not imagine that the clinical mind of the surgeon enables him to leave the miner behind when it comes to catching fish. This is by no means the case. So much brilliant and innovative development has sprung from anglers with very little educational achievement that one is forced to ask why. My answer, for what it is worth, is motivation. For many, the challenge of this fascinating sport provided them with motivation for, probably, the very first time.

Since that time the specimen hunting movement has grown at a tremendous pace, with ever-increasing interest in specialist organisations devoted to the capture of particular species. There are, for example, three organisations devoted solely to carp: the British Carp Study Group, the Carp Anglers' Association, and the Carp Society. Then we have the Tenchfishers, the Pike Anglers Club, the Chub Study Group, the Barbel Catchers, the British Eel Anglers Club, the National Anguilla Club, and umpteen others which do not spring quite so readily to mind.

We are now beginning to see what coarse fishing really is; not a single sport, but a collection of minority interests which sometimes have almost nothing in common. This collection of minorities comes under one fairly loose heading – organised angling. If there *is* a majority, it is the 'disorganised anglers' who fall into none of the other categories. These people just go fishing, anything from once or twice a year while they are on their holidays, to once or twice a week all year round.

It is impossible to describe what motivates them, since there are almost as many reasons for fishing as there are anglers. I have known a few for whom being there is quite sufficient. One memorable eccentric I once took tench fishing removed his bait after catching one fish 'because I don't want my peace disturbed any longer'.

Generally speaking, disorganised anglers simply want to catch, or try to catch, whatever is there, and they do not take it very seriously. 'Proper' anglers tend to regard these freewheelers with great disdain ('butterfly anglers' and 'noddies' are two derisive descriptions) but their importance should never be underestimated. They are really the rock upon which a great sport and a massive industry are founded.

Add together the memberships of all the known angling organisations and, even with no allowance for a considerable number of dual memberships, the figure one ends up with is vastly short of the 3·5 million thrown up by the NOP survey.

Disorganised anglers make up the rest, and one can only guess how much they contribute to the staggering sum of at least £633 million we anglers are said to spend each year. Think about that figure for a while. Imagine how it translates into jobs, and how crucially important angling is to the economy in large areas of the country.

It is not just about the tackle trade, the factories, and the shops. Where would the coastal fishing industry be without the angler? The fish farmers and the hotels and boarding houses in angling areas – sea, game, and coarse? Newspaper, book, and magazine printing? I could go on for pages without saying it all, but one comment from a small shopkeeper sums it up. Much of the weekly exodus from Sheffield passes a newsagent's door in Worksop, and half seems to stop there, stocking up with papers, drinks, sweets, and even baits like sweetcorn and luncheon meat. 'In the close season,' he once told me, 'I practically starve.'

It is indeed a mighty edifice which a tiny minority of dreary crackpots are trying to undermine, but they will never make it. The strength does not lie simply in our political and spending power, but in the hold the sport continues to take on new generations of youngsters.

It happens for no obvious reason, just as it did with me. The ancient hunting instinct, once vital for survival, is less deeply buried in some than in others. The original necessity has become a sport, which in turn has reverted to a necessity for 3·5 million people. In an age of increasing leisure the number can only multiply.

The few who oppose us may multiply too, and we who fish must tolerate and understand them. They are, after all, merely people whose own hunting instinct has surfaced in a different form, however much they may hate to admit it.

My last words should be about this guide. It is not the sort which enables the reader to turn up a river and learn which clubs control how many miles, and where day tickets are to be obtained. That would simply produce a mass of statistics and information which is already available in other excellent books, like *Where to Fish* or the various guides produced by Beacon Publishing.

The coarse fishing available in every region of England and parts of Scotland and Wales is properly summarised, with enough information to get the angler started, but the main aim is to take a detailed look at the major species of coarse fish. I have recruited a team of expert anglers to write about their favourite fish – history, records, distribution, and one or two reliable methods of capturing them.

My thanks to them for so promptly setting about their allotted tasks. I found their contributions a delight to read, and have learned a great deal. Not least I have learned that I am still vulnerable to the influence and inspiration of expert anglers.

Pike

Colin Dyson

EVEN PEOPLE who know nothing about fishing think they know something about the pike. It is the one species of coarse fish which makes the pages of the national newspapers from time to time. It captures the imagination simply because it is a large predator with a fearsome set of teeth, and over the years it has achieved in folklore and mythology a place comparable with that of the shark.

The pike is portrayed as a vicious killer, a bully boy which terrorises almost every other creature, fish or fowl, unfortunate enough to share its habitat. It will take lumps off unwary bathers and bite the noses of drinking animals. Sadly perhaps, the legend is based on precious little truth.

One thing which is certainly true is that the pike is a deadly and efficient predator. It has changed not at all since prehistoric man first began to draw on the walls of caves; only man has changed. It is we who have learned about savagery, greed, and mindless killing. It is we who have invented reasons and excuses for all the dubious things we do, and we tend to credit nature's creatures with our own failings.

In any comparison with the pike, or even the shark, we come out very badly. All the pike does is look for food when it is hungry, and take what is available. In normal circumstances that means other fish, including its own kind, but many other creatures too – frogs, birds, and all manner of aquatic animals, including water-rats and voles.

The pike plays scavenger as well as predator, taking dead prey as readily as live; the sick, diseased, and dying in preference to the fit and healthy. I say 'preference' with heavy qualification. The pike does not seek them out because it *knows* they are diseased or dying; it simply finds them easier to catch. In fulfilling its own needs, it contributes to the health of its environment, a role which is not well understood, even among anglers.

Why this should be so is difficult to understand, for the function of pike as scavenger and predator is no different from that of the lion and the hyena. David Attenborough's brilliant televison programmes have taught the masses how they fit into nature's complex jigsaw and how every creature exploits some sort of food resource and is itself exploited. He has also demonstrated, with chilling clarity, the terrible consequences when man or some natural catastrophe interferes and breaks the chain.

Underwater, much the same applies. The pike is the supreme freshwater predator, vulnerable only to larger specimens of its own kind and the amphibious animal predators such as the otter (sadly, increasingly rare) and the mink (rapidly, and regrettably, increasing). Animal rights protesters, who have released mink in large numbers, have learned nothing from Attenborough. Would they release tigers in a shopping precinct? Introducing mink into the wild is an equally devastating

Opposite: Dave Plummer with a splendid brace of Broadland pike

15

Gord Burton from Southport admires one of his many fine pike from Loch Lomond

prospect for the inhabitants of hedgerows, woodlands, fields, and streams.

It is the sheer size of the pike which has captured the imagination of the angler. In British waters only the carp and the relatively rare catfish grow to similar proportions, given the right conditions, but these are relative newcomers compared with the pike.

How big do they grow? In this particular case it is of little use to study the record lists, for they are totally misleading. When the pike bug first bit me, the accepted British record was a fish of 47 lb 11 oz, taken from Loch Lomond by Tom Morgan shortly after the last war.

Research by the noted pike angling historian, Fred Buller, has proved pretty conclusively that Morgan's pike was genuine, as far as the weight is concerned. There were reliable witnesses, and some trouble was taken to weigh it properly before the great fish was given to the inmates of a local refugee camp, who ate a piece of angling history.

Many years later the British Record Fish Committee purged its list, and Morgan's pike was one of the casualties. No explanation was ever given, but informed opinion has it that it fell because it was not taken by acceptable means, by fair rod and line angling.

Morgan was basically a salmon angler and, of course, a Scot. His method of pike angling was to park baited rods on little rocky islands, then retire to a reasonably central point with boat and gillie to await events. He was rowed to whichever rod got into action. In the view of those who were to judge him later, this amounted to gorge baiting. The object of the vast majority of pike anglers is to strike a fish quickly, hooking it in the mouth so that it can be released undamaged. Morgan's method would more often see the pike swallowing baits armed with fearsome trebles – totally beyond the pale today.

None of this should be taken as criticism of the man. Reverence for the pike has emanated almost totally from the south of the border. To the average practical Scot the pike is a menace which eats 'proper' fish like sea trout and salmon. To Morgan it offered a pleasant way of killing time between salmon seasons. He never claimed the record; neither did he grumble when it was taken away.

The real importance of his fish today is that it inspired later generations of pike enthusiasts to try their luck on Lomond. So far nobody has come anywhere near matching his achievement, and there is diverging opinion nowadays as to whether such monsters still exist. That is an argument I do not intend to join, though there is ample evidence that Scottish waters once supported pike much bigger than Morgan's.

In the process of investigating the Morgan story, Fred Buller came across the skull of the now famous Endrick pike. Given the necessary knowledge, it is possible to calculate, from the skull, the probable length of the fish to which it belonged. From the length, the weight can be calculated with a fair degree of accuracy. Variables, including weight variations at different times of year, can be taken into account. Big pike are always females, which can weigh up to 20 per cent heavier when fully in spawn, and they can easily handle a prey fish of around 20 per cent of their own body weight. Buller and his friends did their sums and the great Richard Walker's initial and astonishing estimate did not seem far off the mark. He thought it could have weighed 70 lb, way beyond the comprehension of the average angler.

There are remarkable tales about other Scottish skulls: the Loch Ken pike, the Parton Station pike ... They are awe-inspiring, and Buller's books cannot be too highly recommended for those who wish to delve more deeply into the rich history of the sport. *The Domesday Book of Mammoth Pike* and *Pike and the Pike Angler* (both published by Stanley Paul) are seldom left on my shelf for long.

Continental pike fishing is beyond the scope of this book, but it is relevant to mention it in the context of how large these fish can grow. Scotland, for whatever reason, is not now coming up with the goods, and Ireland's once magnificent pike fishing has been sacrificed in the interests of trout and salmon, but several continental countries are still producing leviathans comparable in size to some of our mythical and not so mythical monsters of the past.

The estimate for the Endrick fish becomes much more believable when we consider the 67 lb 3 oz pike, netted by Arno Wilhelm in his small German lake as recently as March 1983. This fish stood on its head the widely held 'big waters equal big pike' theory, for it came from a lake no more than 150 yards long by 50 yards wide. It was, however, a pike which had plenty of easy feeding and little or no competition.

Within the past few years other continental waters, like the Irr Lake in Austria, have produced pike over 50 lb, and there was also the amazing case of the giants from Switzerland's Bielersee. For as long as anglers have fished for pike, we have seen conduct which has gone far beyond acceptable limits. It is a commonly held view that all anglers lie, cheat, and exaggerate, but the majority are almost boringly honest. There are dishonest ones, though, and pike fishing has attracted more than most.

For whatever reason, the angling world looks up to those who catch big pike, and this may provide the spur for some to cheat. The most common form of cheating is to exaggerate the number of big fish caught, or to claim an extraordinarily big fish without adequate photographic evidence or reliable witnesses. Swiss businessman Jurg Notzli did it the other way around.

Notzli astonished the angling world with a series of huge fish, mostly from waters with no big fish form at all. He did not simply claim them, but produced them as evidence. Fish of 41 lb 12 oz, 49 lb 8 oz, 55 lb, and 62 lb 8 oz formed the tip of the iceberg. In a very short time he became the most successful pike angler who ever lived, but there were those for whom the catches were too good to be true. It was left to my kind to perform one of journalism's more useful functions.

A team of investigative reporters was unleashed on the Notzli case, and it was not long before his fantasy collapsed around his ears. The reporters found he had been buying huge pike, alive, from the commercial netsmen who work the Bielersee. The man had hardly covered his tracks at all, even leaving his business telephone number with one of the netsmen. He took a monumental risk of exposure for a fleeting moment of pike-fishing fame.

I cannot think of a more dramatic example of the pulling power of the pike. Even becoming the sport's biggest cheat is some sort of claim to fame, but Notzli's name will soon be forgotten. What will endure in the minds of pike men will be the sheer size of the fish he bought from the Bielersee.

What have I achieved up to now? I have taken the reader into the upper realms of pike fishing lore and, I hope, stimulated the imagination. Some of you may be feeling much as I did, when Fred Buller took me to the spot where Morgan hooked his monster. Overawed is probably the right word. My own best pike at the time weighed 25 lb, and something nearly twice as big was inconceivable. It still is, somehow, despite the ample proof of even bigger pike, so it is perhaps time to come back to earth.

Most of us are stuck with ordinary pike fishing and can only dream of the extraordinary. My approach is to fish for 20-pounders and hope for my first 30-pounder, though I make no special effort to achieve that goal. It may come in its own good time, but if it never does I shall not mind too much. I am deeply content with the ordinary, which is available to all.

We may never find a small lake capable of producing a pike like that German giant, but it could happen. One pike finding its way into a heavily and regularly stocked trout lake might reach record proportions. There is such a fish in English angling history — the Dowdeswell pike, which could have weighed 60 lb. Already we have seen modern trout waters, including quite small ones, producing fish to nearly 40 lb.

These are unusual, managed waters, where regular culling enables the odd big fish or two to

Deadbait pike ready for the net

Opposite: Half mackerel baits – one of the most effective of the pike catchers

thrive. The waters which produce 30-pounders by more natural means are, on the whole, large fisheries with an extensive food chain. A pike will grow fast if the right foods are easily available at all stages of its development. If it has to expend too much energy in its search for food, or has to compete too hard with other pike, it will not reach a great size.

Traditionally the Norfolk Broads and the lacework of rivers which connect them have been the most consistent of England's big pike waters. They have the necessary food chain, with sizeable bream at the top end. When Morgan's Loch Lomond fish fell from grace it was replaced by a 40-pounder taken by Peter Hancock from Horsey Mere in 1967, and the recent form of Broads like Martham (limited access available via the Norfolk Naturalists' Trust) suggest that it could fall.

Most of the Broads can produce 30-pounders, and they all offer 20-pounders, as do the main rivers such as the Ant, Bure, Thurne, and Waveney. The only English waters comparable to the Broads used to be the fen drains and rivers of Lincolnshire and Cambridgeshire, particularly the latter. In recent years they have suffered from severe decline in the populations of other coarse fish, and the pike have declined in consequence. Do not write these waters off, however. One day they may recover their extraordinary status.

The best general advice on how to find good pike fishing is to seek waters holding plenty of coarse fish, be they rivers, gravel pits, or even quite small lakes. All the great rivers of England have good pike form – Severn, Wye, Hampshire Avon, Thames, Trent, Great Ouse, Yorkshire Ouse, Yorkshire Derwent, and Ure, to name but a few.

For many species of coarse fish the great gravel pits along the major river valleys have assumed considerable importance. They do not offer easy pike fishing, but I find them an interesting and stimulating challenge. Others feel the same way about canals, which rarely offer big pike potential. One of the main appeals of the game is making the best of what you have, but the extraordinary is there for those who wish to seek it out.

It is clear from the earlier parts of this chapter that Scotland has the edge over England where quality is concerned. The reason is simple: the food chain is stronger, incorporating the runs of sea trout and salmon, and Lomond also has a unique species – the powan – in teeming abundance. Lomond will continue to draw like a magnet, but the potential of other Scottish waters has hardly been tapped. While experts believe nothing can quite match Lomond, there are many waters which could produce big pike. Chief among these, probably, are Loch Ken and Loch Awe. Most stillwaters in the border areas offer sport which would be considered good by most English standards. The Dumfries waters are particularly well worth a look, including Lochmaben and Milton Loch.

Each contributor to this book is invited to discuss his favourite methods of catching his chosen

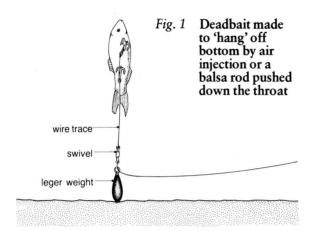

Fig. 1 **Deadbait made to 'hang' off bottom by air injection or a balsa rod pushed down the throat**

wire trace

swivel

leger weight

I think I will play safe by confining myself to two of the methods I find particularly effective, and which can be employed on both rivers and still-waters. The first (fig 1) relies on the pike's scavenging habit, and the bait can be any dead fish. The effective list of deadbaits includes most coarse fish species and trout, but smelly sea fish have the edge. These can be mackerel, herring, smelt, pilchard, and nowadays exotics like snappers and goatfish which are imported for Caribbean immigrants.

Pike use three senses when they hunt: sight, sound, and smell. Clearly, sight and smell are the operative two in the case of deadbaits, and I often opt for presenting a bait off the bottom to improve its chances of being seen. The pike's eyes are set for forward and upward vision and, rightly or wrongly, I think fishing deadbaits off the bottom doubles the chances of a pike finding them. Methods include suspending them below a float, but in my example the fish can be air injected or have a rod of balsa wood pushed down its throat.

species. This places me in some difficulty. Whole books have been devoted to pike angling methods, but they all boil down to one or two basics. The angler offers a fish, alive or dead, or something which can be mistaken for a fish, such as plugs, spinners, or spoons.

Fig. 2

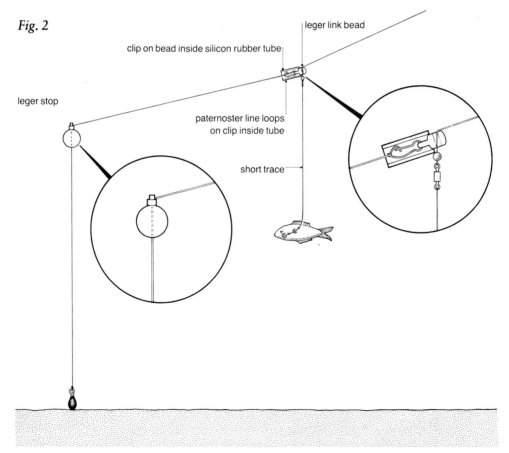

leger link bead

clip on bead inside silicon rubber tube

leger stop

paternoster line loops on clip inside tube

short trace

The drawing virtually speaks for itself, though beginners should note that the wire trace is essential. The pike's needle-sharp teeth can make short work of nylon monofilament line, no matter how strong it is.

The other method is the sunken paternoster, for which both live and dead fish can be used (fig 2). Use of the former is controversial these days, because it is supposed to be cruel. Anglers have to make a choice. My definition of cruelty is the deliberate infliction of pain, and nobody has yet proved that the cold-blooded fish with its primitive nervous system can experience any painful sensations. The argument that hooking a fish as bait is cruel can also be used against angling as a whole, since hooking fish is the whole object of the exercise. I discount it, but respect the right of others to disagree.

Use of live fish brings the pike's third sense into play. It can detect the vibrations of a moving fish and home in with great accuracy. There have been many instances of totally blind pike being caught, in excellent condition. The sunk paternoster method is best with a livebait, and my rig, which may at first glance seem complicated, is basically very simple. It is designed to prevent the fish tangling with the sunken float, and to give line freely when a pike takes the bait. The reel line is usually held in a clip at the butt end of the rod. A taking pike pulls it out and triggers off some form of visual or audible bite alarm. These range in sophistication from a piece of silver paper wrapped over the line to expensive audio-electronics. My clips are on a brightly painted bobbin, tethered to the rear rod rest, which falls to the ground when a pike takes line.

Expect no complicated advice from me about how to time the strike. As soon as a run develops I reel in slack line until I feel the fish. I take a second or two to note which way the pike is running and then sweep the rod back in the opposite direction. It is not a fast, violent movement, for that can break the line. It is a flattish and firm sweep of the rod, and the pike is hard held for a few seconds to ensure the hooks go home.

I always aim to hook them in the mouth, but nobody is infallible. Some pike swallow the bait before they move off, so it is essential to have equipment for unhooking these fish; this is available from most specialist tackle dealers. Another essential is a large landing net, with arms of 36 to 40 inches. Nobody gaffs pike these days. Basic tackle requirements are rods with $2\frac{1}{4}$ to 3 lb test curves, and good line of an adequate breaking strain for the size of pike likely to be caught. I should say 8 lb is the minimum, but I mostly use 11 to 12 lb. In Scotland I would use 18 lb. I always use 18 lb trace wire, but I would step that up for Scotland. As far as hooks are concerned, I used to use nothing but strong size 8 and 6 semi-barbless trebles, but now I am sold on the new VB double hooks by Partridge.

If I have fired your interest to the point where you wish to know more, seek out the books I mentioned earlier. Two other excellent works are *Fishing for Big Pike*, by Ray Webb and Barrie Rickards (Adam & Charles Black), and *Pike Fishing in the 80s* by Neville Fickling (Beekay Publishers).

Mike Wilson with a splendidly conditioned common carp – a descendant of the original wild carp

Carp

Mike Wilson

CARP FISHING as we know it today has a very short history – if the few stalwarts who sought them prior to 1950 will forgive that impertinence. The key words are 'as we know it today'. Historians seem to agree that carp are not an indigenous species, and there is some evidence to suggest that they may have been stocked in Clarendon Palace, Wiltshire, by Henry II around 1271. Alternatively one can accept that they first came to England in the 15th century, a conclusion based on a book entitled *The Treatyse of Fysshynge with an Angle*, credited to Dame Juliana Berners (or Barnes), Prioress of Sopwith, near St Albans, in 1486. Experts on the literature of that period, however, believe this book was a compilation of various manuscripts written around 1450.

What is certain is that the original wild carp was used for food both here and on the Continent for several centuries. The wildie is a golden-brown fish, with large, regular scales covering a slender body. In rich water they can achieve weights in excess of 10 lb, though nowadays there are very few waters containing true wild carp. They can interbreed freely with the faster-growing king carp developed by Continental cultivists for eating purposes, and it was these fish which were to revolutionise carp fishing in this country.

It happened very gradually at first. As the early pioneers of carp fishing were plodding from one milestone to another – and the majority of anglers were convincing themselves that large carp were uncatchable – a time bomb was ticking away in an unknown private estate lake at Bernithan Court, near Ross-on-Wye. It was stocked in 1934 with small carp originating from Galicia, in Poland, and nobody could have foreseen the consequences.

Bernithan Pool, later renamed Redmire Pool,

is a mere 3 acres but it is an extremely rich environment. The carp had already grown to previously undreamed-of proportions by the time anglers (notably members of the Carpcatchers Club) began to fish there around 1950. Events since then are detailed in an outstanding book, *Redmire Pool*, by Kevin Clifford and Len Arbery. Here it is sufficient to say that the catches electrified the angling world, and the carp record shot from 26 lb to 31 lb 4 oz then to 44 lb. This last fish was taken by Richard Walker in 1952 and transferred alive to the London Zoo Aquarium, there to inspire countless anglers before its death in June 1971, by which time its weight had dropped to 28 lb.

It is still the official record, for reasons explained elsewhere in this book, but most carp anglers now recognise another Redmire giant, a 51 lb 8 oz carp caught by Chris Yates in June 1980. The catches leading up to Walker's fish had a profound effect. Suddenly large carp were catchable, and the methods were revealed in a blaze of publicity. Angling clubs were encouraged to stock with carp, and the foundations for the modern carp scene were well and truly laid.

Nowadays 20 lb carp, rarities prior to 1950, are caught more often each season than 2 lb roach, and 30 lb fish are not rare in southern England. They are not, however, as numerous as some seem to imagine, and the importance of careful handling and returning them alive cannot be over-emphasised. Chris Yates' fish, which put on a great deal of weight late in its life, had been caught eight times previously by other anglers. On each occasion it weighed between 38 and 40 lb, and was the personal best for all the anglers concerned. For Yates it was the farewell appearance; the fish was found dead some weeks later.

The monsters of Redmire, and those which now inhabit many other waters, bear little resemblance to the original torpedo-shaped wildie which some anglers believe is still the hardest fighting, pound for pound, of all the carp. One of the results of selective breeding has been variety in the scaling, though there is no biological difference between each type.

There are leather carp, with no scales at all; mirrors, which have a scattering of large, irregularly placed scales around the flanks; linear mirrors, which have a line of large scales along the lateral line; and common carp, which are fully scaled like the wild fish, though the scales are larger. There are two other types, crucian carp and the recently introduced grass carp, neither of which are relevant here.

The main interest is in the big fish, no matter how they are scaled, and in where and how they can be caught. They are generally recognised to be stillwater fish, though they seem to thrive well enough in rivers where they have been introduced. Big fish have been caught in the Trent, Ouse, and Nene, and I believe the Thames holds exceptional fish, if only we could locate them. Their success depends largely upon the temperatures at spawning time. Shallow, weedy waters which warm up quickly are almost essential for successful breeding. Carp have therefore done best in the warmer climes of southern England — Kent and the counties around Greater London having by far the largest number of carp waters. They are caught in the North, where they have been stocked by clubs, but there are few carp waters in Scotland or Ireland.

As Redmire proved, growth rates in the right conditions can be phenomenal. The carp's natural diet includes water plants and all aquatic creatures, with land-borne creatures such as worms, slugs, and caterpillars which find their way into the water from time to time. They can also cope with hard molluscs like swan mussels; twice I have had large carp regurgitate mussel shells which have been crushed up by the powerful throat teeth. On most waters their diet is supplemented by anglers' baits; indeed, they need this on some waters to maintain their weight.

Though primarily bottom feeders, carp will accept baits at all depths and, in some circumstances, food which floats on the surface. As in all forms of angling, feeding habits largely dictate how the fish can be caught, but some preliminary advice should put beginners on the right lines.

Contact with other carp anglers is the usual short-cut to finding suitable waters. Two major organisations cater for both novices and experienced anglers: the Carp Anglers' Association and the Carp Society. Both keep in touch with members through regular regional meetings, national conferences, and top-quality free colour publications — *Carp Catcher* and *Carp Fisher* respectively. The National Association of Specialist Anglers (NASA) has a similar structure, and while it is not a carp-only organisation, many of its members fish for carp. Its free colour publication, *Specialist Angler*, always carries a few articles on carp fishing, and magazines such as *Coarse Angler* take it very seriously. Anyone can join these organisations at modest cost, and it is money well spent.

Tackle for carp angling has developed greatly since the 1950s, especially in the past ten years. The early split cane rods have given way to hollow glass fibre and now carbon fibre. The choice may seem bewildering, but there are two basic types. There are compound taper rods, generally used for ranges up to 50 yards, with a softish action all through, and fast taper models designed to cast much greater distances. Once the techniques are mastered, distances of more than 100 yards can be achieved. Fast taper rods have a very stiff, powerful action, required both to achieve the distance required and to set the hook at long range.

Avoid cheap rods, even if they seem irresistible bargains. Stick with named makes offered by specialist suppliers. The same advice goes for reels. Buy top-quality fixed spools, and with lines and hooks take note of the brands stocked by the specialist firms. It is the same with such indispensable items as landing nets and bite alarms. The

*Chris Yates with his unofficial record carp – 51 lb
8 oz from Redmire*

Battle with a summer carp in a Hampshire pool

game has become so specialised that many ordinary tackle shops do not have the right products for a particular situation and they cannot offer the novice reliable advice.

Carp anglers have gained a reputation for being a close-mouthed breed, and most will clam up if you start asking for details of their latest going bait. However, when you have found your carp water, general conversation with the regular anglers can help you to avoid many hours of fruitless fishing. You would discover, for example, what types of baits the carp respond to. In a particle water, the fish takes small baits such as sweetcorn, tares, maple peas, sultanas, peanuts, and maize.

For this type of fishing you should fish fairly close, say 20 yards. Look for fairly shallow water, 3 to 8 feet, with some sort of feature. This could be a gravel or sand bar on the lake bed, snags such as fallen trees, weedbeds, islands, or a sudden drop-off in the depth; anything which might be a feeding area can be tried. A simple terminal rig for this sort of fishing is shown in fig 1.

Fig. 1

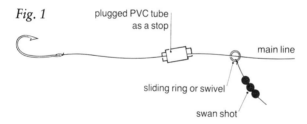

plugged PVC tube as a stop

main line

sliding ring or swivel

swan shot

On difficult waters, where the fish have endured a lot of angling pressure, results can be improved with more sophisticated bait presentation methods. The hair rig, for example, invented by C Alma Baker CBE in 1937 for the capture of difficult big game fish, has been independently redeveloped for carp fishing by Lennie Middleton and Kevin Maddocks. It has had devastating results, and is indiscriminate in the sense that the novice with the right bait has almost as much chance as an experienced angler.

Fig 2 shows the principle – a bait tied to the hook with a short length of very fine line, usually

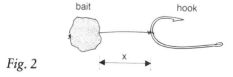

bait

hook

x

Fig. 2

1 lb. There is little for the wary fish to feel, but when it sucks the bait in, the hook (tied to much stronger line) follows it. With the rig in fig 1, the type of bite I have experienced has been a slow, jerky take.

The hair rig produces a fast, confident pull, but there is a different response again to the bolt rig (fig 3), which has an Arlesey bomb between two stops.

Fig. 3

A fish can take only a very short length of line before the upper stop hits the bomb. The rig was developed to overcome the problem of fast 'twitch' bites. With the bolt rig the fish suddenly feels resistance, and its first reaction is to swim off fast, virtually hooking itself in the process.

To return to particle baits for a moment, I have never found them to be instantly successful, and have generally baited-up with them daily for at least a fortnight. The longer I have pre-baited, the longer and more successful the bait has been. On some waters carp can be educated to take floating baits. Bread crust was the most regularly used until the late 1960s. Then anglers began to experiment more, with baits such as marshmallows, cat and dog foods, puffed wheat, and floating protein baits, the ingredients which are now readily available from bait suppliers.

These baits have a number of advantages. They float well and can withstand casting, and the same basic ingredients can be used to produce hundreds of variations simply by the addition of different flavours and food colourings. Where fish are really cautious, even a change of shape and size of bait can pay dividends.

While fish can be caught up top with a single bait cast into the vicinity of feeding carp, the best results are achieved by regular baiting up with surface offerings. This is designed to educate the carp and overcome their natural caution, but take care not to educate the local bird life instead.

Figs 4 to 7 show basic rigs for floating baits. The first is a simple freelined bait, though it can be used in conjunction with a float to add casting weight. Fig 5 shows a surface bait anchored to the bottom, generally used in windy conditions or when the weight is needed to achieve distance. In fig 6 the bait is shown floating off the bottom, anchored by a lead shot, and in fig 7 it is a floating worm. A small amount of air is injected with a hypodermic needle, but take care not to inject yourself: an air embolism can kill you.

Fishing at long range has been found necessary for consistent results on some waters, chiefly the large gravel pits dug in the South to repair war damage or for motorway construction. Constant bankside activity has driven the fish out to less accessible areas, sometimes more than 100 yards away from the angler.

Fig. 4   *Fig. 5*   *Fig. 6*   *Fig. 7*

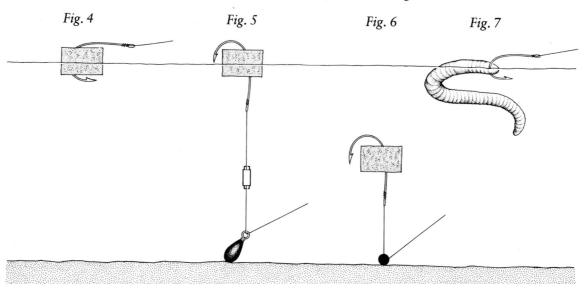

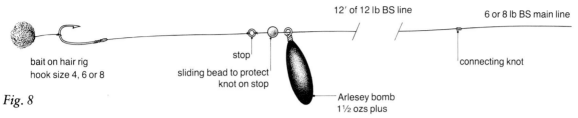

Fig. 8

Fast taper rods with test curves of $1\frac{3}{4}$–$2\frac{3}{4}$ lb were part of the tackle development for this situation. Main lines in general use are 6 and 8 lb, but where the angler has to punch the bait to extreme range a shock leader is required – around 12 ft of 12 lb line tied in at the business end to withstand the force of casting. Fig 8 shows a typical rig in current use, and fig 9 illustrates the best knot for tying in the shock leader.

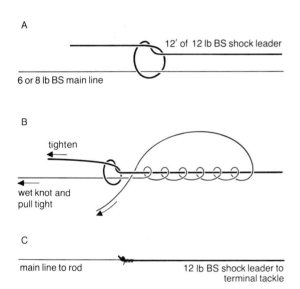

Fig. 9

Clearly, I cannot discuss all baits and all methods, but it may be instructive to examine my approach with one of my favourite and very successful baits – maize. This is pressure-cooked until it is quite soft. Over the years I have caught carp on hard maize, but I have experienced a problem with missed bites. On examining the hook I have noticed that its point has been curled over. It happened so often that it had to be caused by the fish, but if the hook had been damaged by the powerful throat teeth I should have felt the fish on striking.

The answer came from watching fish in my aquarium. I noticed that with small, fairly hard particle baits, the carp picked them up with a quantity of stones, possibly to help crush the food items. I reasoned that I had been striking against the stones in the fishes' mouths. With soft baits the problem was not so noticeable. I fished them on 6 lb and 8 lb line on size 4 to 6 hooks, sharpened and dipped in thin cellulose dope (the type used for model aircraft), then allowed to dry. Six inches from the hook I have a stop made from PVC tubing plugged with a piece of cocktail stick. A link leger is made from a short length of Biro tubing and 3 inches of 10 lb line, with five glass beads attached for casting weight (fig 10).

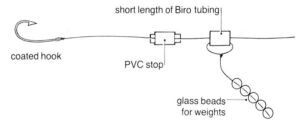

Fig. 10

Why cellulose dope and glass beads? On 'hard' waters, for large fish, I avoid using bare metal in defence of my theory that two dissimilar metals (steel hook and lead) in an electrolyte (lake water) sets up a small electrical field, rather like that of a car battery. Carp learn that certain baits are dangerous. A fish that has detected an electrified field in the past prior to being hooked will, I think, also associate this with danger. I cannot prove that this method has dramatically improved catches, but it certainly has not reduced them.

Back to the maize. Under certain conditions I insert a piece of yellow polystyrene between the maize and the eye of the hook, trimmed until the bait just sinks. I have found this important on hard-bottomed gravel pits, where the carp appear to vacuum-up the food from a few inches off the

John Wilson admires a small carp from a Norfolk pool

bottom. Without the added buoyancy from the polystyrene the weight of the hook can prevent the bait being sucked in.

Good bites are the purpose of every bait. This brings me to the question of bite detection. Bites are shown by a visual indicator on the line, backed up by an audible bite alarm, which is commercially available. There are two basic types. One involves sideways line movement caused by the line tightening against an offset antenna, thereby closing an electrical circuit. The other has the forward movement of line driving a wheel which activates the electronics. Their function is to alert the angler, who could be dozing if he is night fishing.

The visual indicator tells him which rod is in action, if he is using more than one, and the most commonly used is the monkey climb set-up (figs 11 and 12). The indicators can be bought or simply made from various diameters of plastic tubing. Herb containers are often ideal. Forward movement of the line causes the indicator to climb a metal rod, usually placed between the reel and butt ring. Provided the top of the metal rod is above the level of the line between the reel and the butt ring, the indicator will rise and fall in response to a continuous run from a fish. The main purpose of the metal rod is to stop the indicator blowing around in the wind. The set-up can be used with the bail arm of the reel open or closed, but if it is closed, make sure the reel is free to backwind or the rod will be pulled in.

Many carp anglers wait for full-blooded runs which get the indicator rising and falling or the reel handle spinning, but I usually strike at any movement. It all depends on your style and method of fishing. Timing the strike comes from experience. Initially I would recommend striking only when the line is moving. If the bail arm is open you must either close it or, as I often do, clamp a hand over the spool to stop line leaving. Point the rod at the fish and, as the line tightens up to the rod tip, sweep the rod back firmly, still trapping the line on the spool, of course. It is unlikely that the hook penetrates properly during the strike. It goes fully home when you are playing the fish on a tight line.

Many factors are involved in setting the hook – line stretch (1 foot for every 10 feet of line out); water resistance; slack line; hook point possibly masked with weed or, more frequently, the bait;

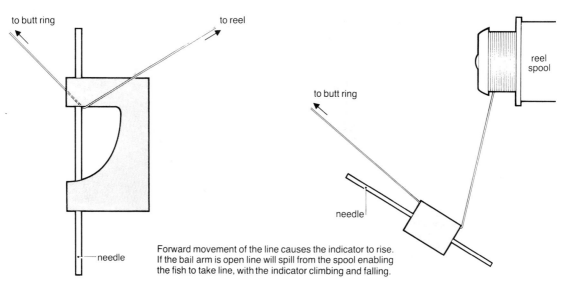

to butt ring

to reel

reel
spool

to butt ring

needle

needle

Forward movement of the line causes the indicator to rise.
If the bail arm is open line will spill from the spool enabling
the fish to take line, with the indicator climbing and falling.

(Note: Thin steel rods known as needles are used to stop the wind blowing the indicators around).

Figs 11 and 12

position and weight of lead; position of hook in the mouth; and the direction the fish is travelling. All can affect the success or otherwise of the strike.

Similarly there are many factors involved in playing a fish. To the novice I would suggest that no attempt should be made to stop the initial, fast run; that takes experience. Let the fish take line, either off the slipping clutch or by backwinding, but brake the release of line by finger pressure on the spool or on the back of the bail arm housing. Fish held on a tight line tend to kite in towards the bank. Sideways pressure with the rod is the only way to overcome this.

Never attempt to net a fish until it is well played out. Inexperienced anglers often lose fish at the net, the most common reason being loss of hook-hold. During playing the hold can become weaker, and the change of line direction at the moment of netting causes the hold to give. Where possible, I like experienced anglers to net my fish. Instead of lifting the rod to shorten the line I like to

take a few paces backwards, keeping at least 20 feet between me and the fish.

Having caught your fish weigh it and return it as quickly as possible. Where the rules permit, carp sacks can be used to retain fish for a short time while photographs are organised, but make sure you get the right type of sack. Some mass-produced ones are best used for onions, not fish. The carp must not be able to see through the sack. If they can, they will struggle and damage themselves. It follows that keepnets are unsuitable for carp. In my view they are unsuitable for all fish for longer than a few minutes.

Carp fishing is a fascinating branch of angling, and in such a short chapter only some of the basics can be covered. Recommended books, for those who wish to study further, include *Stillwater Angling*, by Richard Walker; *Drop Me a Line*, by Walker and Ingham; *Quest for Carp*, by Jack Hilton; *Confessions of a Carp Angler*, by BB; *Carp*, by Jim Gibbinson; *Carp Fever*, by Kevin Maddocks; *The Carp Strikes Back*, by Rod Hutchinson; *Carp for Everyone*, by Peter Mohan; and the specialist magazines mentioned earlier.

Roach

John Wilson

I HAVE WRITTEN before, but do not apologise for repeating myself, that if I were to pick just one freshwater species my choice would have to be the roach. Strange maybe, because most fish fight harder and certainly grow much larger, but I like roach because it is the fish I grew up with. I respond to its inquisitive, gentle, and sometimes fickle nature; the subtle colour change from its summer brassiness to its winter wardrobe of silver scales tinged with blue, and pert, deep-red fins.

I love the deep-bellied hump-back shape of a specimen roach, caught mint, in the peak of condition. I love to see a shoal of roach topping in the early morning mist, whether they are sucking in midge pupae from the surface film of a huge gravel pit, or simply jumping for joy (as I am sure they do quite often) in a fast-flowing tidal river.

For these and countless other reasons I find roach the most challenging species of all. It may lack the charisma of specimen carp and pike, but the roach will always be the backbone of our freshwater sport. It is by far the most popular of fish, and certainly the most common British freshwater fish. Throughout England and much of Wales there is scarcely a pond, pit, lake, reservoir, or river which does not hold roach, and several of the Scottish salmon rivers like the mighty Tay and Tweed breed roach of a good average size, as does Loch Lomond.

Fortunately for anglers, roach are prolific breeders, even from three or four years. During the mating season the males, like all cyprinids, are easily distinguished from the females by the small pimple-like spawning tubercles on their foreheads. Spawning itself takes place in late May or early June, depending on water temperatures and weed growth. Then roach arrive *en masse* in the shallows (a lovely sight) to deposit their eggs.

As with most species the males substantially outnumber the females. Often as many as five or six attendant males will be trying to fertilise the orangey-pink eggs of one ripe female. In really shallow water, the splashing and shuddering noises of spawning roach can be quite loud and will, if the temperature suits, continue well into the hours of darkness. The eggs adhere to bottom-rooted weeds and the fibrous matting of sub-surface roots beneath overhanging willow and alder trees. They take about two weeks to hatch.

In river systems where temperatures could stay low during an unusually cold spring, the spawning period may not have been fully completed before the season starts on 16 June. In my local river Wensum, for instance, I can recall one year when the roach did not spawn until the first week in July, but such a late date is rare. A bad spawning season, when roach shed their eggs late, results in the fry being smaller and much weaker than they need to be for survival during their first winter.

These events would certainly help to explain the cycles of prolific and then suddenly poor sport with roach. This pattern has become almost the norm in many river and reservoir systems during the past couple of decades. Of course, the national roach disease which drastically affected fish stocks all over the country in the late 1960s did not help. I believe that inconsistent weather patterns linked to the present changing climatic conditions hold the key to many modern angling mysteries, but when Mother Nature gets it right, she creates magnificent fishing.

It is in the largest of lakes, pits, and particularly reservoirs where the largest roach are found. They grow big, often in shoals of a hundred fish or more, because they have a constant and abundant food source in the masses of zooplankton (such as daphnia) and aquatic insects which nourish them at every stage of life. A 2 lb roach from a rich reservoir may be only six or seven years old; a fish of the same weight from a water less rich in regular food supplies may be eleven.

For several decades, reservoir roach from the southern counties dominated the big roach lists. The former record of 3 lb 14 oz, caught on bread paste by Bill Penney in 1938 from Lambeth reservoir, was joined in the net by another of 3 lb 1 oz on

Close up of the roach – the most popular of all coarse fish

the same day. The previous record of 3 lb 10 oz was held by Wilf Cutting with a fish caught in Hornsea Mere in 1917, and throughout the forties, fifties, and sixties, 19 out of 20 roach breaking the 3 lb barrier were caught from reservoirs.

In 1964, Bert Brown caught a roach of 3 lb 14 oz from a Lincolnshire gravel pit. This equalled Penney's 26-year-old record, although many thought the fish was a hybrid. Eleven years later, in 1975, Richard Jones, who was tench fishing with lobworm at the start of the season, broke the record with a mammoth roach of 4 lb 1 oz from a Nottinghamshire gravel pit. Many now consider this the most difficult of all records to break, because this particular fish was late in spawning and heavily swollen with eggs. More than 9 oz were removed from the fish when it was examined several hours later. One can assume that in its normal state it would have been a roach of somewhere between 3 lb and 3 lb 12 oz.

At around the same time during the mid-seventies my local Norfolk rivers, the Waveney, Bure, Yare, and particularly the upper reaches of the Wensum, were producing hundreds of roach over 2 lb, with a few topping 3 lb. Fish over 2 lb 8 oz were by no means uncommon, but unfortunately, like all eras of big fish in numbers, this one was not

to last. It finished quite suddenly towards the end of the decade.

Perhaps the big river roach cycle will eventually be repeated. I hope so. For the present, however, there are still numerous rivers and large pits, particularly in southern England, which can still produce roach in excess of 2 lb. These waters include the Wensum. Ironically, in 1984 I took the largest roach I have ever caught from this river. It weighed 1½ oz under 3 lb.

The Hampshire Avon and Dorset Stour immediately spring to mind as the main producers of roach in the south. Their adjacent tributaries, the Allen and Nadder, also breed roach of a high average size. Berkshire's river Kennet has in the past produced some monster roach from its crystal clear high upper reaches, and no doubt there are some left in the private, isolated trout stretches. The Thames itself is too big to tackle with just big roach in mind, but numbers of fish between 2 lb and 2 lb 12 oz are caught from several of its tributaries, principally the upper reaches of the Windrush, Cherwell, and Evenlode.

Kent, perhaps more famous in recent years for its carp fishing, contains big river roach. The Kentish Stour, and even the Medway – although not a patch on its pre-1960 condition – still breed some big ones, but the pride of Kentish roach fishing must surely rest on the shoulders of the tiny river Beult. During the winter of 1983 it produced roach of more than 3 lb for Nigel Wilham.

In the Midlands, the river Ise in Northamptonshire is hard to beat. For more than a decade it has produced a whole string of roach between 2 and 3 lb. The Great Ouse Relief Channel, before the water authority emptied most of its stocks into the Wash during the winter floods of 1977, was full of big roach between 1 lb 8 oz and 2 lb 8 oz. For sheer numbers of fish, some of the larger Midland rivers like the Trent are unbeatable.

Strangely enough, and despite the boats, odd bouts of run-off surface pollution, and the difference between tides, some of the best fishing for good bags of quality roach is to be had in the lower tidal reaches of the larger rivers. The lower Thames, for instance, and the Kentish Stour take some beating. The fast-flowing tidal reaches of my local rivers Yare, Waveney, and Bure offer superlative roach fishing despite the boats. A similar situation exists on the tidal reaches of the Avon.

Returning to thoughts of big roach, I wonder if the London reservoirs will ever produce the roach they once used to. The Tring reservoir group certainly still holds some surprises with monster fish of most species taken each year, including roach to over 3 lb. For a really huge one, as for big pike, future prospects must lie in one of the massive and well matured trout reservoirs. Here coarse fish are regularly culled, leaving those remaining to grow extra large.

Clean roach of over 4 lb without spawn have been netted from the giant Grafham, and while coarse fishing is not permitted there at present, I am optimistic about the future. Ardleigh reservoir near Colchester has opened its gates from October onwards, with promising results, and others will surely follow.

To describe in detail every method by which roach can be taken would require a book in itself, but I believe in two basic methods. Trotting with a stick float and quiver tip legering will stand you in good stead for river roach wherever you fish. Both methods, of course, may be adapted to the roach of stillwaters, simply by using an antenna or waggler type of float, fixed bottom end only to beat surface tow, or, in legering, by swapping the quiver tip bite indicator for one more sensitive to stillwater, such as a swing tip or clip-on leger bobbin.

For the fun of hooking into roach on light tackle, no more than a couple of rod lengths out in a steady paced river, reel line is around 2 to 2½ lb, with a 1½ lb bs hook length if the water runs on the clear side. Hooks will range from size 14 for bread crust or two maggots, down to a 20 or 22 for a single maggot or caster. When the bait is presented further out or the surface is choppy, the stick float should be replaced by a waggler.

If the surface is calm we can over-shot the float so it almost sinks, and set it a little overdepth, after plumbing the swim. Enough of the tip will be visible above the surface to distinguish bits, providing a fairly tight line is kept from float to rod. Allowing the current to pull the float along and take the line smoothly from the reel (one reason why I prefer a centre pin), slowing its passage downstream, is called 'holding back'.

Trotting with a stick float allows you to trundle the bait along close to the bottom at the same speed as the current, which in deep rivers is nowhere near as fast as at the surface. Throw some maggots into a clear river and watch them. For a few yards they get whisked along at surface speed, but as they sink further they start to slow. This is the problem facing the angler who trots for roach. His

Lincolnshire's Upper Witham — a small but productive roach river

Opposite: Match fishing for roach, when it is often quicker to land by hand

float is going at one speed while the bait, several feet below where the roach are (usually within 2 feet of the bottom), will be going at another.

Choice of float size depends on current speed. You may require a 5 no 6 stick for really slow swims, a 5 BB heavy stick for medium to fast water, or even a 5 AA balsa stick for long trotting the really fast swims, but for all of them the shotting pattern is quite similar. You try to graduate the shot at regular intervals to act as a keel for holding back (see fig 1), with the smallest shot nearest the hook. You first decide on the amount of shot required to

Fig. 1 **What happens below the surface during float fishing with stick floats**

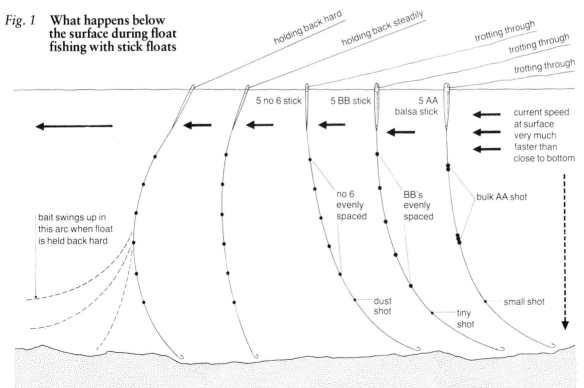

holding back hard

holding back steadily

trotting through

trotting through

trotting through

5 no 6 stick

5 BB stick

5 AA balsa stick

current speed at surface very much faster than close to bottom

no 6 evenly spaced

BB's evenly spaced

bulk AA shot

bait swings up in this arc when float is held back hard

dust shot

tiny shot

small shot

present the bait slowly, then choose the float, always remembering to use too much rather than too little lead if you are in doubt.

Even a big balsa stick can be over-shotted and made to fish effectively in quite slow water, but the converse, when there is insufficient lead to keep the bait down when you hold back in a fair current, generally produces nothing. Very small fish may even be attracted to its unusual speed and compete with each other; you sometimes see the tiny taps while you are settling the float at the head of the swim.

Roach of the stamp to bang the rod tip over and put up an enjoyable scrap – fish of, say, 6 to 10 oz and more – can prove difficult to please, particularly in hard fished waters. Hold back on the float harder than you normally would, and the bait rises unnaturally above their heads. If you send it unchecked through the swim, dragging the bait too quickly behind, bites will be few and far between. The way to induce bites is to achieve the steady balance of tackle by which the float glides down

Trotting with a centrepin reel is often a deadly method for the better quality roach

smoothly, yet noticeably slower than the flow. Every now and then, hold back for an instant to swing the bait tantalisingly upwards a few inches, in the way that loose feed around it is trundled along by the current, and watch out for a sudden snatching bite just as the float re-settles. If there is more than sufficient float showing above the surface, do not be afraid to add more lead till it is only a blimp, and try fishing as far over depth as the flow will allow before catching bottom. You will catch many more fish (particularly during the winter months in low water temperatures) from bites which you would not have seen with $\frac{1}{4}$ inch of the tip showing.

My favourite method of stick float roaching is trotting directly downstream from a dinghy anchored out in the river. The float can then be shotted all the way down without fear of it rearing off line and out of the swim when it is held back hard – a constant problem when one is bank fishing with the stick.

Loose feed may be introduced by hand or catapult, well upstream of the swim so it reaches the bottom before the end of the trot through, on the 'little and often' principle. Six maggots every other

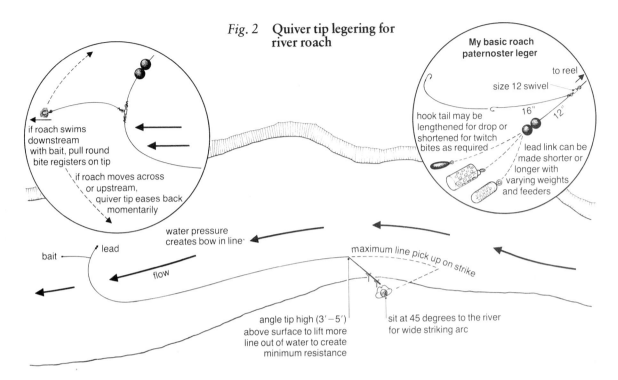

Fig. 2 **Quiver tip legering for river roach**

My basic roach paternoster leger

to reel

size 12 swivel

hook tail may be lengthened for drop or shortened for twitch bites as required

16"

12"

lead link can be made shorter or longer with varying weights and feeders

if roach swims downstream with bait, pull round bite registers on tip

if roach moves across or upstream, quiver tip eases back momentarily

water pressure creates bow in line

maximum line pick up on strike

bait

lead

flow

angle tip high (3'–5') above surface to lift more line out of water to create minimum resistance

sit at 45 degrees to the river for wide striking arc

trot through often prove more beneficial than a handful at irregular intervals.

In very deep, fast water, a bait dropper set with a lead line to open and deposit the maggots or casters 2 or 3 feet above bottom can prove deadly, grouping the shoal into a nice tight area.

Whether you use a screw-in quiver tip or a specially built rod with a spliced-in tapered tip, the secret of hitting bites which other anglers seem to miss on the tip (particularly at range) is always to follow through on the strike. This helps to pick up surplus line held in a bow by the current between rod tip and bait.

Many anglers miss bites not because they strike too late but simply because they do not pick up enough line to move the bait, let alone set the hook. This is an elementary but most important point, and one reason why I prefer a long 11 to 12 foot built-in quiver tip rod. Another reason is that a long rod allows me to sit well back from the water's edge, hidden in the reeds, yet still having enough rod over the water to keep the line well out. I also prefer to sit facing downstream and across at an angle of about 45 degrees to the water and usually have the tip angled upwards 3 to 4 feet above the surface, placed in two rod rests, so maximum line is picked up in a long arc on the strike.

Line strength depends on whether you will be tossing out large, fully loaded swim feeders into a fast, wide river, when a 5 lb bs would be needed to prevent snap-offs on the cast, or using a two swan shot leger at close range. Here a line of $2\frac{1}{2}$ to 3 lb (with lighter hook length) is suitable.

The end rig should be simple (fig 2), made with one tiny size 12 barrel swivel. I prefer the simple paternoster leger because it is most effective for changing from one length of hook tail to another, or from a feeder to bomb or swan shot leger, all of which can be done in seconds. Make sure both reel line and hook length are connected to one end of the swivel and the lead or feeder link to the other. This avoids tangles and keeps you in contact with the roach if the swivel breaks.

Without question, the most difficult thing to do when quiver tipping for roach or any other fish is to interpret movement of the tip. Movement can indicate that the leger is merely rolling or resettling in the current, or it could be a bite. You have to decide which very quickly indeed, or the fish will have gone. I rarely encounter simple tap-tap bites followed by the tip pulling round and holding. In fact, I would say I have caught far more roach by hitting those tiny, often insignificant movements, where the tip eases back for a split second before re-tightening, than from obvious pull-round bites.

It all depends how a roach sucks in the bait on the day. For instance, a real clonking pull round would indicate that the fish has simply gobbled up the bait and immediately turned off downstream with it. This often happens; when a small shoal of very large roach are competing against each other and quickly make a getaway, for instance. Chub often bite in the same manner.

Consider a huge shoal of roach close to the bottom, where feeder upon feeder full of maggots have been deposited. The fish have no reason to make off with a single maggot. It is sucked in on the spot and chewed with the pharyngeal teeth to extract the juices, while the roach moves upstream or across the current to the next maggot. Just before the lead or feeder is dislodged and the roach feels resistance, the angle from lead to tip is altered slightly, only enough to register on the fine quiver tip as a gentle relaxing of pressure. Perhaps a second later the tip will noticeably spring back as the lead repositions itself, after being moved by the roach continuing in the same direction. Of course, you will strike to an obvious bite.

Often roach feel this build-up of pressure and spit out the maggot skins. This is more or less what has happened when you reel in a hook containing nothing but skins, without having had an inkling of a bite. Everything depends on interpreting even the slightest movement of the quivertip, and relating that movement to what is happening underwater.

When bites prove difficult to hit, try progressively altering the hook length by anything from 3 inches to 6 feet. Starting with the hook length a few inches longer than the lead or feeder link (about 16 and 12 inches respectively), shorten the tail if sharp tap-like bites are regularly missed; lengthen it if there are no bites at all. Really spooky roach will usually succumb to a bait presented on the drop. Tighten up quickly after casting and be ready for an immediate indication of some sort on the tip. Two dark casters or a small cube of bread crust are ideal for encouraging bites on the drop as they are naturally buoyant. A step down in hook and tail sizes might also be worth a try when bites are not forthcoming from fish which are known to be in the swim.

Be careful, however, of change for its own sake. Roach, particularly when their numbers are being steadily depleted, sometimes vacate the swim for a few minutes or even hours, drifting downstream or up-river. In addition to trying all the variables, cast around both up and downstream to stay with the shoal.

One of my favourite methods of taking whopper roach of more than 2 lb from my local rivers Waveney and Wensum is to use tackle and baits which only a fair-sized roach, say of 1 lb or more, is capable of taking. You cannot beat a large, twopenny-sized lump of breadflake concealing a size 6 or 8 hook tied direct to a 3 lb hook length, helped along every so often with small balls of mashed bread groundbait. This is shark tackle, perhaps, to a match angler who talks of size 24 hooks and has to extract roach from a sluggish canal – but if you are after shark-sized roach...

Perch

Vic Bellars

EACH SPECIES of fish has its own aura. A fresh-run salmon, covered with sea lice, exudes the mystery of great oceans. Look a pike in the eye and you can see a ruthless killer in those yellow-ringed depths. The perch, with dorsal fin rigidly raised, contrives to look much bigger than it really is, emanating an air of aggressive importance. Tiger barred, spiky, bristling, and with the whole effect set off by vivid orange/red ventral fins, a large perch has an aura of magnificence.

I sensed this as a boy, long before I ever caught a big one. The hordes of little fish I hauled from little ponds grew in my imagination to roughly the same proportions as the giants continually reported from Oulton Broad, then a magnet for perch fanatics.

For many years the record was 5 lb 15¼ oz from the Suffolk Stour, but I know little about this fish. Evidently the Record Fish Committee did not know enough, either, for it was one of the casualties of the famous purge of 1968. In its place went a 4 lb 12 oz fish caught at Oulton in 1962 by the late Syd Baker, from Norwich. When I recently approached Syd's widow she could remember every detail: North Bay in the last hour of daylight; bait, a small liphooked perch livebait; hook, size 8; line, 3½ lb; tackle, a roving float.

Many Oulton perch came close to that one, but what of the 5 lb 4¾ oz perch reported nearly 50 years before, from Stradsett Lake, near King's Lynn? It took only one telephone call to establish that the angler, Herbert Green, was still alive, and one letter to establish that he, too, had total recall. It was November 1936, and he was pike fishing with a 3 inch perch livebait on a size 2 hook to 8 lb line. Again it was roving float fishing, with cane rod and Aerial centrepin reel. The bait was suspended 3 feet deep in 8 to 9 feet of water. Herbert also remembered other perch of 2 lb 8 oz to 4 lb, still burned into the memory 48 years on. That is how perch fishing grips its enlightened enthusiasts.

The great days of Oulton are over, and we hear little now of Stradsett lake. They fade into the memory as a new era emerges, an era in which almost anything can happen. Disease drastically thinned Britain's perch populations in the 1960s, but this means that the remaining fish grow bigger. In the past few seasons we have had increasing reports of fish of more than 3 lb, some more than 4 lb. We felt that something dramatic was about to happen, but nobody would have been fool enough to predict what did occur.

On 4 March 1984, Syd Baker's record was broken twice, on waters many miles apart. Both events were flukes. Bill Weatherhead was legering maggot for carp in the Jubilee Pool near Ombersley, Worcestershire. The bait was taken by a perch weighing 4 lb 14 oz, but his reign as record-holder was to last precisely 2½ hours. In Hampshire, that same day, a 63-year-old granny, Ethel Owen, was after carp in a 1-acre puddle called Kings Lake, near Romsey. Floating crust is perhaps the least likely method of catching a perch, but her offering was taken by a monster of 4 lb 14¾ oz. She became the first woman to hold a coarse fish record.

Policeman Charles Williams returns a 4 lb 11¾ oz
perch to a Leicestershire lake

Neither method figures in the instructional section of this chapter, but the events that day prove how impossible it is to predict where big perch might be caught. Freak conditions can throw them up almost anywhere, though there are many venues which, before 4 March 1984 at any rate, I would have backed more heavily than Kings Lake and Jubilee Pool.

So, with inspiration springing from both angling history and recent events, let us take a closer look at this fascinating predator. The pike springs from camouflaged obscurity as an arrow leaves a bow, but the perch is built for stamina, not speed. A shoal of perch will harry prey to exhaustion with the tenacity of a wolf pack.

Very large perch are often solitary. This is not from choice, I think, for the shoaling instinct is inherent, but because its companions have succumbed one by one to predators or disease. Old age also takes its toll until just one fish remains, the sole survivor of a particular year class.

Perch can thrive in many environments – the great lochs and loughs of Scotland and Ireland, lakes, rivers, reservoirs, gravel pits, canals, drains, and tiny ponds. Pond perch can grow surprisingly large. Perch can exist in muddy waters, but they thrive best in clear ones where they can catch their prey with ease, for they are sight feeders. In brackish or slightly saline water, they will thrive as nowhere else.

Little perch are suicidal, hence my success with them as a boy. As they increase in size they become far more circumspect, and the larger they become, the longer the odds against catching them with regularity. The problem lies in the fact that there are relatively few big ones. If you hope to catch a big perch, from 2 to 5 lb, by far the greatest problem is that of location. Perch can weigh 7 lb or even more, and I am certain that such fish are present in a few of our waters, almost certainly in the larger trout reservoirs. However, unless you know exactly the areas such fish frequent, locating one or two huge ones in such a vast expanse of water is virtually impossible.

Until late October, or when water temperatures fall rapidly, perch prefer water of medium depth, up to 12 feet or so, and may well shoal at mid-depth, underneath the level of their prey. Like chub, perch prefer cover. Lily rafts, weedbeds, sub-surface bars, overhanging vegetation, and fallen trees make good perch holding areas. In the warm months perch will be on the move, stalking and hunting. In high summer, main feeding periods will generally coincide with dawn or dusk and, more rarely suspected, on bright moonlight nights. In winter their behaviour pattern changes and perch shoal tightly in a comparatively small area, invariably the deepest water available.

Once perch have reached about 6 oz in weight they will turn almost exclusively to the fish diet necessary for rapid and sustained growth. It seems logical that as large perch feed mainly on other fish, and can swallow a fish one-third of their own size, the most likely bait to tempt one is a small fish. At times, however, particularly in winter, a large lobworm is effective and is the only bait that will survive the change of pressure as it plummets into the depths.

By far the best livebait is a small perch, 2 to 4 inches long. Rarely used, but nearly as good, are ruffe, certainly in clear water and bright conditions. Gudgeon make superb baits. Roach, rudd, bleak, dace and minnows, two at a time, all have their day. Stone loach seem very attractive, and years ago I had great success with them.

Reservoir trout anglers using lures or streamer flies catch large perch up to and over 3 lb. Angling writer Richard Walker told me that at Hanningfield he located shoals of big perch by echo sounder, and had great success with a fly dressed to represent a small perch – his Hanningfield lure.

Apart from worms – and deadbaits, which are not half so effective as some people think – the next best thing to a livebait is an artificial lure intended to represent a live fish. Small spoons, spinners, and plugs are most effective, but nowadays lure fishing for perch is a much neglected art, and few if any anglers are aware of the correct technique.

To spin effectively it is necessary to understand how a perch attacks its prey. It will launch the assault from below and behind, chasing and harrying, grabbing at the prey's tail fin so as to cause damage and restrict its swimming capacity. By such tactics the prey can be caught and engulfed. It stands to reason that a perch will attack a spinning lure likewise. Most lures are fitted with a treble hook behind the blade, and this is what the perch will grab. If the hooks are razor sharp there is a possibility that the perch will be hooked, but it does not happen as often as might be expected.

Suppose a good perch has hit the treble and not been hooked. Invariably it will break off the attack because it has mouthed metal, not soft flesh. The perch must be encouraged to continue the attack until it *is* hooked. Instead of hard metal it should encounter soft, succulent flesh.

The solution is simple: substitute a single hook for the treble and bait the hook. A lure with a blade 1 inch long is the largest that should be used, though generally ¾ and ½ inch seem best. The hook size can vary from No 8 to No 4 and may be baited with a section of lobworm or fish strip. It is essential to use reasonably long-shanked hooks.

The worm section is threaded on the hook up to the eye, and the point and bend must not be masked. The amount of worm trailing behind the hook bend is critical. It should not exceed ½ inch, otherwise a perch will nip off the morsel, pause to swallow, and lose interest in the departing lure. I have proved over and over again that if the hook is correctly baited a perch will follow, striking time after time, and will eventually get hooked.

Worm sections can slip down the hookshank and mask the point of the hook. This is easily overcome by whipping a short length of line, about 8 lb bs, to the hookshank just behind the eye, so as to leave a tiny stub or bristle, about ⅛ inch, which, when bent upwards, holds the bait in position. The colour of a worm closely resembles the caudal fin colour of a small roach, rudd, or perch, the natural aiming point for an attacking perch. The fish will not be suspicious because worm section feels natural.

Thin strips of fish without too much flesh adhering to the skin also work well. The lighter undersides of mackerel, herring, or sprat may be used, or slices from roach, rudd, or perch. Once again, very little should trail behind the hook bend. The amount that does trail should be dyed warm orange to provide the all-important aiming point.

When one is using fish strip it is necessary to use a hook to which has been whipped a small hook, size 16, to prevent the bait slipping down to the bend. The eye or spade end of this little hook is cut away before whipping, and it is positioned on the larger hook just behind the eye with the point towards it. Two fish strips, skin outwards, flutter attractively and seem a marginally better bait than a single strip.

All the advice that I have ever read on spinning has said that the speed of retrieve should be varied, the rod swung from side to side to make the lure make sudden changes in direction, and even when a pluck is felt the lure should be speeded up to make the quarry think its prey is about to escape. Knowing how a perch chases a little fish, you must spin so

that the lure can be caught, and caught easily.

If you spin as is always advised you are making that more difficult, so spin slowly, at an even pace and in a straight line. If you feel the odd pluck, continue the retrieve without any variation. Angle the rod tip to the line of retrieve so that you can see a pluck as well as feel it, and carry on spinning until the rod tip pulls round. This signifies that the perch has a firm hold and your response should be a gentle strike to set the hook, usually well inside the perch's mouth.

The only feasible lure for this method of spinning is a bar spoon (see fig 1), by which the blade revolves around the central axis of the bar. Bar spoons have the added attraction of producing strong vibrations, and many varieties are weighted which helps in long casting; up-trace weights are an abomination. The best perch lure I have encountered is the Abu Droppen, closely followed by the old-fashioned fly spoons which have to be modified into bar spoons. Others well worth using, all in the

Fig. 1   **Baited bar spoon**

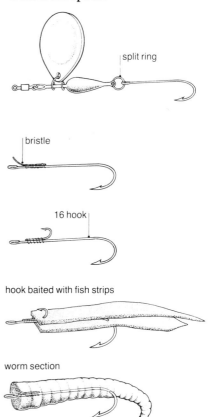

split ring

bristle

16 hook

hook baited with fish strips

worm section

smaller sizes, are Mepps, the Mepps Aglia, the Mepps Adour, the Ondex, and the Abu Colibri.

One piece of advice with which I am in complete agreement is to use a dull lure in clear water and bright conditions, and a bright one in deep water or dull conditions. All my lures are matt varnished to eliminate excessive flash.

The baited spoon is an exciting method but, as perch are not selective, fish of all sizes will be caught. However, it seems far more effective than an unbaited lure where the larger specimens are concerned. My best perch, over 4 lb, succumbed to a worm baited lure. A small livebait is more likely to appeal to a huge perch than any other bait. A perch will swallow a large fish but you will get far more runs on small ones, 2 to 4 inches in length. Besides, large baits cause difficulties in timing when to set the hook, let alone mounting them on the tackle.

Livebaits should be lip hooked, small baits on a size 8, medium baits on a 6, and 4 inch baits and over on a 4. Contrary to all you may have read, perch are not strong fighters, so the hooks can be fine in the wire. Heavy forged hooks can make little baits nose-heavy and restrict their movements. The hook should be passed through both lips, top lip

Perch fishing in a weedy corner of Slapton Ley in Devon – a water once famous for monster rudd

first so that the point protrudes forward of the bait's nose. Inserting the hook through the muscle in the region of the dorsal fin may be tried with the larger baits, but they do not seem to last or remain as lively as one lip hooked.

Livebaits may be presented under a float, set at any depth, paternostered, or legered on the bottom. I have found that the free roving technique, whereby a bait can swim where it will, suspended under a float, is best when perch are on the prowl. The paternoster is designed to tether a bait in a small area.

Large perch are intolerant of resistance, and the serious perch angler should make sure that a livebait can be taken without the predator feeling any drag. Even when you are float fishing, a big perch should be allowed to run off with the bait, so the reel bale arm should be open to allow line to peel off the spool unhindered. More big perch are lost by the angler striking quickly than for any other reason.

45

No hard and fast rule can be laid down as to how long to wait before setting the hook. There are too many variables. For instance, there is no way of knowing the size of the perch which has taken the bait. Some days the bait will be swallowed quickly, but more usually a perch will run off for some yards before starting to swallow.

As a general rule, the larger the bait the more time should be given. For gudgeon-sized baits, 10 seconds should result in the perch being hooked. If not, allow a little more time on the next run. Sometimes the only way to connect is to wait even longer. For 4 inch baits even 15 to 20 seconds may be necessary. If a run develops, then stops and recommences, strike at once, for the perch has started to swallow. The times I have suggested may seem inordinately long to some, but it is a long time since I deep-hooked a large perch.

Before I elaborate on perch rigs, a few words on general tackle: while I prefer to use Avon rods, 11 feet long, any rod with a 1 lb test curve will do nicely, and an ordinary match rod is adequate. Even light, soft action carp rods may be pressed into service and, except for long range work, when fast taper rods are an advantage, a medium taper rod will cope with most methods and situations. The Avon can be used for spinning, but I think a more specialised tool is better and I now use a light medium action 9 foot rod with which a lure can be flicked out one-handed. A fixed spool reel is essential.

Lines should be light. I rarely go above 3 lb bs for float fishing, 4 lb for legering and the paternoster, and 5 lb for spinning where lines are more subject to wear and tear. Only in excessively weedy or snag ridden waters should heavier line be contemplated.

The roving livebait rig (see fig 2) is simple, consisting of the hook, a single shot, the float, a small snap link swivel, a bead, and a sliding stop knot. The line is threaded through the bead and passed through the eye of the link swivel; then the hook is tied on. The shot, which may be one AA or a swan shot, depending on float capacity, is positioned 18 inches above the hook to allow the bait freedom of movement. The snap link swivel is clipped to the eye at the base of the float.

Floats should be slim and ideally should have no more than 1 inch showing when supporting the bait and shot. I make my perch floats from $\frac{1}{4}$ inch diameter balsa rod in various lengths from 4 to 6 inches. Some have a cut-down plastic dart flight

inserted into the tip for extra visibility at long range and to catch the wind when it is necessary to drift a bait long distances. Apart from the coloured tip, these floats are painted to camouflage pattern in two tones of green, the finishing coat of varnish being matt. There are times when perch are feeding near the surface and the bait may be suspended within a foot or two of the float. Brightly coloured shiny floats scare fish.

The link swivel facilitates instant float changes without having to break down the tackle, and the bead lodges against the stop knot, which would otherwise slip through the eye of the link swivel. The sliding stop knot tied with heavier line than the reel line, 6 lb bs, should be tightened so that it will hold its position, but slide when required. When

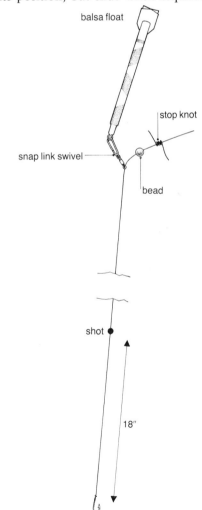

Fig. 2 **Roving livebait on worm float rig**

Fig. 3

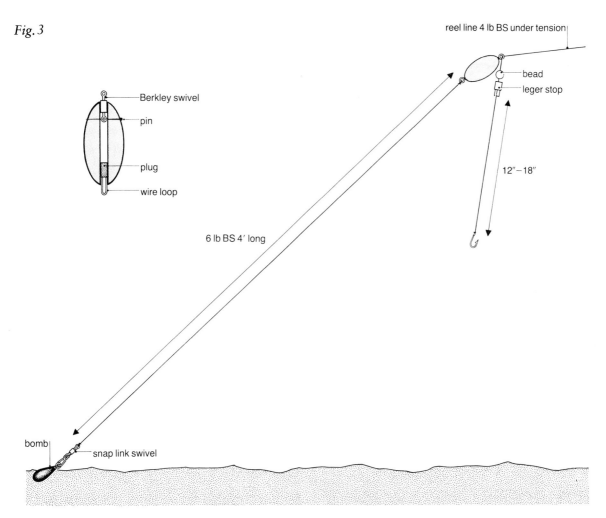

reel line 4 lb BS under tension

bead
leger stop

12″–18″

Berkley swivel
pin
plug
wire loop

6 lb BS 4′ long

bomb
snap link swivel

you are sliding the knot to alter depth, the line should be wet or it could become weakened. Leave both ends of the stop knot at least an inch long, then the knot will pass through the rod rings smoothly.

Rigging a float slider fashion enables water of any depth to be fished without casting difficulties, for the float rests against the shot prior to casting. If the bait is to be suspended 14 feet deep, the stop knot is positioned 14 feet above the hook.

Normally this roving float rig is used with a well greased line so that the line floats. This is particularly important when you are drifting a bait out on the wind. If a cross-wind forms a bow in the line and the float is dragged along, the line should be treated with detergent so that it sinks quickly. This reduces the problem, but in really strong cross-winds it is best to dispense with float fished baits and leger or paternoster instead.

One of the most efficient perch rigs is the sunken float running paternoster (see fig 3). This allows a bait, preferably a livebait, to be presented well clear of the bottom, and is virtually tangle free. The sunken float is made from a small balsa float body, incorporating a swivel with the eye free to revolve. A short piece of fuse wire bent into a U is inserted into the base and secured with a cane or matchstick plug secured with Araldite.

To overcome the possibility of the swivel pulling out of the sunken float when you are casting with a heavy bomb, a dressmaking pin can be pushed through the balsa so that it passes through the buried swivel eye. This is easier than it sounds; any length of pin protruding can be cut away and the remainder filed down.

Some 4 feet of line, heavier than the reel line, about 6 lb bs, is knotted to the wire loop, terminat-

The river Ouse, near York, which sometimes produces quality perch

leger rig. After the hook has been tied on, the leger stop is plugged from the hook side 12 to 18 inches from the hook.

The running paternoster is fished under tension to the rod tip, so that when the bomb is holding on the bottom and the rod in two rests, the line is slightly tightened to the bomb and the paternoster link is at an angle. The greater the tension, the nearer to the bottom the bait will be suspended. By tensioning to the bomb, the hook link is less likely to tangle with the paternoster link. A livebait presented on this rig will try to swim to the bottom but the sunken float resists the downward pull. However, a lively bait will keep on trying, sending out visual as well as vibratory signals which are attractive to perch.

When the bait has been taken line will run out and the bomb will not move, so there will be minimum resistance. One of the simplest ways of keeping the line under tension is use an adjustable Gardner line clip, fixed to the rear rod rest so that it is positioned directly beneath the reel spool. It is most important that the line is only just held, so that the slightest pull will release it from the clip. If it is held too firmly the resistance will cause a large perch to eject the bait.

ing in a small snap link swivel to which a bomb can be easily attached. The line is passed through the swivel eye at the top of the float, through a small bead and the barrel of a small leger stop, as in the

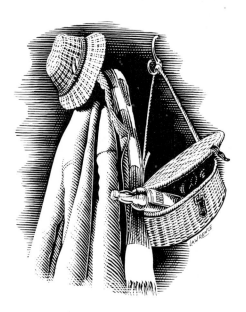

Bream

Graham Marsden

IT IS quite obvious from a study of the 50 biggest bream ever caught that the mid-1970s were a significant turning point in the fortunes of big bream anglers. Suddenly, or so it seemed, huge double-figure bream were being caught from a number of fisheries.

The truth is, however, that one particular gravel pit in Oxfordshire has been largely responsible for producing these big fish. It has acquired several names, but is probably best known as the TC pit. The not so well informed have been given the impression that several different waters have been producing giant bream. Despite the misleading information, there has been *some* increase in the numbers of big bream taken in recent years from waters other than the TC pit.

One or two of these fisheries have been one-offs. They are not really big bream waters at all, but by some freak of nature have managed to throw up one bream far above the average size in that water, if, indeed, there are other bream present. One such water is Beeston Hall Lake in Norfolk where Mike Davison, from North Walsham, took the official record bream of 13 lb 9 oz in July 1982. He tempted it with sweetcorn. It is believed to be the only bream in the water, and has been taken a number of times at weights over 10 lb.

While this book was being written, two other waters have produced reports of huge bream which, for one reason or another have not been claimed as official records. Stoke-on-Trent angler Anthony Bromley reported a 15 lb 6 oz bream from an unnamed Cheshire mere. Alastair Nicholson, from Banbury, reported a 13 lb 14 oz bream from Queenford Lagoon (an Amey Roadstone Corporation fishery in Oxfordshire, but not the TC pit,

which is at Wolvercote). Over the next few weeks he was to report three more monsters from the same water. They weighed 15 lb 6 oz, 14 lb 14 oz, and 14 lb 12 oz.

Neither angler wished to subject his fish to the ordeal of waiting for British Rod Caught Record Fish Committee verification. It may be that one or both may gain acceptance by the National Association of Specialist Anglers, which also keeps a record list with slightly different rules. Whatever happens, the best bream catch in history, as far as I am concerned, was achieved at the TC pit in September 1983.

Alan Wilson, from Blackpool, fished there for two weeks but in one memorable night he netted four bream over 13 lb, the exact weights being 13 lb 2 oz, 13 lb 6 oz, 13 lb 8 oz, and a record-breaker of 13 lb 13 oz. Alan had personal reasons for not claiming the BRCFC record, and was content to have it recorded by NASA. Official or not, there is no doubt that his 13 lb 13 oz bream was the biggest caught in Britain at that time. It was well documented, photographed, captured on video-tape, and witnessed by a number of experienced, honest, and authoritative anglers.

The night Alan caught the bream the water was flat calm, with no fish rolling at the surface. He had baited his swim, a gravel bar rising from 9 to 6½ feet, with brown bread crumb laced with hemp and chopped lobworms. Using a running leger, 5 lb line, and an 8 hook baited with lobworm he cast in and waited until 11.15 pm for his first bite. The 13 lb 8 oz fish was the result, his first ever double-figure bream. The second bite at 2 am produced the 13 lb 13 oz fish. At 3.45 am he caught the 13 lb 2 oz bream, and at 6 am the net slid under one of 13 lb 6 oz. Four bream for 53 lb 13 oz. It is difficult to imagine it ever being bettered.

The bream is a deep-bodied, narrow-backed fish varying in colour from almost black to a golden-bronze when mature, but usually silver-sided when immature. Young bream weighing up to 8 oz or so, popularly known as skimmers, can often be mistaken for the quite rare species called silver bream rather than the immature common bream.

Common bream, or bronze bream as they are also known, are true shoal fish and basically bottom feeders. In the small to medium sizes, up to 5 or 6 lb, it is not unusual to find them in shoals numbering 100 or more. They can grow well into double figures, but these are exceptional fish from exceptional waters, and it is as well to bear in mind that the average bream weighs less than half the record weight. A bream weighing more than 8 lb is a really big fish.

Bream are a very popular fish with most coarse anglers, mainly because they are so widely distributed and within reach of almost everyone. When a shoal of bream has been located it is possible to amass a very large catch over some hours, providing non-stop sport on the right day. Furthermore, big bream provide a most interesting and demanding challenge, which the all-round specimen hunter has come to appreciate.

Although bream are widely distributed, there are certain areas in the country where they habitually grow to specimen size (more than 8 lb). The gravel pits of the South are known for big bream and so is my own area, the meres of Cheshire and Shropshire.

What constitutes a good bream fishery? The water must exceed 5 acres in surface area, and preferably be much larger. Whereas large carp can be found in comparative puddles of no more than $\frac{1}{2}$ acre, bream never do well in small waters. Other factors are that the water should be rich in natural food, and the population of fish, of any species, should be less than the water could actually support. Most of the really good big bream waters that I know have poor spawning sites, and so do not encourage the bream to overbreed. They also have a

variety of predators, such as eels, perch, and pike, which ensure the spawn and fry of a successful spawning are well thinned before they can grow to any size and reduce the natural food supply.

The behaviour of bream is unusual in some ways. Not only do they mass in large shoals, they also feed as a shoal, all competing for food in one comparatively small area. This is why it is often possible to catch a large number of them at a sitting. They establish feeding routes to which they adhere day after day, week after week, and often for many seasons. About the only time they stray from these routes is when they spawn, usually at the end of May, when they seek out the shallow, weedy margins. There they remain for two to three weeks laying eggs and milt and cleaning off.

One of their most endearing and helpful habits is rolling at the surface, which they do during a feeding spell. They cleave the surface – sometimes just their dorsals in evidence, sometimes half their depth – now and again with a distinct splash, but most often as quietly as a butterfly settling on a flower.

No one knows why they do this, but my theory is that they are taking in extra oxygen from the surface in between spells of feeding among the maelstrom of muck and mud the shoal is causing on the bottom. There are a few waters where the bream do not roll, but these are usually waters that hold comparatively few very big ones. I think that is further evidence that my theory is right. A few bream do not stir up a lot of mud when feeding, therefore there is no need to seek extra oxygen at the surface.

The most reliable method of locating the feeding areas of any fish is to observe them feeding. We know that rolling bream are feeding bream, so if we can observe bream rolling, we know where their feeding areas are. They feed most often through the night and in the early morning, so the best time to visit a water to spot bream rolling is at first light.

It usually takes several visits to establish the complete path the bream are taking. Before long we will know the general area where they begin to roll, where they cease rolling, and the pattern the route takes. This can be a straight line of 50 yards or so, or an L covering a path of several hundred yards.

I am always pleased to discover a feeding route that veers off at a tangent, for more often than not the point where the bream turn will be an excellent hotspot. Otherwise, on a straight line or simple curved routes, the point at which the bream cease to

A 7½ lb bream from the Colne – a big fish for a river

roll should be chosen. This is not always best, however. I check the whole route for any distinct variation in bottom features, particularly deeper holes, or sharp rises, for such features are usually very attractive to bream. In these places they do most of their feeding. If no such distinct character can be found, there is no alternative but to fish on a trial and error basis along the whole route over a period of time. Somewhere along the length of even a featureless route there will be one area which the bream favour more than any other.

There are, I know, anglers who do not believe in pre-baiting. They say it is totally unnecessary if you have chosen a good swim, for the fish will visit the swim anyway, without the attraction of numerous helpings of free feed. That is true enough if you think pre-bait is nothing more than an attractor, but the main purpose as far as I am concerned is to re-establish the fishes' taste for a proven bait or to

51

wean them on to a bait they have not seen before. Pre-baiting can do that, as well as instilling confidence into the fish that a bait is readily available and safe to take.

I have dabbled with new baits for bream, including the protein packed, high nutritive value ones that have proved successful for carp. There have been isolated successes, but I have come to the conclusion that the old favourites, maggot, caster, worm, and bread, are still the best on the vast majority of waters.

If the water is private or semi-private and little fished, such as an estate lake, I try bread and worm to begin with. If the water is well fished, and particularly if matches are held on it, the first choice has to be maggot and caster. The amount introduced each time depends on the population of bream and other fish. Generally, on each visit a pint each of maggot and caster packed into as little groundbait as possible is adequate, or 50 or so chopped worms in half a 2 gallon bucket of mixed groundbait or soaked bread.

How often do we pre-bait, and for how long? The short answer is every day for as long as possible, except on the days you fish. Often my friends and I will pre-bait every day for several weeks before we fish, and then continue baiting two or three times a week after we begin fishing. It is difficult to pre-bait too often and for too long, but very easy not to do it often enough and for long enough.

It is important to pre-bait exactly the same spot each time. The best way of ensuring this, particularly in distant swims, is to position a marker at the far edge of the swim. This marker can be a small block of polystyrene to which you anchor a stone or chunk of lead with the appropriate length of line.

Most of the Cheshire and Shropshire meres are like saucers, with shallow margins and deep water towards the middle. For this reason, and because bream generally prefer to feed some distance from the margins, most feeding routes will be found at least 30 yards from the bank. There are some waters, however, notably gravel pits, where deep water can be found right under the rod end, where the bream will feed close in.

The distance from the margins at which the bream feed will be the main deciding factor as to which method – float or leger – you can use; that is, unless you have the use of a boat. I much prefer to float-fish whenever it is practicable, not only for its greater sensitivity in detecting bites and delicate presentation of a bait, but because I derive much pleasure from catching good fish on float tackle.

One of the main advantages of float fishing is that if the swim is close enough to reach with a float, it is close enough to loosefeed with a catapult without the using of groundbait as a carrying agent. More of that later.

Most of my float fishing for bream is done from a flat-bottomed punt in swims that lie 40 to 50 yards from the bank. The depth of the swims I fish average 9 to 11 feet, which means that my 13 foot match rod is long enough to allow me to use a fixed float. I do not use more than one rod when float fishing, for the second rod, with the line to the float running just below the surface, can cost more fish than it catches when a fish runs into it.

My 13 foot carbon match rod is a very delicate weapon, allowing me to use a 3 lb reel line confidently and, at least to begin with, a $2\frac{1}{2}$ lb hook length. If bites are hard to come by I do not hesitate to drop down to a 1·7 lb hook length, and so far I have landed scores of bream over 8 lb, many over 9 lb, without losing one through breakage. Believe me, on a short line a sizeable bream can fight very well indeed.

Maggot and caster are my chosen hookbait when float fishing for bream. They are ideal as loosefeed and allow me to use small hooks, which seem to be a decisive factor when the bream are biting shyly. I usually begin with 14s, but generally go down to 16s, and sometimes 18s when things get tough. A bronze, round bend, forged spade-end hook is my choice. In calm conditions I prefer a straight peacock float with a cane insert, shotted as in fig 1, but when there is a chop on the surface, generally the best condition for bream, I choose a Drennan Driftbeater float shotted as in fig 2.

When you are boat fishing it is wise to tackle up at the side and lay everything out within easy reach before you row out to the swim. When you get there, you have only to lower the anchors gently at each end of the boat and sink the keepnet, or carp sack, over the side of the boat facing away from the swim. Then you feed the swim, using about six catapult pouchfuls of casters for every pouchful of maggots. The first feed should be the largest at any one time. On my waters it is usually two pints of casters and about a quarter pint of maggots.

From then on you feed according to how well the bream are responding, firing two or three pouchfuls of casters and the odd one of maggots every time the bream show signs of going off feed.

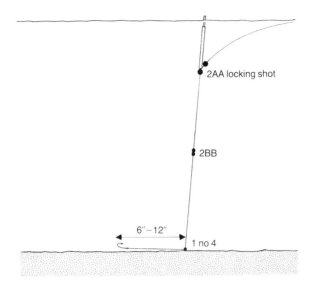

Fig. 1 **Straight peacock with cane-insert float**

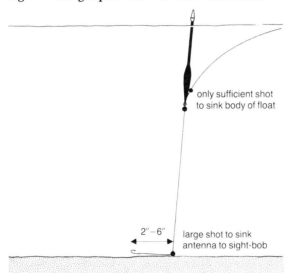

Fig. 2 **Drennan Driftbeater float**

When they are feeding well I easily get through six pints of casters and a pint of maggots in a day. This relates mainly to big bream of more than 8 lb, when I hope to catch six or a dozen in a session. A bigger shoal of smaller bream will need much more bait than that.

Most often the hookbait will be maggot, one, two, or three on the hook, depending on whether the hook is, respectively, an 18, 16, or 14. Every so often you may find the fish have developed a preference for caster, so when bites are hard to come by, do not hesitate to try caster, or a sandwich bait of maggot and caster.

Bites on the straight peacock float usually begin with a slight lift, then a total disappearance when they should be struck. On the Driftbeater float the long antenna will rise steadily out of the surface and then move off very slowly. Strike at that point, when the antenna reaches its maximum lift and begins to move.

Legering is almost the standard method for catching bream, probably because most bream swims are too distant to be tackled efficiently with a float. The rod I prefer for this is an 11 foot medium taper, of approximately 1 lb 2 oz test-curve, fitted with a screwed end ring to take a swing tip or quiver tip. It is easily capable of casting a $\frac{1}{2}$ oz bomb 50 yards, and can cope admirably with a $\frac{3}{4}$ oz bomb when I need to overcome cross-winds or cast to more distant swims.

As with float fishing, my reel line is 3 lb, with a $2\frac{1}{2}$ lb hook length (or 4 lb and 3 lb respectively for big fish). The terminal tackle I prefer is a fixed paternoster, tied as in fig 3 with a long hook length, or in fig 4 with a long bomb length, if the bream are feeding hard on the bottom. The long hook length

Fig. 3 **Long hook-length paternoster**

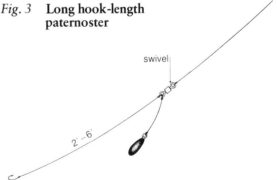

Fig. 4 **Long bomb-length paternoster**

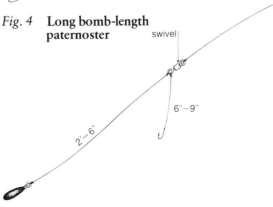

The rowing course lake at Holme Pierrepont, Nottingham, is noted for producing large match catches of bream

paternoster is generally the most productive, for the bream invariably begin to intercept food while it is still sinking when they are well on feed, and the long hook length allows the bait to sink slowly.

Bread flake's natural buoyancy makes it an excellent bait for fishing on the drop. It should be fished on a long-shank, eyed No 10 or 8 hook, the flake being squeezed lightly around the shank and left fluffy around the bend and point of the hook. The same effect can, however, be achieved with floating maggots. The way to produce them is to cover the bottom of a bait box with water about $\frac{1}{8}$ inch deep and drop in a handful of maggots. Eventually most, if not all, of these maggots will become floaters. Keep them to one side for use as hookbait only.

The type of bite indicator I use depends on whether I am fishing for a large bag of medium sized bream or one or two big ones. When I am fishing for a lot of fish I generally swing tip, for with this indicator you can cast and be instantly ready to register bites the moment the tackle hits the water. It is also a most sensitive indicator, revealing even the tiniest of bites. The quiver tip can be similarly used, but I prefer one mainly when fishing running water.

When my target is big bream and I am not expecting many bites, I use an electric bite alarm combined with some kind of bobbin clipped on a loop of line between reel and butt ring. This combination allows me to relax and scan the water for rolling bream, knowing I shall get an audible warn-ing the moment the bobbin begins to move.

When legering a distant swim you have to rely on a catapult to introduce the feed. This should be a fine pure bread groundbait if you are fishing bread flake, liberally laced with chopped worms if worms are your hookbait, or laced with caster or feeder maggots if your hookbait is maggot or caster. The groundbait should be mixed in a shallow bowl, adding groundbait to water until a fluffy mixture is obtained. It should be of a consistency that will readily squeeze into a tight ball, but will break and dissolve easily when it breaks through the surface. Caster and feeder maggots will not break the ball in flight, as will hookbait maggots. It is better to fire in half a dozen small balls of bait than one or two large ones which can unduly disturb the swim. Ground-bait a compact circle, introducing about a dozen balls of bait to begin with, and then top up when the fish show signs of going off feed.

Never be content to sit and wait for bream to bite. It is far better to cast regularly, especially when flake fishing, to maintain the buoyancy in the bait, and continually present them with a slow-falling bait. I am sure the movement of the bait goes a long way to tempt bream to bite, so even when you are sure the bait has settled on the bottom, it can be a good ploy to twitch it along several times before finally retrieving for another cast.

Bream can arrive in a swim very suddenly, but can just as easily depart if you disturb them or fail to maintain their interest with sufficient feed. The secret of successful bream angling, is efficient hook-ing and landing of fish without loss – for a hooked and lost bream can spook the whole shoal – and introducing just the right amount of feed at the right time, which is something only experience can teach you.

Tench

Tim Marks

FOR MORE years that I can remember, anglers have spent countless misty summer dawns fishing for the distinctive olive-green tench. Regulation tactics for this fascinating species involved simple float tackle, with bread or worms for bait. These methods still succeed in the right situation, but tench fishing has changed radically during the past decade or so. The seventies saw the adoption of the swim feeder as the number one tench producer and recent years have witnessed the extension of special bait techniques from carp to tench angling.

The reasons for this rapid advance in techniques tie in with the gradual increase in big tench captures which has taken place over the past 15 years. The realisation that tench were definitely getting bigger (for a variety of ecological reasons) attracted large numbers of specialist anglers to tench fishing. This opened the way for a revolution in both water choice and fishing methods.

The 1950s and '60s saw most tench fishing carried out on natural lakes with heavy groundbait and big baits. Thinking anglers such as the Taylor brothers and Dick Walker refined this approach. They used smaller baits where necessary, and the deadly lift method was developed by Fred Taylor. At this time 5 lb tench were regarded as real specimen fish, and even an angler as well regarded as Frank Guttfield did not catch his first 6-pounder until 1966.

At this time the record stood at 9 lb 1 oz — caught by John Salisbury from a gravel pit (ahead of its time) at Hemingford Grey, and it was not beaten until 1975. The new record fish, which broke the 10 lb barrier by an ounce, came from a Peterborough brick pit. By this time the phenomenal catches of Tenchfishers member Len Head

were making headlines. Len proved that given the right water (a pit), consistently to catch tench in excess of 7 lb was a real possibility. More and more anglers turned to the pursuit of super-tench, and gravel pits became the major focus of their attention.

Since that time, every June has seen predictions that the record will be shattered by a fish well into double figures. In fact, the national best now stands at 10 lb 2 oz, only 1 oz up on Lewis Brown's 1975 fish. The current record holder is Eric Edwards who caught his fish on 17 June 1983, on sweetcorn. The fish came from an Oxfordshire gravel pit, thus re-emphasising the potential of gravel pits as the country's premier big tench waters.

Paradoxically, the current record has twice been exceeded, but in neither case was a claim registered. The biggest fish, weighing 10 lb 10 oz, came from a Cheshire mere in 1981 and fell to Dennis Kelly. The fish was heavy with spawn, and rather than wait for witnesses to come to the water, Dennis chose to return it. The other record beater

Swingtipping for tench in a large Lincolnshire lake

A 3 lb tench from a Nottinghamshire pond

Being particularly hardy fish, able to survive pretty adverse conditions, tench have a tendency to breed rapidly and ultimately to exhaust the available food supply. This is reflected in the large number of waters (usually natural lakes) with huge populations of stunted tench. These fish are fairly easy to catch, simply because of the relative lack of natural food available, and usually weight around 2 to 3 lb. Typically, this type of water is mud bottomed and therefore coloured and lightly weeded. Fishing these waters generally requires a dawn and dusk approach, as the shallow water makes catching fish in the middle of the day difficult.

Gravel pits have become the most likely haunts of big tench because they are often too big to suffer from over-population. They have fairly clear water and lots of natural food for the fish; in these conditions fast growth is possible. Gravel pits have been dug all over the country and because of their favourable geology (in river channels) they can support big tench regardless of their geographical location. Thus pits in Yorkshire and the South West contain tench as big as those found in the generally more favourable South East.

The future of tench fishing lies more and more with gravel pits as they continue to be excavated (albeit at a reduced rate) and the existing natural waters get overfished or overstocked. Other waters that produce big tench with some regularity are the meres of Cheshire and Shropshire, and some of the old established estate lakes in East Anglia. In both these cases the waters are naturally very rich and so are able to breed big fish. What is then required is minimum competition for the available food or some form of curb on the tench population, to keep the overall numbers of fish down and so raise the growth potential.

Once a possible water has been located, the way to find the tench (barring talking to other anglers) is to watch the water. Tench are prone to rolling on the surface around dawn and dusk, close to where they feed, and likely looking swims can soon be pinpointed. If the water is very calm, rough guesses of the size of the fish can be attempted – but do not be too optimistic.

A far better way of judging a water's potential is to ascertain the size of the male tench present. Males are easily distinguished by their oversized pelvic fins and pronounced pelvic bones. They run much smaller than the female of the species, and a male of more than 4 lb indicates a fairly good water.

came from Wilstone reservoir in Hertfordshire, again in 1981, and registered 10 lb 4 oz. Unfortunately for its captor, Richard Francis, the fish was foulhooked and so did not qualify as a record.

Dennis Kelly's fish points the way into the future and many well qualified observers still predict 11 and 12 lb tench as realistic targets. My own view is that while such fish probably do exist, the chances of one coming from a recognised tench water are slim indeed. I see it as far more likely that a really exceptional tench will come from a quiet gravel pit and will probably be caught by a carp angler.

Tench have been present in Britain for hundreds of years and were bred for culinary purposes by monks in the Middle Ages. They are widespread in the South of England and slowly thin out as you move north and west. There are a few good tench waters in South Wales, some in Lancashire and Yorkshire, and almost none at all in Scotland. Tench are primarily stillwater fish and so are found in all manner of ponds, lakes, pits, and reservoirs. Canals and sluggish rivers are also worth fishing; I have taken some useful fish from the river Lea in Hertfordshire. The Irish record tench also came from a river – the Shannon at Lanesborough in 1971. It was caught by the legendary Ray Webb and weighed 7 lb 13¼ oz.

A 5 lb male tench is pretty rare, but catching one indicates the probable presence of very big female tench. A 6 lb male is almost unheard of.

Catching tench regularly demands a versatile approach, treating each water on its own merits. No single method can be guaranteed to succeed on a particular water, so it pays to experiment with different baits and techniques. Attention must also be paid to the prevailing weather conditions and their likely effect on the fish.

Generally, tench are fairly easy to catch at the start of the season and sport remains good throughout June and July. The abundance of natural food available in high summer (late July and August) often makes fishing difficult, as the fish become partially preoccupied. With the arrival of September and cooler weather, the fishing improves again, and if the shoals of tench can be located, big catches are possible at this time of year.

In the past it has been assumed that tench do not feed during the cold winter months. However, the recent upsurge in winter carp catches has prompted some anglers to attempt winter tench fishing. Fish have been caught with some regularity, especially from southern gravel pits, and this trend towards all the year round tench fishing will slowly gain acceptance. Fishing through October until the first heavy frosts can be very productive, and a warm spell in late February or March is likely to bring the fish on to the feed.

Tackle for tench fishing depends entirely on the specific water and methods that are to be used. For the traditional type of float fishing and simple legering, an Avon or heavy float rod and 5 or 6 lb line will suffice. Tench fight tenaciously, and using light tackle close to weedbeds or other snags should be avoided at all costs. Some heavily fished waters become quite difficult in mid-summer and lighter tackle is then required. A standard match rod, 3 lb line, and sensitive float tackle are usually the best bet in this situation – but only when there are no snags close by.

The recent switch to swimfeeder fishing demands a specialist approach with well designed rods and tackle. For feeder fishing, an 11 to 12 foot medium to fast taper rod of about $1\frac{1}{4}$ lb test curve is the usual choice, with something a bit more powerful for long range fishing. Carbon fibre has now replaced glass as the premier rod-making material and a well chosen carbon rod will be significantly more versatile than a glass one of the same test curve.

It is now possible to buy a 12 foot carbon blank with a medium action and a test curve of between $1\frac{1}{4}$ and $1\frac{1}{2}$ lb and use it for any form of tench fishing. The extra length will suit float fishing and hitting quick bites while using a feeder, and the progressive power of such a rod will cope perfectly with the heavier line and leads required for distance fishing. A rod like this will cost upwards of £50 – but as it would require at least two glass rods to do the same jobs, the extra expense is well worth while. Do not be tempted to cut corners and buy a cheap carbon rod, as they are notoriously unreliable; it pays to stick with a recognised top-class supplier.

Reels, lines, and hooks are largely a matter of personal choice. Any good fixed spool reel and full spools of various breaking strain lines will suffice. Hooks need to be chosen with particular care as they must be both reliable and strong. In the smaller sizes forged hooks should be used; the new Peter Drennan range can be recommended. If you prefer spade end hooks, try VMC 9284 or Mustad 39853 patterns. All these are good strong hooks, reliable down to size 16. With bigger hooks the wire thickness is not so critical, as the size of the hook provides strength. The Drennan eyed hooks can again be recommended, as can the Mustad 496s – a very nice short shank spade end hook.

Other specialist items of tackle the serious tench angler should not be without include catapults for both loosefeed and groundbait, swing tips or butt indicators for registering finnicky bites, and a supply of block-end and standard swim feeders of varying sizes.

On any tench water, the probable early season location depends on the weather. Tench do not spawn until the water temperature reaches at least 18°C (64°F) and the bigger female fish tend to stay in fairly deep water until the shallows reach the required temperature. Thus if the early season weather is warm and the water temperature is high, the fish are likely to be in pretty shallow water and close to spawning. Once spawning has occurred, the fish will roam around the shallow areas of the water, gradually moving into deeper water as summer passes. If, however, the early season water temperatures are low, then the fish will probably be in fairly deep water (up to 10 feet) but still close to the preferred spawning grounds.

By September the tench will have moved into pretty deep water (if such exists) and on gravel pits I would concentrate on water of at least 12 feet deep and sometimes considerably more. At this time of year the fish tend to form into large shoals and stay in fairly well defined areas. Much of the water can be barren, so it pays to move around trying various swims until the fish are located. Earlier in the

A tench on the float from Pickmere

season the fish are considerably more nomadic and the best policy is usually to pick a likely spot and stick to it, hoping that the fish will find the baited area.

Within any likely area of lake – containing water of the correct depth and showing signs of tench activity (rolling) – bottom features and weedbeds are worth particular attention. In natural lakes, margin weed often draws the fish close to the bank and creates possibilities of good close range fishing. Conversely, gravel pits with deep margins often have recognised tench patrol routes along the marginal shelves.

Fishing at longer range on pits usually involves locating a specific feature – bar, channel, small plateau and so on and then repeatedly casting into one small area. On natural lakes the usual lack of bottom features (apart from weed) makes a wide range of approaches possible. One obvious method is to cast to one particular area, hoping to build up an area of feed, and then hold the fish in a confined space.

An alternative approach involves using a swimfeeder and casting around the swim trying to locate individual browsing fish. The idea here is that one big fish can consume all the contents of a feeder and so will take the hookbait, whereas if only one fish finds an area that has been heavily baited, the chances of hooking it are much reduced. I tend to favour the latter approach, particularly on waters containing few fish. Groundbaiting can be very useful early in the season, but generally does more harm than good if used in excess.

This approach goes directly against the traditional 'heavy ground baiting for tench' tactic, which relies on large numbers of fish to warrant really heavy baiting. Anyway, the fish learn to avoid white carpets on the bottom soon after the season starts.

The aim of any groundbaiting or loosefeeding should be to hold the fish in the swim for as long as possible, without feeding them too much. The longer the fish are held in the swim, the greater the chance of the hookbait being taken. Thus cereal groundbait can be cut to a minimum and in some cases dispensed with altogether. What is required is some kind of particle bait for which the fish will grub around without satisfying their appetites. Casters and hemp are good examples of this sort of bait; they are difficult to find because they are small and dark, and they do not feed the fish too much. Once the fish are present in the swim, standard

60

baits fished over this carpet should succeed. Worms and sweetcorn work particularly well when used in conjunction with hempseed.

Hookbaits for tench are legion and vary in size from whole swan mussels on the one hand to single maggots on the other. The best policy is to begin the season with as big a bait as the fish will comfortably accept, and then scale down as the season progresses. I see little point in heavily pre-baiting with maggots during the close season and then being forced to use size 18 hooks and 2 lb line after only a few weeks. Bread, worms (lobs and red-worms), and sweetcorn are reliable early season baits with single grains of corn, stewed wheat, maggots, and casters coming into their own as the fish get wise to bigger offerings.

The rate at which the fish go off certain baits is directly related to the angling pressure on the fish. On lightly fished waters tench can be caught on big baits throughout the summer; all that is necessary is a selection of worms, bread, and corn. On harder fished lakes the fish soon learn to avoid certain baits, and progressive reduction of the bait and accompanying hook size through the season is usually the answer.

For close range fishing, loosefeeding is quite adequate, using a catapult as the distances to be cast increase. For medium and long range fishing, leger tackle is the best bet, with swim feeders used where necessary. For maggot fishing, Drennan feederlinks are the most suitable feeders. They can be adapted for long range fishing by the addition of drilled bullet weights. Used upside down, feederlinks make superb (small) open-ended feeders and only need to be replaced by standard open-ended feeders when large quantities of bait are required.

Experience has shown that leger tackle fishes best when using a fixed paternoster rig (fig 1). Standard link leger rigs can be used early in the

Fig. 1 **Fixed paternoster feeder rig**

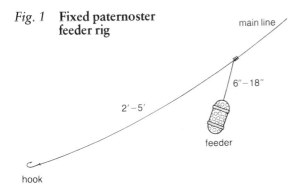

season when the fish are feeding confidently, but bites soon became finnicky and the paternoster is much the more sensitive of the two rigs.

Length of the hook link should be varied according to the type of bites being received. Generally speaking the longer the link the better the bite registration. I would recommend using links of at least 2 feet in length and going up to 5 or 6 feet when the fish are not feeding confidently.

Bite detection when you are using small baits can sometimes lead to problems. The best solutions are swing tips or butt indicators. Personally I favour butt indicators as they have less effect on casting. Mine are 12 inches long and made from fine gauge aluminium tube. They are taped on to the rod under the butt ring using a length of silicone tubing as a hinge. They can be replaced by shop bought swing-tips which will perform the same job if the screw thread and intermediate ring are removed (fig 2). Used in conjunction with the Optonic bite indicator, they are most efficient.

Fig. 2 **Butt indicator**

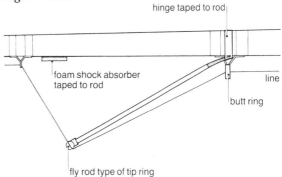

When fishing at close range and having reasonable expectations of success, I generally choose to float-fish. Float fishing has several advantages over legering, including the ability to use lighter tackle to register the slightest of bites. Much of my float fishing involves fishing off the bottom (fig 3) using an antenna type of float. This method has the added advantage that the bait can be moved at will without snagging the bottom. I set the float to fish the bait a couple of inches off the bottom and then twitch it towards the bank every few seconds. This method can score very well and the fish often take the bait just as it is dropping back in the water after being moved. As tench are particularly inquisitive fish, it is the movement that stimulates the bite.

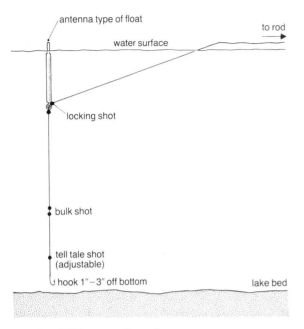

Fig. 3 **Off bottom float rig**

Standard bottom fishing is best accomplished using the lift method (fig 4). This rig (devised by the Taylor brothers) simply employs a buoyant quill

Fig. 4 **'Lift' method**

float and a heavy shot used as an anchor. By fishing the bait close to the shot (2 to 4 inches) the fish moves the shot as it picks up the bait, so releasing the float and causing it to rise in the water. The rig was designed for fishing small baits when the fish are shy, but it can be easily adapted to early season fishing. All that is necessary is to increase the distance between shot and hook, thus reducing the sensitivity of the rig. Tail lengths of over a foot can be used with big baits early in the season. The shot is moved closer to the hook as the season progresses.

Float fishing requires intense concentration and the use of only one rod, so it is best confined to expected feeding spells. I generally fish 90 per cent of the time with leger tackle and then switch to a float when I think the chances of fish are highest. On natural lakes this usually works out as float fishing for the first and last hours of the day, as bites are usually concentrated around dawn and dusk unless the weather is particularly favourable (cloud and mist or drizzle), in which case the fish may feed all day. On gravel pits the fish can feed at any time and it will take a few sessions to get an idea of the best times. No hard and fast rules can be laid down, but many pits have a feeding spell around late morning and some produce fish in the dark.

Using boiled baits for tench is a relatively new technique and one that has filtered through from carp fishing circles. Carp anglers developed the

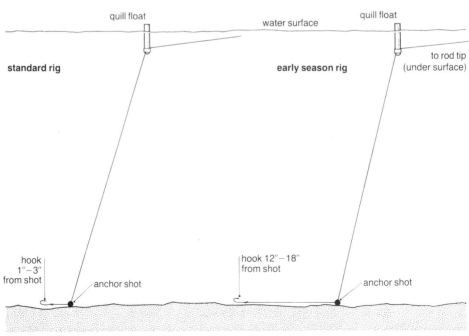

method of mixing varieties of paste baits with eggs, rolling them into balls and boiling them to make them hard. The intention was to make them unacceptable to other unwanted species – including tench. Tench will take them, though it seems to take them much longer to learn that boilies are valuable food offerings.

Fishing this method specifically for tench is best practised on waters that have been carp fished for several seasons. Generally speaking the accepted method employs 6 to 8 lb line, a lead of at least an ounce, a 2 foot tail, and a longish hook with the bait being side or top hooked. In essence the technique involves a bolt rig, so called because the fish feels the hook or the weight of the lead (or both at once) and bolts as a first reaction to danger. It runs with the bait, and either hooks itself against the weight of the lead or is easily hooked by the angler.

For bait, any standard base mix can be used, with the individual adding his own combination of colour and flavouring. Because tench are known to like sweet flavours, these are worth a try, as are others such as maple and buttercream. This style of fishing is fairly limited in its application and is likely to be rewarding only on big fish waters. Heavy

pre-baiting is likely to be necessary on waters that have not seen similar baits before. The method is really a last resort.

Baits should not be too hard or too large, $\frac{1}{2}$ inch diameter being about right. Using a paste rather than a true boiled bait might prove more successful in the short term as the tench would take less time to learn to accept it. Carp anglers are streets ahead when it comes to designing new tackle rigs and experimenting with flavoured baits. The next five years will see many changes in tench fishing based on the further application of the boiled bait and advanced terminal tackle ideas, most of which will have been directly learned from innovative carp anglers.

Successful tench fishing is all about adopting a versatile approach. Once a decent water has been chosen, some serious thought on fish location should isolate the most likely areas. It is then up to the angler to choose a suitable tackle rig, bait, and feeding programme. There is no point in slavishly adopting the currently fashionable method just because it is catching big tench from a few hard fished gravel pits. Think for yourself, weigh up your own water and *then* choose a method and a bait, not the other way round.

Eel

Brian Crawford

More than 3500 papers have been written about it by zoologists, biologists, and the like. They cover all aspects of the biology of this fish, and yet many secrets have still to be uncovered. If you had not read the chapter heading would you have guessed I was talking about the eel?

The unconverted majority of anglers have not taken to the eel quite so readily as the scientists, but there are some who fish for nothing else, and the number seems to grow every year as more people realise what an exciting challenge the eel can offer. Catching a big one is perhaps the most difficult of all angling achievements.

They have fascinated me since I caught my first of more than 4 lb while fishing for tench in a small reservoir. I was impressed by the brute strength of that fish, the tenacity of its fight, and its awesome appearance when it hit the net. I have felt the same about every big eel I have encountered since.

That original encounter had a profound effect, leading me into avenues I then scarcely knew existed. I began what has become a lifelong pursuit of this strange and enigmatic species (*Anguilla anguilla*), and in 1969 I joined the National Anguilla Club, determined to learn as much as I could. Inspired by similarly dedicated eel fanatics I have amassed a wealth of information about this snake-like scavenger/predator.

I have probably read all those 3500 or more scientific papers, paying special attention to those of particular relevance to angling. Several of these have emanated from Christopher Moriarty, one of the top research scientists in the field, who works in Ireland, but it was a Danish naturalist, E J Schmidt, who first observed that eels appeared to originate in the depths of the Sargasso Sea.

The eel has a remarkable life-cycle which, if fully understood, would encourage even those who do not like the eel to treat the species with more respect. Mature eels spawn in the Sargasso and then die. The eggs hatch into tiny transparent leaf-like larvae called leptocephalus, which are carried by the Gulf Stream to the shores of Europe and the Mediterranean Sea.

This journey takes about three years, during which the infant eels grow to about 3 inches in length. On arrival, the transformation is complete. The flat leptocephalus has become an elver – a tiny, still transparent baby eel. The elvers reach our shores by the million. Many stay in estuaries and waterways by the sea, but many also ascend rivers, canals, streams, dykes, and any trickle of water they can find.

Eels nearer the sea generally remain small, up to $\frac{1}{4}$ lb, and are predominately males. These stay in this region for 5 to 8 years, growing slowly to maturity. Then there is the powerful urge to return to the Sargasso, the long one-way trip to perpetuate the species.

Most females and a few males push upstream, seeking ever-cleaner water, tasting food traces and scents coming downstream. Eels dislike light and need to be in bodily contact with mud, gravel, or clay as they follow bottom contours on their travels. Occasionally, they take up residence in suitable areas of rivers such as weirs, deep holes,

Mike Wilson with a specimen eel

sunken trees, boats, and collapsed banks. The annual elver run on the river Severn in the spring is still a very impressive sight. These muscle-powered shoe-laces can travel almost everywhere, even up vertical concrete walls of locks if the walls are wet. There is an elver eating competition at Frampton on Severn each Easter where 1 lb of elvers – more than 1000 – are eaten in about 20 seconds.

When eels reach suitable growing areas inland, they stay for 10 to 20 years, feeding and storing protein for their long return travels. Female eels can average 2 to 3 lb in suitable waters such as weedy, clear, shallow gravel pits, where warm water encourages a large quantity of weed, with the masses of crustaceans and small fish for the eels to feed on. The warmer the water, the more eels feed and the bigger they become.

Typical examples of suitable waters are the large country estate lakes such as Westwood Park Lake near Droitwich, famous for the catches of big

eels by John Sidley. This is a large water holding vast weedy areas, reasonably shallow, and with large amounts of food. Other types include reservoirs like Abberton, near Colchester, most of the large Midlands lakes, and the famous meres of Shropshire. Almost all waters contain eels, but the closer they are to rivers, the smaller the eels. All the best eel waters I know are some distance from rivers and are reasonably shallow, with much weed.

Eels' heads are of two types. There are the large, round, broad head of fish-eating eels, and the small pointed head typical of those concentrating on crustaceans. Both types can be present in a water, but usually one type is more common. When you catch a few you can decide whether to use large hooks and fish portions for the large-mouthed eels or smaller hooks and worms for the small-mouthed types.

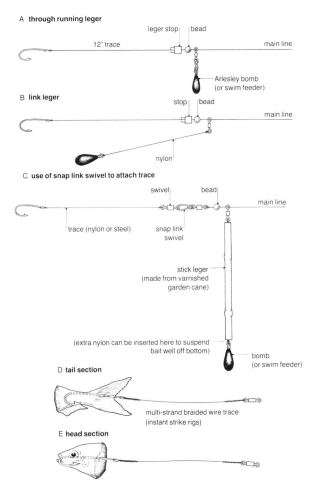

A **through running leger**

leger stop | bead

12" trace

main line

Arlesley bomb
(or swim feeder)

B **link leger**

stop | bead

main line

nylon

C **use of snap link swivel to attach trace**

swivel | bead

main line

trace (nylon or steel)

snap link
swivel

stick leger
(made from varnished
garden cane)

(extra nylon can be inserted here to suspend
bait well off bottom)

bomb
(or swim feeder)

D **tail section**

multi-strand braided wire trace
(instant strike rigs)

E **head section**

Small pointed-head eels in very clear water often have very large eyes. These indicate that they are daylight feeders grazing in the weeds for crustaceans and possibly fish fry. If there are many of this type present, daylight eeling offers good potential.

The British record eel is a magnificent 11 lb 2 oz, caught by Stephen Terry from Kingfisher Lake, Hampshire, on Friday 24 June 1978 at about 11.30 am on 6 lb bs line and size 8 hook baited with worm. Stephen was seeking carp when the giant eel struck and on the light tackle, gave a tremendous fight. The eel unfortunately died and is at present on display in the bailiff's hut at Kingfisher Lake. A replica is on display at Nimrod tackle shop, Bournemouth.

Two former record fish of 8 lb 8 oz and 8 lb 10 oz are both on display at Veal's tackle shop in Bristol. Another great eel of 8 lb 10 oz, caught by

John Harrison in July 1983, is on display at Tom Haynes' tackle shop, Stafford.

A big eel which did not make the historical record list was one of 9 lb 8 oz reported from the Grand Union Canal in 1969. It was almost accepted as a record but Dr Terry Coulson, then chairman of the National Anguilla Club, intervened. He discovered the freshwater eel was actually a small conger (these grow to well over 100 lb).

Many waters hold eels which are possibly big enough to smash the record. Double-figure eels turn up from time to time, unfortunately not for serious anglers, so the facts are lost to posterity. More big eels are being caught each year. Looking at the 'Top 50 big eel list' published by *Coarse Angler* magazine, we can see this pattern for eels over 7 lb 1 oz:

Before 1950	4
1951–60	5
1961–70	8
1971–80	26
1981–83	8 (4 in 1983).

There are now many specialist anglers actively fishing for big eels, and they are being more successful as relevant information becomes available.

Tackle for eels is relatively simple. It is best kept so; the use of complicated rigs can be disastrous. Any reasonable carp or pike rod of 10 to 12 feet long and 2 to $2\frac{1}{2}$ lb test curve will do. The action required of the rod – slow, medium, fast or ultra-fast taper – will depend on the water fished, the bait to be used, and the distance to be cast. Soft baits need soft action rods, hard baits can be used with faster rods. Lines should range from about 6 to 11 lb bs, again depending on the rod, water, bait, and distance. I have a selection of rods and spools of line to attempt to cover all variables. I use Mitchell 300s, but almost any similar reel can do the job. Avoid plastic geared models, for eels can put terrific pressure on the reel and the plastic gears will collapse under the strain.

Typical eel rig terminal arrangements can be a simple running leger or link-leger, as illustrated. Variations can include stick legers and swim feeders or extended link legers. Surface float rigs can be used in styles similar to pike fishing, but using much smaller baits. Swimfeeders can be filled with a large assortment of items – chopped worms, maggots, casters, cat or dog food, cotton wool soaked in any liquid attractant/appetite stimulator as sold by specialist bait dealers, or any possible filler the angler can have available, remembering that eels in general hunt by scent or taste.

Hook sizes can be between 1 and 8, depending on bait type and size. I use Partridge extra-strong hooks and Jack Hilton carp hooks, which have not yet let me down provided they are kept sharp and are discarded at any sign of rust or damage. I generally use braided multi-strand wire (not the nylon covered type) for hook traces, but 10 lb line can be used with instant striking, when eels should be lip hooked.

Eels tend to give steady to fast runs and should be struck as soon as possible by closing the bail arm, pointing the rod towards the eel, and gently retrieving the line until a firm pull is felt. The rod is brought steadily upwards in a firm strike. Keep pressure on the eel at all times, but not too much. Wind down, bringing the rod to an angle of about 45 degrees to the eel and carefully and gently pull the rod up to about 85 degrees. Keep up this continual winding down and pumping up action without straining the tackle too much, and the eel should be brought to the net completely under control. If you are unable to pump or wind down,

continue to keep a steady pressure with the rod about 60 to 70 degrees, allowing the rod action to bring the eel to the surface.

A large triangular, micromesh landing net should be used. It needs to be sunk well under the incoming eel which is drawn right over the net until its tail is past the stretcher cord. Raise the back of the net slightly and allow the eel to swim backwards into it. Lift the net so that the arms are above water, then grip it, lifting it well away from the water. Try to unhook the eel while it is still in the net, using long artery forceps and a large cloth to hold the eel. If you cannot see the hook, cut the trace as near to the eel's mouth as possible.

Eels of 2 to 3 lb should be returned to the water at once. They do not like light and may suffer if kept too long. Single large eels can be kept in a large black carp sack. If they must be kept for photographing, use a small-mesh keep net. Do not leave them in a sunny spot or they will quickly die. If you

It's a long way from the Sargasso Sea to a landing net in Nottingham!

must take eels home to eat, take only those well under 2 lb or those which are obviously damaged.

Photographing a big eel is the most difficult and frustrating experience of all. I confirmed this when I took photographs of a friend's magnificent eel of 5 lb 15 oz caught in May 1984 in a Lincolnshire gravel pit. I told my friend, David Taylor, to take the eel out of the carp sack where it was put at 10 pm during the all-night session. It had been in the sack for six hours and was fully recovered, very strong and lively. We placed the eel on its back, supported by the carp sack, for five minutes or so to quieten it down while David took its measurements of length and girth and I prepared our cameras and decided on a suitable background for the photograph. It is best to have water, trees, or bushes framing the subject, not a car, bike, or untidy tackle.

When all was ready, Dave held the eel in a variety of positions while I took about 24 pictures. Sometimes Dave was in charge of the eel and sometimes the eel took charge of Dave. The final couple of shots showed the eel being released and swimming away very strongly. Eels can and do survive being kept out of water for longer than other fish, but do return them as soon as you can. If there are problems, return the eel to the net for a while and do not grip it harder than you need to or you may rupture an internal organ.

There is no greater moment for the dedicated eel angler than to see a superb eel swimming away, with snake-like action, back into the depths — perhaps to be re-captured by some other lucky angler, or to swim free and migrate back down river to the sea, thence to its birthplace to spawn and die.

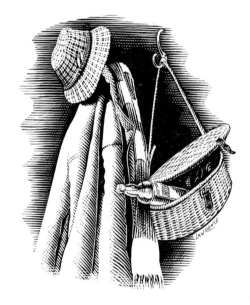

Zander

Neville Fickling

I WONDER IF the 9th Duke of Bedford ever imagined that the 23 zander stocked into his lakes at Woburn would become the nucleus for a large and ever growing population of these predatory fish. The aliens, then known as pikeperch, arrived in January 1878 after a long sea journey from Bothkamper Lake in Schleswig-Holstein. Further introductions in 1910 aided the establishment of the zander, and over the years additional waters received a stock of these fish.

By the early sixties zander were still limited to waters in the Bedfordshire and Buckinghamshire area. This all changed in 1960 when Norman Mackenzie, then Fisheries Officer for the Great Ouse River Board, authorised the transfer of mature zander to the Board's stockponds at Hengrave Hall, Bury St Edmunds, in Suffolk. There they spawned and in March of 1963 100 small zander of around one and two years of age were netted and taken to the Great Ouse Relief Channel at Stow Bridge. There 97 were released, three having failed to survive the journey. For several years little was heard of these fish, but one was caught in 1965. In 1966 it became evident that the zander had spawned with great success as anglers started to catch numbers of around 1 lb to 1 lb 8 oz. The zander started a steady and somewhat controversial march through the Fens of East Anglia and beyond.

For those who were involved, 1968 to 1977 was the decade of the zander, and we will never forget it. In 1968 Woburn claimed the record with an 8 lb 8¼ oz fish. It was topped the following month with a 9-pounder from the Relief Channel, and reclaimed by Woburn in September with a 9 lb 2 oz fish. Then came the first double-figure zander,

10 lb 4 oz from the Relief Channel in November 1968.

From then on Woburn was right out of the picture and the Relief Channel really took off. Between November 1969 and February 1971 the record was topped five times, with me in the act twice. Bill Chillingworth had the best fish in that spell, at 15 lb 5 oz, but it was more than 5½ years before somebody caught one bigger. It weighed 16 lb 6 oz, and although not claimed as a record it was widely accepted as genuine. It came from the nearby Cut-off Channel, and was not topped until Dave Litton had a 17 lb 12 oz fish from the Relief Channel in October 1977. That fish still reigns supreme. It took a strip of bream, legered in 13 foot of water, and in classic zander style it was taken at dusk.

Throughout this period and ever since there have been many other zander in double figures, but since 1978 nobody has topped 14 lb. The big fish boom ended because the two key waters, the Relief Channel and Cut-off Channel, went into decline. The big zander ran out of prey fish, and either died or lost weight. No other water has yet proved rich enough to stage a repeat of that glorious era, and we may not see it for a number of years. For the moment what seems to be happening is the steady establishment of the zander way beyond the original points of introduction.

Today they are to be found in many waters in England. The fenland fisheries remain the focus of attention, but many other waters are now attracting interest. If you wish to catch a zander however, the Fens are probably the best bet, particularly the drains of the Middle Level system – the Middle Level itself, Sixteen Foot, Forty Foot, Twenty Foot, and Bevills Leam. The zander in these waters have been subjected to a lot of persecution, but it is still possible to catch fish in excess of 10 lb, if you are

lucky. The original zander water, the Relief Channel, has continued to decline and is now fairly unproductive as regards zander, but it will no doubt return to something of its former glory in time. The same can be said for much of the Great Ouse river, though the middle reaches around Huntingdon are still worth considering.

If you live in Suffolk or Essex, you will find zander in the river Stour and Abberton reservoir. They arrived in these waters through a water supply pipeline, such is the invasive ability of this fish. At present little is heard of these zander, but Abberton reservoir will soon become a favoured venue, producing some giant fish in the next decade.

In Surrey you can fish Old Bury lake for zander. The fishery manager introduced them, and has been fairly pleased with the result. One or two other

Close up of a zander from Old Bury lake in Surrey

waters in the London area also have zander, mainly because of illegal introductions.

One of the biggest concentrations of zander in the Midlands is to be found in and around Coventry. Coombe Abbey lake has already produced fish to 13 lb and has a healthy stock of zander averaging around 4 lb. The nearby Coventry and Oxford Canal also has them, though they do not grow so big. Both populations are the result of illegal introductions, as are the zander now found in the Leicester area, river Severn and river Nene.

Despite the restrictions placed on the movement of zander, it appears that little can be done to halt their spread. This prospect is met with cries of terror from match and club anglers, concern from pike anglers, and glee from zander specialists. Whether or not any of these emotions are justified remains to be seen.

The biology of the zander helps us to understand why this introduced alien is feared by many anglers. It is the largest member of the perch family, a native of Eastern Europe and the USSR, but now common throughout Europe where it is very much appreciated as a sportfish and for its eating qualities. The zander also has a relative in America, the walleye, which is extremely popular.

One look at the zander's head tells the observer that this fish is a predator. It specialises in the capture of small fish which it seizes with its stabbing teeth and swallows tail first. Its specialised eye, which enables it to see well at night or in coloured water, gives it a distinctive glass-eye appearance.

In this country zander grow up to 17 lb 2 oz. In Europe fish of this size are caught regularly and some grow as big as 25 lb. Thirty-pounders have been noted.

Angling experience has shown that zander are shoal fish and it is usual to catch several once one has been caught. Sizes of the fish in a shoal can vary, but generally they will be similar. Bigger fish do turn up with smaller ones, though many captures of really big fish have been solitary achievements.

The size of a zander pack varies from water to water. Some are very large; I have caught as many as 26 fish from one such shoal in a 50 yard section of drain. Finding these packs is the main problem facing the zander angler. Most drain and stillwater fisheries which are good zander waters tend to have more than 6 feet of water and are rather featureless. Finding concentrations of fry and slightly larger fish is a good bet, if these potential food fish are resident for more than a couple of weeks. Even

then, the zander cannot be relied on to be right in the middle of the food fish concentration. However, somewhere in the area will be a holding spot, where the zander spend much of their time in between feeding forays.

It pays to fish a number of different swims, until the holding spot is located. This involves trying different areas each session, and working around or along the fishery during a session. A big pack of zander will nearly always have a few individuals which will be willing to feed. Once a fish has been taken, a more concentrated effort may yield further fish.

Zander can be very easy to catch on some waters and very difficult on others. Almost the only reason for this is availability of natural food. Waters where prey fish are hard to come by are the easy ones from which to take zander of all sizes.

Shortage of prey fish is usually caused by poor spawning success among the roach and bream population in the water. The zander run out of food and fall much more readily to angling methods. On the other hand, where prey fish are numerous, zander can be very difficult to catch, requiring as much application and care as any other fish species living in a food-rich environment. If you pick the hungry waters you will catch plenty of zander, but for a really big one you should head for a water which has plenty of food fish.

Fishing for zander does not require specialised fishing tackle, but to enjoy the sport to the full it is better to fish with balanced gear. I would choose 11 foot carbon or glass fibre rods of around $1\frac{1}{2}$ lb test curve. These should be of slow to medium fast taper and capable of casting leads and baits with a combined weight of 2 oz. For heavier leads and baits a 2 lb test rod would be better. A good fixed spool reel loaded with 150 yards of 10 lb line would complete the basic equipment.

Hooks are usually size 10 or 8 Partridge outbend trebles, the semi-barbless variety, mounted on an 18 inch 10 to 15 lb braided wire trace. Fig 1 shows the basic arrangement I prefer. For bite indication I use a couple of electronic bite indicators, the Optonic and the MM1, an indicator which uses a mercury switch to activate a buzzer. These are very useful for a long session, and help to make it a relaxed form of fishing.

Fish baits are the norm for zander fishing, though artificial lures have limited uses. The lures I have found to be most useful for zander are $\frac{3}{8}$ oz Toby spoons and a variety of revolving blade spin-

Fig. 1   **Basic zander end tackle**

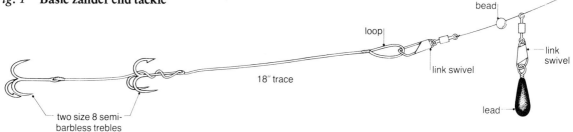

two size 8 semi-barbless trebles | 18″ trace | loop | link swivel | bead | link swivel | lead

ners. All must be worked along the bed of the swim, as slowly as possible. I have also taken a few zander on wobbled deadbaits fished in a similar manner. A good method for small roach is a tandem treble hook rig so that the fish is bent and revolved slowly.

Live and deadbaits are, however, the premier method for zander. My preference is for deadbaits as these are very effective and much easier to obtain (from the freezer) and transport. Almost any small fresh fish will take a zander, though for some reason sea fish baits such as herrings, sprats, and mackerel are generally ineffective. I say 'generally' because there have been odd periods when big zan-

der in particular have had a mad fling, taking herrings and half mackerel in preference to other baits. Smelts are quite a good bait, though they tend to go off quickly in warm weather.

If I had a choice of baits I think I would select small dace and chub. These are a nice slim shape, and zander can deal with them easily. Usually I end up fishing with rudd and roach, because of the difficulty in getting other fish. I prefer fresh baits as they are firmer and cast better, although frozen baits have taken many zander. The ideal bait size is about 4 inches, though larger baits can be cut in half and used as head and tail half baits.

Eel section looks unlikely, but is a very effec-

Fig. 2   **Basic sliding paternoster fished sunken**

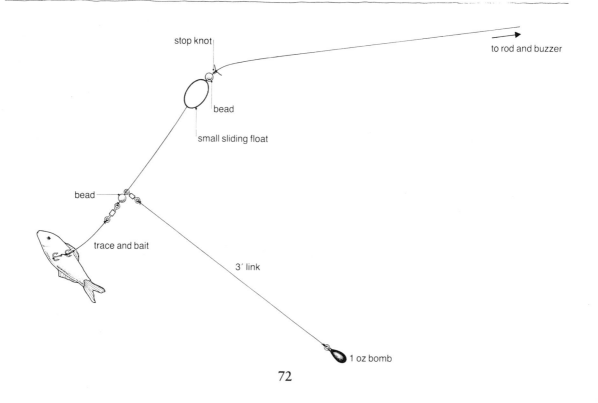

stop knot | to rod and buzzer | bead | small sliding float | bead | trace and bait | 3′ link | 1 oz bomb

tive zander bait. I have lost count of the zander to over 12 lb which I have taken this way. All you need is one 12 inch eel and there you have three baits. The eel's tough skin means that each bait usually comes back each time, so several zander can be caught on one bait. Some pike anglers take the eel section home after a days fishing and use it again. I do not need to do this, because eels are easy to obtain in the summer.

An eel section can be mounted on a large single hook by threading under the skin with a baiting needle or in the usual manner with two trebles. Deadbaits are invariably fished on the bottom, and a running lead employed to provide casting weight. Most situations require $\frac{1}{2}$ to 1 oz of lead, although when a river or drain is in flood as much as 2 oz could be used. The lead is attached to the main line by a link swivel, enabling a quick change in lead to be effected without breaking the line. Sometimes float legering is used. Here a small sliding float is set overdepth with two or three swan shot just above the trace to hold the bait in position.

Most livebaiting uses the float paternoster rig. I prefer chub and crucian carp for this style of fishing as they do not tangle things up in warm weather. The sunken paternoster shown in fig 2 is a favourite of mine. Once again the electronic bite indicator is used to give instant warning of a run. Sometimes a legered livebait can be very productive; this is fished in the same manner as the deadbait.

Usually two rods are used for zander fishing. This enables the angler to fish a live and a deadbait in the same swim. On some days deadbait is preferred; on others livebait produces most of the action.

Weather and time of day have a big influence on success. There are no set weather conditions which produce the fish on all waters. Similarly, the best time of day varies from water to water and from month to month. Most zander fishing is done in the autumn, particularly September and October. This is the ideal period for quantities of zander, with the prospect of a big one thrown in. Of course it is possible to make good catches at other times; June and March are also favourite times of mine.

On most waters the dawn and dusk period sees zander hunting for food, and it is important not to miss this spell. You must be on the water before dawn and fish into the dark. Often a number of runs will come very quickly, and that is your lot. On

Returning a zander catch to a Cambridgeshire drain

73

A brace of zander to 8 lb

some waters a bright sunny day and clear water will see brief periods of sport, but the angler must fish efficiently to catch any number of fish. I like to have a couple of spare rods set up so that I can be back in action immediately after a catch.

A dull, overcast day with strong winds can cause the zander to feed much longer on some waters. Sometimes, when conditions seem all wrong – flat, calm, hot, sunny days being one example – zander feed all day. These fish are not hunting, but resident in large numbers in one particular swim. If you drop on to this pack of zander and it is willing to feed, a memorable day is possible.

It is worth fishing for zander at night on some waters, but you really have to fish them first to find this out. There is no way that I know to predict whether zander will feed at night on any particular water. I have taken several double-figure fish at night and have found that the period around 1 am is a good time to expect a run. Night caught zander are generally less numerous, but tend to be of a good average size. With buzzers it is possible to sleep, yet be ready to strike the fish before it has gone more than 10 yards.

If you happen to arrive at a river or drain and find that it is in flood, do not despair. In these conditions your chances are increased tenfold. Zander can be caught at all times of the day in these conditions, for dirty water encourages them to hunt far and wide for food. The problem with floodwater conditions is keeping a bait out in the water and avoiding all the debris which is washed down with the current.

The best method in these conditions is to fish very close in with as much of the line out of the water as possible. You need only have the bait in more than 6 feet of water under the rod tip to stand a good chance. Even with these tactics you will need to make regular checks on the bait to make sure that

74

Fig. 3   **Possible zander swims on a fen drain**

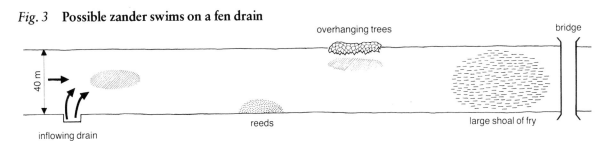

overhanging trees

bridge

40 m

inflowing drain

reeds

large shoal of fry

Hatched areas are typical holding areas where zander may spend much of their time. When hunting actively they can turn up anywhere.

weed and debris have not covered the bait and line. If you can fish in a flood in any month, but particularly in March, your chance of a big zander is quite good.

The actual take of a zander when it picks up a bait is quite positive, with the line running from the open reel spool at a fair speed. With two trebles and a small bait, the strike can be effected as soon as you reach the rod. There are frustrating days when zander drop the bait. The only cure for this is to reduce the bait size and strike even sooner.

Zander can be very sensitive to resistance, particularly when there is plenty of natural food about. Hungry ones are usually less discerning and seldom drop the bait. The fish do not fight in a spectacular manner, but do put up a solid dogged resistance. The aim is to land them as quickly as possible as they can completely exhaust themselves in a long struggle.

I like to put nearly all my zander back alive, mainly because too many people are killing them indiscriminately. Small ones up to 5 lb make very

good eating, and when they are numerous I will take one. However, I have little time for anyone who kills big zander.

To put them back alive, I net my fish on landing and pick them up under the chin. Hooks are removed using forceps and the fish weighed in a sling immediately. If I want a photograph I give the fish a breather in the landing net for five minutes while the camera is set up. Then it is back to the water and held until ready to swim off strongly. Generally, the warmer the water, the quicker you have to be.

For me, the magic of zander fishing is typified by a summer's evening as the sun sets over the flat fenland horizon. The small fish are flipping casually on the surface and the surface of the water gets darker by the minute. Sometimes a run comes, sometimes it does not. The expectancy is very much a part of the enjoyment. This is only exceeded by the thumping of a weighty fish as darkness falls, and the bent rod silhouetted against the starlit sky . . .

Chub

Dave Plummer

Chub is without doubt one of our most popular fish. Your idea of chub fishing might be a hectic day on the Trent or the Derbyshire Derwent, filling your net with half a hundredweight of 1 to 3 lb chub in a match. Another angler would be more interested in getting a bait to a particularly large and wary fish resting under an overhanging willow tree. Then again, the reader might enjoy both aspects of chub fishing.

My own interest is the pursuit and capture of the larger specimens. By 'large' I mean fish over 4 lb. A 4-pounder is a specimen chub and only a few waters hold large numbers of fish of this size. Five-pounders are rare enough to require a lot of effort, and fish of 6 lb and more are very rare indeed.

This was not always the case. In the past hundred years quite a few chub of 6, 7, and even 8 lb have been reported. Some are unlikely to have been genuine, though a few are indisputable. The reduced number of big fish must be attributable to the overall decline of many of our rivers, since angling ability has never been higher. Abstraction and land drainage work have served to make the environment less favourable for chub.

To grow big they need a regular supply of good food and plenty of cover. Chub, perhaps more than any other fish, enjoy cover, be it an overhanging tree, undercut bank, or bridge arch. Much of this vital cover has been lost on many fisheries, and the poorer water quality caused by trout farming and various other forms of pollution have served to prevent chub from growing to monster sizes.

Weed cutting is thought to have increased infestations of parasitic worms which live attached to the gut of the chub, reducing their ability to grow. Yet all is not lost, for chub seem to have adapted to a life in stillwaters. A few unpublicised gravel pits in the Oxford and Gloucester areas contain some very big chub. As time goes on, more of these waters will be stocked, increasing the chances of a 7 lb chub.

Meanwhile, most of us have to set our sights lower. For most anglers catching a chub of more than 4 lb will involve a trip to one of the known big chub rivers. The most northerly chances of a big chub are offered by the border rivers such as the Annan. Several of the rivers in that area have produced fish of more than 4 lb, with the occasional 5-pounder. In Yorkshire, nearly all of the rivers have produced big chub, but only two offer a realistic chance of the exceptional – the Derwent and lower Ure/Ouse.

Both these large, deep rivers have numbers of 4-pounders, but in my experience a 5-pounder is almost impossible. Near Hull is the river Hull itself, a difficult water, but one which has produced some very big fish. Whether it is still capable of producing a 5-pounder I am not sure, but reports suggest that any chub is an achievement at the moment. The nearby Barmston drain was polluted a few years ago and is probably no longer worth considering.

Down in Lincolnshire, the upper Witham and Welland are certainly capable of producing 4-pounders, but again periodic pollutions have not helped matters. In the Midlands, the rivers Eye and Leam are good prospects. The Trent itself does not, at the moment, seem to be a big chub water, though weighed 4-pounders and occasional 5-pounders do get caught, especially in the tidal section. The problem is sorting the big ones from the small.

The same goes for the Severn and its tributaries. The nearby Wye is said to have specimen chub potential, though little is known about it. Restrictions placed on angling by salmon fishing interests tend to make the capture of big chub difficult.

Skipping across country we come to Norfolk, at present the base of my chub fishing operations. Number one in the Norfolk big chub stakes must be the river Wensum. Here 4-pounders are fairly common and a 5-pounder is a realistic possibility. The river Waveney, too, in its upper reaches has produced some good fish. Little is heard these days of the river Wissey so it is perhaps no longer a big chub river. The little river Nar near King's Lynn has one or two good chub, but finding them is extremely difficult.

The Thames is a very good chub river, though it takes a long time to get to know the right areas to fish. The middle and upper Thames can certainly produce 4- and even 5-pounders. Its tributary, the Cherwell, is an excellent chub water and well worth a visit. Down towards the very south of the country are perhaps the two most famous chub rivers. The Hampshire Avon, though nothing like the river of the past, still has some nice fish, and the Dorset Stour is still good for numbers of 4-pounders.

Before fishing, it pays to get to know your river. Walk the banks in the spring and try spotting big chub. They may later disperse and return to their normal haunts, but weedy areas of gravel will attract chub at spawning time towards the end of May. Chub can be caught throughout the fishing season, in almost any type of water conditions. Few fish species are so responsive.

Chub fishing in winter and summer needs a mobile approach, so the angler should try to avoid being hampered by large amounts of fishing tackle. One rod only is required. I favour an 11 foot Avon type of about $1\frac{1}{4}$ lb test curve with a nice through action. Carbon rods are more pleasant to use and mine has a really sensitive tip, with a screw-in attachment should I wish to use a quiver tip. I also use a lighter rod of 11 feet 3 inches with built in quiver tip.

Any good fixed spool reel can be used, but it must have a finely calibrated clutch. There are many good reels with stern drag mountings which allow easy adjustment of the clutch. Lines are around 4 to 6 lb depending on the swims being fished. Fairly open water allows the use of the lighter line while snags will require the extra strength of the 6 lb line.

Hooks are large, as befits the size of the chub's mouth; a size 6 is about standard. The only other items required are a landing net, container with shot, spare hooks, forceps, scales, weighing bag, and camera. With a few tins of bait, you are ready to go.

Choice of baits is wide, but usually only a few are required. Bread crust or flake is a superb bait, and I always carry it. Lobworms, slugs, and crayfish are also used regularly. A variety of paste baits are worth using, my choice being a cheesepaste or one of the Richworth range developed specially for fish such as chub. The match angler will place much

Mouthful for a chub

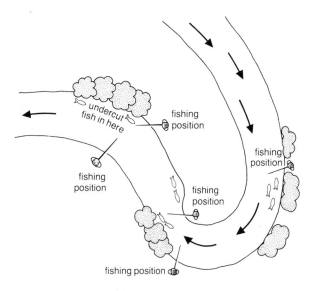

Likely locations for chub

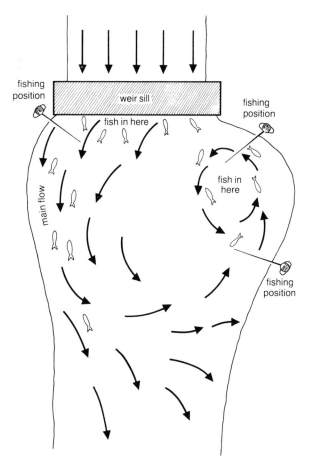

greater emphasis on small baits such as caster, maggot, and wasp grub, though there are times when trotting these baits under a float will also account for some big chub.

Basic chub fishing methods are very simple. The most common tactic is to leger baits such as bread flake and crust with a couple of swan shot pinched directly on to the line or with a link leger with swan shot or a $\frac{1}{4}$ to $1\frac{1}{2}$oz bomb. The heavier weights may be required when fishing mid-river on some of the faster waters.

The rod tip is set at right angles to the line as it enters the water and the tip watched. Chub will usually make a few initial plucks before belting the rod tip round. It is these, not the plucks, that you strike at. Sometimes chub will rise to free offerings of floating crust. Then it is a simple case of freelining a bait to those fish, using a piece of crust dunked in the water to add to the casting weight.

By far the most exciting form of chub fishing is stalking them in the summer. When the water is clear and the weed growth heavy, chub can be spotted and cast to. Common locations include overhanging trees and the associated rafts which build up under them, fences which stand out into the river, undercut banks, extensive weedbeds, and slack areas just off of the main flow in a weirpool. The secret of catching these fish is getting near enough to cast a bait without scaring the chub. Do this and your chances of catching are good.

Sometimes you have to be selective. Big chub often live with numbers of lesser fish, so you have to remove the little ones without putting the big ones off. Several dodges can be employed, the best being to bait up with mashed bread, just upstream of the chub shoal. The smaller fish are invariably the first to leave their sheltered swim, leaving the bigger and more cautious fish for you to try to catch. If a smaller fish should appear in the swim just as you get a bait to the big one, you must try and pull the bait away from the little one. It is surprising how well this works sometimes.

Once one fish has been extracted from a swim, you must decide whether or not it is worth trying again. Sometimes it is better to put some more mashed bread into the swim and move to another spot. I generally have several swims baited in this manner, allowing me to move from each primed

A nice catch from the Aire, a fast improving chub river

78

swim to the next in the hope of creaming off the better fish each time.

When an individual large fish is spotted it is often possible to drop a natural bait such as a slug or a crayfish nearby and to evoke an instant response. At other times you will not see the chub as they are well hidden in dense beds of streamer weed and reeds. In this situation crusts drifted down through the swim might draw them up on to the surface. A freelined hookbait can then follow the free offerings down to the waiting chub.

As you get to know your particular river you will find that certain areas produce few fish but generally larger than average. These areas are best fished at the peak times for chub activity, before and just into darkness. I like to try the big fish swim last of all. Here the presence of only a few big fish reduces your chances of a bite during the day. As dusk falls, prospects improve; this is a good reason to move into the swim and sit and wait.

I suppose that the magic of summer chub fishing is the unspoiled countryside to be found around rivers which hold big fish. Crowds are unlikely, for the majority of good chub waters are not the easily

Chub sometimes fall to small plugs

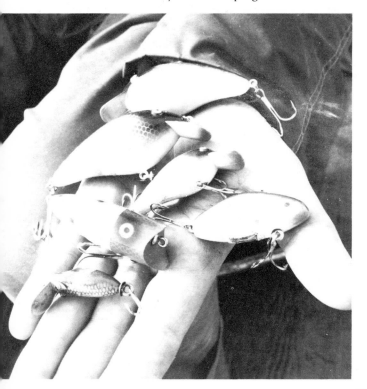

accessible waters most anglers favour. Another attraction is that the angler has to become the hunter, rather than merely a trapper who sits and waits for the fish to come to him.

Winter is probably the best time for catching a big chub. They tend to be a bit flabby and out of condition during the summer and cannot be expected to weigh their heaviest at this time. In winter they have recovered from spawning and are starting to prepare for the following spring. They are deep bodied and firm. Few weather conditions rule out the capture of chub in winter. The only one I avoid is when the river is full of snow water. Then the water is coloured and cold; it contains salt and a variety of debris washed from the land and roads. Ideal conditions are when the river has started to drop after a flood.

If the weather is mild so much the better, but the key is the state of the river. When the water has a bottle green tinge, there is a good chance of many chub bites. Fishing during the winter is not as selective as it can be during the summer, but this is compensated for by the likelihood of more fish from certain swims, for chub tend to congregate in larger numbers during the winter.

Baits like flake, crust, or soft pastes are again the standard. A number of swims are pre-baited during the winter. Those which produce the fish are often near to the summer areas. Again, rafts and any form of cover may hold chub. Snags in the larger deeper rivers can produce numbers of chub, but you will need to use a fair amount of lead to hold out in rivers such as the Yorkshire Ouse.

Other swims, such as the long steady glide, are less obvious. These initially featureless swims can be tackled by searching them out, working along them, or simply putting in mashed bread and drawing the chub up to your fishing position. Deep, featureless glides are not usually the most productive chub swims, but they can turn up the occasional good fish. By getting to know the river in winter, you should soon be able to read the water and predict where the chub are likely to be. By watching the current, you can locate the chub-holding slacks.

Though it is good sense to fish for chub long and hard when the river is dropping from flood conditions, such opportunities do not come every week. Chub will oblige in far from ideal conditions, provided certain weather patterns have prevailed for several days. A very cold spell will see the chub adjust to lower water temperatures. The chub will not be as keen while the temperature drops, but some good sport can be had when it has stabilised. The water may well be low and clear, but chub will respond despite this. My best chub, a fish of 5 lb 10 oz came on a day when ice floes were floating down the river.

For some reason, the very biggest chub will sometimes feed in the worst conditions, and here the angler's approach must obviously be a little more refined. Free offerings or mashed bread groundbait have to be reduced, otherwise the chub will be overfed. Paste baits, such as cheesepaste, have to be made softer, otherwise the cold water makes them too hard, preventing good hook penetration. Bites will not be numerous in these conditions, so you must be on the ball and hit each one. The opposite condition to low water − a river in flood − makes for difficult fishing, but there will always be a few slacks, many of which are usually dry river bank. Here the chub will be holding station with the minimum of effort and can again be caught, provided the amount of debris on the move does not prevent a satisfactory bait presentation.

Stillwater chub behave differently and become very difficult to catch. Some stillwaters contain fish of upwards of 7 lb, most of which have become predatory. The biggest stillwater chub have been caught on deadbaits initially intended for pike, and a few keen chub anglers have set about catching big chub on deadbaits, mainly at night during the winter; sardines have proved a popular bait. Such fishing is very slow indeed. Other stillwaters contain more chub of smaller sizes, and these can respond to a stalking approach. Casting freelined flake or small deadbait such as minnows or bleak in the path of patrolling fish is probably the best method here. In many ways this type of fishing is similar to river fishing, with the constant need for stealth.

Though stillwater chub are not common, there seems to be a general increase in the numbers of pits which have them. There is some evidence that chub can breed in these waters, so such populations may be self sustaining. In the future the already considerable variety to be enjoyed in chub fishing is likely to be increased. At the moment, though, the going is hard, and the chances of beating records are slim.

The two record fish lists have two different fish at the top. The reason for the difference is that the BRFC rules insist on seeing and weighing the fish. The National Association of Specialist Anglers, will in some circumstances accept the evidence of photographs, preserved remains, and the testimony of known, reliable witnesses.

The NASA record chub is an enormous specimen of 8 lb 4 oz caught by G F Smith from the Hampshire Avon's Royalty fishery in 1913. The glass-cased fish is in the study of London journalist Gerry Hughes, and at a length of 25 inches there could be little doubt of its immense weight. All the evidence suggests that the fish was caught on rod and line and was of the claimed weight. NASA's Record Fish Committee therefore accepted the fish. The British Record Rod Caught Fish Committee does not, however, recognise the NASA fish. Its record is another Avon fish of 7 lb 6 oz taken by Bill Warren in 1957.

There have certainly been many bigger chub than 7 lb 6 oz, but the list of big chub contains many dubious fish. This continues to be the problem facing those who would attempt to record chub fishing history. None of the double-figure chub on record can be substantiated, even those caught recently. The 10 lb 8 oz Annan fish caught by Dr Cameron in 1955 was for a considerable time the BRFC record, but eventually this fish and several others were thrown out. The story goes that Dr Cameron's fish was eaten by his cat. Was it a big cat or a small lion?

Grayling
Colin Dyson

BEAUTY, OF COURSE, is in the eye of the beholder, and in any group of anglers at least one would advocate the charms of the grayling. Certainly it is a most handsome fish, with the long dorsal fin waving over mailed flanks, the accusing eye, and the uniquely shaped mouth. There are probably more mysteries about the grayling than about any other freshwater fish. The present record of 2 lb 13 oz bears no relation to what has been caught in the past, though at least one legendary monster, which held the record for some time, was unlikely to have been a grayling.

There are many instances of rivers holding far larger grayling than ever were caught, and on one memorable occasion I saw one myself. For a couple of years I had a permit for the Hartington section of Derbyshire's delightful river Dove. We fly-fished where we could and bait-fished where it was too overgrown to cast. I was fishing one day with Paul Cobbold, now a tackle dealer in Sheffield, and made the fundamental mistake of telling him of one swim where I had 'never failed to catch a trout'. On this occasion, of course, I did fail. The bait was ignored, and I climbed an overhanging tree to see if any trout were present.

There was one, swimming with a small shoal of big grayling – five of them, if memory serves me right – and the biggest was gigantic. It had to be 4 lb, and one of the others looked 3 lb plus. Paul and I were due home for Sunday lunch, but it was 5 pm when we remembered. We spent the whole day up that tree, gazing in awe at the grayling directly below in a crystal clear water, so shallow that the dorsals of the two bigger fish were breaking surface. The Dove had a reputation among other syn-dicate members for producing the odd big grayling (2 lb plus) when it was up and coloured, but these fish were the only ones I ever saw.

We tried to catch them, of course. I fed loose maggots, only to see the fish move to one side and allow them to trundle past. If they would not take free offerings there was little chance of them having one with a hook attached, but it did not stop us trying. We fed and fished worms, and bits of worms, with the same results. I even tried dangling artificial flies and nymphs, and naturals grubbed from the river bed some distance downstream. They were immune to everything except, perhaps, one of us dropping from the tree and grabbing one. I was tempted to try that, stationing Paul at the head of the pool with a net in the hope that one would bolt straight in.

Weighing even the smallest would have been an interesting exercise, to say the least. We have only our estimates – and disbelieving looks from

Netting a grayling from the river Wharfe, near Kilnsey, Yorks

our friends. Yet there have been others telling similar tales. The late and much respected Yorkshire angling writer, T K Wilson, spoke of 5 to 6 lb grayling among spawning shoals in the river Aire. They disappeared after spawning, never to be seen again until the same time the following year. Grayling actually caught in the Aire rarely reached half the size of Wilson's top estimate.

Wilson's sightings on that river helped to convince him that the 7 lb 2 oz grayling caught by Dr Jock Stewart in Scotland's river Melgum in July 1949 might have been genuine. He had seen a very bad box camera photograph of the fish, which he said looked every ounce of the claimed weight. Later experts were to disagree, not so much about the weight but about the species. My late colleague and co-editor of *Coarse Angler* magazine, Colin Graham, got hold of a copy of the old photograph, and we published it. The fish looked nothing like a grayling, and Colin found two experts who believed it was a late salmon kelt. The conclusion of an interested party who had interviewed Dr Stewart before he died was that he had made a mistake. He was not the sort of person who would deliberately deceive. It is interesting to note that the Melgum is a tributary of the Isla, which has produced big grayling. When the 7 lb 2 oz fish was dropped from the record list in 1968 the record was declared open for claims.

Years later a salmon-fishing friend caught a grayling over 3 lb from the Isla, deep-froze it, and brought it back to Sheffield. He did not know he had a record fish, nor did he much care. It was *not* as big as the one we had seen in the Dove. I planned to go and fish the Isla, but before I went I was told that the river had been poisoned to get rid of 'unwanted' species. What a tragedy, if that was so.

Many people have caught record grayling without knowing it. Somebody rang me last year to report a 3½-pounder from Yorkshire's Rye, but he had already eaten it. Record-breakers have been stocked into the Driffield canal, in Yorkshire. Agonisingly for the grayling purists, several over the record mark have been caught in Lymmvale, a remarkable stillwater fishery developed by the go-ahead Cheshire club, Lymm AC. Lymmvale has produced record orfe as well, and it is believed to hold tench into double figures. The idea of an upland stream fish growing to such great proportions in a lake is hard to accept. It is even harder

A splendid bag of top quality grayling

Typical grayling from a southern river

to believe that they also breed there, but the club insists its members have caught smaller grayling than have ever been stocked.

That is a mystery for the biologists to unravel, but the fact of Lymmvale's big grayling, and the umpteen other tales of fish of more than 3 lb, make it easier to believe in some of the 4 lb and bigger fish taken from southern chalk streams late last century and early this century. Dr Sanctuary's 4½-pounder from the Wylye was the record until the Melgum fish came along, and it is reasonable to assume it was genuine. The southern streams are fine fisheries today, but how much better were they before we invented agricultural pollution and other environmental disasters? After the 1968 purge none of these old fish were reconsidered by the Record Committee. Dead men could not come back and obey the new rules. It was like disbelieving the result of the Battle of Hastings because William the Conqueror could not return and make a claim; so said the great Richard Walker, pithily accurate as usual. Although we know 3-pounders are still possible we must accept a much lower norm. A 2 lb grayling is a very good fish, and on most of the grayling waters I fish I am grateful to catch them over 1 lb.

Water authority area summaries indicate the complete distribution of the species, but apart from the southern chalk streams, the key areas for good fish are Wales, Yorkshire, Derbyshire, and the border rivers of Scotland. If you disregard the embarrassment of Lymmvale, they are creatures of clean, pacey water. They will happily share the environment of other coarse fish in the middle reaches of the rivers they inhabit, but the fishing is best higher up, where they have only trout for company.

Grayling fall to all the basic methods – float fishing, legering, and fly fishing – and are none too difficult with any of them. Legering I like the least, for they bite with such enthusiasm they are likely to take a legered bait too deep. Some days, however, legering is the only way to get a bite, though I have never really worked out why.

Normally the grayling is a free and fearless feeder, and on northern rivers I have often caught them within feet of my waders. Favourite swims are where fast shallows suddenly drop into deeper pools, the crease between fast water and an eddy, and long, steady glides. Long trotting with maggot, redworm, or gilt-tail worms was the method about which I read most before I fished for grayling myself, and it always seemed to be done in the depths of winter, with snow on the banks or the ground bone hard with frost. I came to learn that grayling can indeed be caught in those conditions. Of all the species this oddball salmonid is least deterred by low water temperature, but I have to say my better grayling days have not been in extremes of cold. On my rivers they almost disappear in summer, reappearing as if by magic as soon as water temperatures drop in latish autumn.

Once they start to feed they can be relied upon

for the rest of the season, if you know where to look. Rivers vary in this respect. Rocky upland waters are much easier to read than some of the more even-paced waters that grayling inhabit. Perhaps for that reason I have done much less of the long trotting than most who have written about the grayling. On my favourite river they tend to congregate in the pools, and dozens can sometimes be caught without trotting more than 20 yards. The first dozen are often caught within 5 yards; that appeals to me much more than the weary business of trotting 30 to 40 yards of fast glide. All that reeling back is hard work, and I go fishing to relax.

Even close-range grayling fishing is not a particularly sedentary occupation. The conditions call for close control of a dumpy, buoyant float. I can see mine right now; it is set a couple of feet above the hook, usually a 16 baited with maggot, or worm if it is very cold. It is cast into the inches-deep water and held on a tight line as it rolls into the pool. It starts to cock as the shot begins to register in the deeper water, but it has gone before the operation is completed. The vermilion tip can be seen arrowing sideways in the crystal clear water, but by then the thumping rod tip has also signalled the bite.

That is nearly always how the first fish is taken, and maybe two or three more. Then it gets tough. I have to get full control of the float and trot it for a yard or two. The distance increases as the shoal diminishes. If I stayed long enough I would end up fishing in accordance with the textbooks, but I am at heart a lazy man. It is easier to go and find another pool, and start again.

There is magic in every swim, magic I preserve by rationing my grayling fishing to a few trips every winter. I can go for weeks and months without thinking about the grayling, then one day just being where they are is suddenly more important than anything else the sport has to offer.

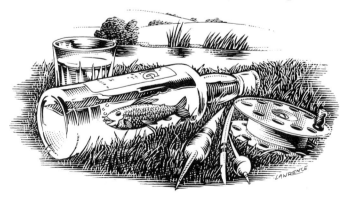

Rudd

Colin Dyson

T HE LONGEST-STANDING coarse fish record is that for the rudd. It was established in 1933 by the Rev Edward C Alston, who died in November 1978. His specimen of 4 lb 8 oz was taken a year before the walleye record, unlikely to be beaten, of 11 lb 12 oz. The only fish which pre-dates Alston's rudd in the freshwater list is Miss Ballantyne's famous 64 lb salmon from the Tay in 1922. That probably will not be beaten either, but will Alston's rudd? It is beginning to look very unlikely, with the apparent decline of some of the waters which used to produce big fish.

Ringmere, near Thetford, Norfolk, which produced the Alston record fish, no longer exists, but its story underlines the unusual circumstances in which big fish are sometimes taken. The area had a very low water table, and Ringmere had a habit of drying up about once every 20 years. It was thought to hold no fish at all when Alston stocked it with 50 rudd weighing between 12 oz and 1 lb, and clearly they thrived with the lack of any competition for the food supply.

Alston forgot all about them until he heard of a local youngster catching a rudd over 3 lb. When he fished it he had one of the great catches in angling history – about 30 fish between 2 lb 4 oz and 4 lb 8 oz. His best and second-best (weighing 4 lb 4 oz) were set up by the famous taxidermist, Cooper. As far as I can discover, only nine rudd over 4 lb have ever been claimed, and some of these may not have been genuine. To catch two in one session is an amazing achievement.

It is possible that I saw a record rudd in the 1960s, when the late Ted Grant was night fishing with me on the lake at Wolterton Hall, near Aylsham, Norfolk. He shouted for me to come and see a fish he landed just after midnight. I had taken a rudd of more than 3 lb from another water that summer, but the one he was holding seemed huge in comparison. We were never to know what it weighed, for it wriggled from his grasp and back into the water. Big rudd were sometimes taken from Wolterton at that time, usually on legered bread flake in the first hour after dark, but never as big as that one. Ted was heartbroken. Astonishment at the proportions of the fish had made him careless, but he was never down for long. 'Well,' he said, 'God had to be on the side of the Revd Alston!'

Wolterton was to produce a 3 lb 3 oz rudd in 1974 – the bottom fish in *Coarse Angler* magazine's 'Top 50 rudd' list, but little has been heard of them since. That seems to be the pattern with the species. They frequently peak and then disappear, especially on smaller waters like Wolterton and Bridge Farm Lake at Lenwade, Norfolk, which produced a run of good fish around 1980–81. Now it is believed those fish were hybrids, though it takes minute scientific examination to prove that.

Rudd hybridise so well with roach and bream that some believe there may be few true rudd left, and that all the bigger ones may be hybrids. Hybridity has been proved on several of the waters which have produced big rudd and this tends to throw doubt on past achievements. Even Slapton Ley, Devon, is in that position, but it is more than 30 years since Slapton produced a really big rudd. Since the pollution in the 1960s nothing has been heard of the rudd which ran to more than 3 lb in the Upper Thurne area of the Norfolk Broads. Other species have made a comeback, but not the rudd which offered superb sport on places like Hickling Broad.

Opportunities for the exceptional are now very limited, though the distribution of the species is pretty widespread. Rudd are present in every water authority area, but the key areas are the Lake District and the North West, Wales, the South West, the fenlands of Cambridgeshire, Norfolk, and most southern counties. Anywhere in one of these areas we might see a freakish situation like that on Ringmere, and the record could go.

If it happens, though, I will be a little sad. Alston's feat was so great it should last for ever. At

Opposite: Golden scaled rudd from a lake in East Anglia

Below: 12 oz rudd from Trawsfynydd

about the same time he caught his 4½ lb rudd, he equalled the current tench record of 7 lb. Although he was a considerable angler, almost nothing was known of him until Fred Buller wrote a touching obituary in *Coarse Angler* in 1978. I think of Fred's 'gentle Englishman' every time I see a rudd, but I wonder whether I will ever see another over 3 lb.

My only fish in that category was a fluke at a lake at East Carleton, Norfolk. I saw a fish bulging in a lily bed, thought it was a carp, and cast a freelined lobworm to it. The bait landed on a lily pad, half dangled into the water, and the rudd sipped it in. Most of the rudd over 2 lb that I have taken have also been accidents, taken on legered bread in the first two hours of darkness when I have been fishing for tench. The same bait, method, and time have produced a big rudd for many other anglers, making nonsense of the idea that rudd are exclusively surface feeders.

Early writers noted the underslung mouth of the rudd and concluded it was designed for surface feeding. They coupled this with observations of rudd feeding up top, and the myth was born. The truth is that rudd can be caught anywhere from surface to bottom, though catching them off the top with floating baits is the most satisfying. On Hickling in the sixties we used to locate them by drifting bread or floating casters downwind until we spotted surface activity.

The trick was to get a bait to them without scaring them. Big rudd are not tackle shy, but they are as easy to frighten as big chub. I still remember the withering look I got from the great Frank Wright when we had located a shoal and were all set to fish ... and I knocked a maggot tin into the bottom of the boat, and the rudd bow-waved off in all directions.

They manage to avoid me almost completely these days, which is a pity. Big roach are beautiful fish, and I agree with the old broadland angler who once told me: 'Big rutch may be boo'iful boy, but rudd is rutch in Sunday clothes...'

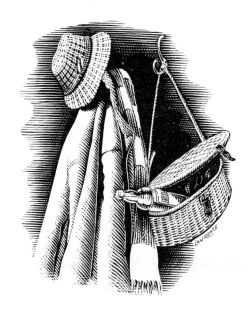

Dace

Dave Thomas

PRACTICALLY EVERY coarse fish species has a history. Tales of splendid deeds by legendary characters have been handed down the years: Alston's rudd, Morgan's pike, Bill Penney's roach, Walker's carp . . . but where is the history of the humble dace? Nobody bothers to keep record lists for a species which seldom grows to more than 1 lb in weight. Nobody makes a name for himself by catching great numbers of specimens. Almost nobody has said anything particularly memorable about the dace, except for Fred Taylor's dry observation that we can 'spend our lives trying to catch a pounder, and when we do it'll be a little chub!'

In that sense I am less fortunate than the other contributors to this book, but there the misfortune ends. For me dace are the most important of all species. I became a world champion largely because of them. They gave me the skill to compete successfully on the big match circuit, which in turn gained me selection for England. Dace can give anyone the basic skills required to catch many of the other species discussed in this book, so maybe I am justified in making this chapter more instructional than most of the others.

First, though, I would like to dwell a little on the nature of dace fishing, and why these lightning-biting little blighters are so special to me. Learning on them, as I did on the Yorkshire rivers, is a bit like running before you can walk, but I have never tired of catching them. They have given me endless pleasure over the years. The fishing is fast and furious; this is the thrill of it.

Find a shoal of dace and you have an almost guaranteed continuous response. There are very few quiet spells, and if it does go quiet you can be pretty certain that there is continuing activity under the surface. The fish are still looking at the bait, snapping up the loosefeed, more than likely mouthing your bait however briefly, even if no bite is apparent on the float. No other fish demand quite the degree of concentration or the exactness of control and presentation, not to mention the reflex reaction to a bite.

Being able to observe the movements and responses of dace in the shallower stretches of the Yorkshire rivers such as the Wharfe, Nidd, and Swale, has given me an awareness, a fish sense, which has been an invaluable asset in my pursuit not only of dace but other fish too. Bridges make excellent observation posts and I have spent endless hours over the years simply watching the reactions of dace to loosefeed and to anglers' tackle and bait trotted down the swim.

Those observations taught me that although the float may not indicate a bite, this does not mean nothing is happening. Anything up to half a dozen fish may not only have mouthed the bait but had it right in, and the angler need not be doing anything very wrong for this to happen. It has to be seen to be believed. I have stood on the bridge at Boston Spa on the Wharfe watching my friends fishing a slow-falling maggot into the slack water behind the centre structure of the bridge, and counted as many as six dace taking and rejecting the bait before it reached the bottom. They can do it without so much as a flicker of the float. We overcame this problem as youngsters by the observer anticipating or seeing the fish take and calling 'Now!' to the one fishing, who would promptly strike. Something like four out of every ten calls hooked a fish. Of course, this is a most unsatisfactory and unsporting practice, tantamount to cheating, but it taught us a lot.

This situation would occur not only with the fish taking on the drop. Watching from a bridge as a friend fished the river Nidd, I could see that the swim was full of dace greedily gobbling up the loose maggots which were being fed in. However, as it

Dace fishing on the Thames at Bell Weir Lock

was February and the water cool, they were not so inclined to come off the bottom. The right tackle was being used, anything up to four fish every swim down were taking the bait and even holding it long enough for a bite to register and be contacted, but not a flicker on the float was evident. My friend could not believe it. As far as he was concerned the swim was devoid of fish. I had to prove otherwise by adopting the old call system. He began hooking fish, but not before several adjustments had been made, on my instructions as observer, to the depth and shotting of tackle. Eventually we got it right. The next six bites were positive and every one hooked without any difficulty. If all this can happen in $2\frac{1}{2}$ to 3 feet of water, think of the possibilities in, say, 8 feet.

The dace waters which offer the sort of challenge I am talking about are the more heavily fished stretches of the ones where dace are plentiful but not over-abundant. On some of the game rivers like the Wye and Cumberland Eden, dace are so numerous that they can be caught much more easily, and they are of a bigger average size. Catches run to

Small dace like this can build big match catches

40 lb regularly; even 100 lb is not impossible. On lesser waters, like those in Yorkshire, the situation is different. The fish are still quite plentiful but quickly become educated, especially on the popular stretches. Catches of 8 to 10 lb can be good, 15 to 20 lb, exceptional on most stretches, although I have often taken much bigger ones. Other difficult dace rivers are the Warwickshire Avon and the Bristol Avon. On the upper Trent the dace are not particularly easy but their abundance means a fair catch is always on, even if you end up with 15 lb where you should have caught 25 lb.

The most popular baits for dace are maggots and casters. Depending on the river, and sometimes

the swim, both can be equally effective or one more so than the other. Casters in general are more suited to the steadier glides; in anything like a fast glide or a rapid, maggots are favourites. Dace need slightly more time to snatch a caster going by than a maggot. I know some waters where casters tend to sort out the better-quality fish, especially where there is a mixed shoal of, say, 3 to 8 oz fish feeding.

Mixed feeding with both maggot and caster would be acceptable in most cases; then the two could be alternated on the hook. However, care

must be taken not to introduce floating casters into the swim, for dace love to follow them downstream. Feeding, whether it be maggots or caster, is of the utmost importance in dace fishing, the idea being not to overfeed them. Little and often is the rule to get the fish competing for those free offerings which, fed in the correct way, will keep a dace swim producing for an indefinite period. The competition created in this way will induce the shoal to come as near as it dare to the source of food. Overfeeding has the reverse effect. If the shoal was not big enough or hungry enough to intercept the number of maggots introduced, the fish would be inclined to chase downstream after them, reducing the angler's chances of taking a good catch.

By feeding little and often, I mean *every* cast. I soon learned in my early days as an angler, fishing the popular day-ticket stretches of the Wharfe at Tadcaster and Boston Spa, that no maggots in the swim meant not a dace to be seen. The only way to get a bite was to throw in a few maggots and cast into them, making sure the hookbait was going down with the dozen or so loose maggots. That way a bite could be guaranteed.

In many cases a dozen maggots every cast would be far too many, and the swim would quickly die if that much feed was introduced. I know some stretches in Yorkshire where double-figure catches can be made by feeding no more than six maggots every cast; you can keep the shoal responding for hours by minimising the offerings in this way. Many times in matches I have seen an angler kill his swim within seconds of the start by throwing in a handful of maggots. It can be disastrous where dace are concerned.

One of the best examples of feeding for dace came while I was practising for the world championships on the Warwickshire Avon at Luddington. The tendency here was to feed for chub, but I was convinced there was a considerable head of dace in the river. One day I decided to find out for sure by reducing the feed to a minimum, feeding about half a dozen maggots every cast. It worked. Four hours later I had put 18 lb in the net and the fish were still coming thick and fast, competing for the loosefeed right at the head of the swim.

I knew I could have kept them coming indefinitely then, but decided to find out what would happen if I stepped up the feed rate – as if I did not

Trotting for dace on the Yorkshire Derwent at Stamford Bridge

know. I introduced a much larger quantity of maggots and, sure enough, next cast I caught a dace halfway down the swim, then one at the end of the swim before they vanished completely, as I expected. That is how easy it is to kill a dace swim.

The fastest bites in dace fishing are the ones that come on the drop. If you have seen dace attack a falling bait you will see why. They dart up, take

Small fish – big bait!

the bait, turn in a flash and dart away again. This is when they feel the resistance of the tackle and reject the bait. It all happens so quickly that by the time the angler reacts to this lightning bite, the fish has gone. It is at times like this when dace can be the most frustrating, exasperating fish. They are im-

Shallow water (2½ – 4 feet) Less depth means fewer shots down the line

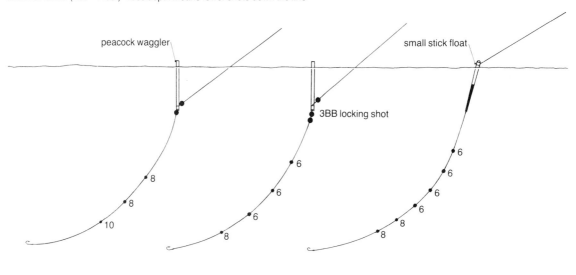

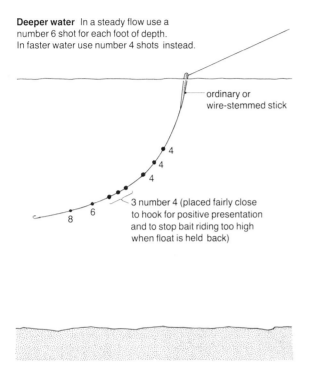

Deeper water In a steady flow use a number 6 shot for each foot of depth. In faster water use number 4 shots instead.

ordinary or wire-stemmed stick

4

4

4

3 number 4 (placed fairly close to hook for positive presentation and to stop bait riding too high when float is held back)

8 6

possible at times, but a challenge to test the skill of any angler.

It is usually in summer when dace are in this mood, coming off the bottom, but the more difficult they become the more determined I am to catch them. I always believe that if the fish are accepting the bait they can be caught, and this is where presentation is essential.

The manner and speed with which these dace take mean that it is not possible to connect with every bite, but using the correct float, shotting, hook size, and depth will produce a greater proportion of hittable bites. The fish, feeling less resistance, will hang on to the bait a split second longer. If you are quick enough there will be another fish in the net rather than another missed bite. Floats need to be streamlined for this on the drop fishing. A small quill, if the fish are near enough, is ideal, or a slim stick float, wire stem stick, or tiny balsa. A small, straight peacock waggler can be as good as anything at times.

Effecting a natural fall, acceptable to the fish, calls for light shotting, three or four number 6s down the line, or even dust shot. The more shot you can get away with, the more positive the bite. The most important shot is the tell-tale, usually a number 8 or smaller, and its position in relation to

the hook is crucial. This tell-tale is the one which lets you know you have a bite, so the nearer the hook the quicker the indication.

Unfortunately, that is not the end of the story. The distance between shot and hook affects the behaviour of the bait (usually called the presentation). Placing it further from the hook can result in a better bite. Nearer than a foot can be too close; further than 2 feet can be asking for trouble in the shape of a burst maggot, or not bite registering. Getting it right is often a question of trial and error. I am constantly making minor adjustments to get the tackle exactly correct.

There is only a split second between hitting a bite and missing one. Control and a tight line are essential for the quick bites and a size 20 or a 22 to 1 lb line is about standard. Sometimes an 18 is acceptable, maybe even bigger with caster, since the hook can be buried. It depends how hook-shy the fish are. Ideally, I like to get those dace on the bottom, and sometimes in summer I resort to groundbait mixed hard to go straight down. The dace will usually follow it and feed on the bottom, which makes for much easier bites, although not all waters will respond to groundbait. It works in Yorkshire on rivers like the Ure and certain stretches of the Wharfe. A golf ball size is all you need with a few maggots or casters. In really shallow swims I have been able to see the ball of groundbait on the bottom and the fish moving over it.

Another river where groundbait is essential to pin the dace down is the Bristol Avon, especially on the deeper parts of the river. Here there is anything from 8 to 14 feet of water and to attempt to catch by loosefeeding, when the fish could be at any level in mid-water, would be quite impossible at times. By introducing small hard balls of groundbait at regular intervals the fish can be caught on the bottom where the bites come more positive. Sliding floats are often employed with the bulk shot as much as two swan to get the bait down quickly where it can trip the bottom over the groundbait area. When practising for the last National Championship on this river, I had one of my best sessions with the dace on the pole using a bristle float and number 7 olivette in 8 feet of water, and the bites were really positive.

Talking of bites . . . after an open match on the Wharfe at Ulleskelf, the England international Kevin Ashurst was heard to ask one of the top Leeds anglers, 'What do you do when you're getting a

smashed maggot every swim down and never see a bite?' The typically dry-humoured Yorkshire reply was, 'Keep quiet about it.'

I love dace fishing in autumn and on the milder days in winter. If you can find them at these times of the year they really can be fun, less inclined to come off the bottom, somewhat easier to catch than during the warmer months, but still formidable opposition. There can be real problems in unfavourable weather. Wind is the biggest enemy, when the dace are playing hard to get; a downstream wind is particularly difficult.

One answer is to decide where the bites are coming and try to control the float at that point in the swim, before the wind forces a bow in the line, which in turn drags the float and ruins presentation. Another trick is to check or draw the float back and then let it run with the flow. Often the bait is accepted as it reaches bottom, and these are usually good bites. I know one swim on the Nidd in some very shallow water where I have taken a dace almost every cast doing this, when simply going through the retrieving at the end of the swim produced nothing.

As you may have gathered by now, dace fishing is not for the lazy angler who likes to sit back and take things easy. It is hard work which, if you stick at it, will improve your skill as well as proving that you only get out of something what you are prepared to put into it. Having learned on dace, I tend to be a maximum effort angler. I have noticed many times in matches on rivers like the Trent that my work rate is twice that of anglers around me, but it pays dividends. I have dace to thank for that.

My successes on the Warwickshire Avon, although I rarely fish the river, are also attributable to my dace efforts, not least of course my world championship win at Luddington. This stretch of the Avon, being fast and shallow, was tailor-made for me, and it was not surprising that I started favourite to win the title, even though I caught chub and not dace. That is another point about being a dace angler: if you can catch them, the rest come easier.

There can be no other fish more responsive than dace. If you can get the better of them, give yourself a pat on the back, but if you finish up throwing your tackle in, don't say I didn't warn you.

Barbel

Archie Braddock

I T WAS more than twenty years ago that I caught my first barbel, from the river Stour in Dorset, yet I can vividly remember every detail of that fish. Long and streamlined, with its huge dorsal fin erect and the dark hue of its back shading into a beautiful dusky gold on the flanks, to me it seemed a creature of awe-inspiring beauty and mystery. I had lived on that river for most of a week, sleeping rough on the bank within feet of the water. I had seen barbel everywhere, some of them big ones; I had been at them from the grey light of dawn until well into darkness, yet my reward was one bite which gave me a fish of 3 lb.

Why would the barbel not take my carefully presented baits? What was I doing wrong? It was to take the next two decades to find the answers, and along the way I made a thorough study of the fish themselves. I delved into their history, distribution, and growth rates. I experimented with brainwashing to persuade them to eat what I wanted them to eat, in preference to their natural diet. Of course, I also studied where they can be found.

Eons ago Britain was joined to the European continent, and major rivers like the Trent, the Thames, and the Rhine all flowed into one mighty waterway known as the North Sea River. *Barbus barbus*, to give the fish its scientific name, occurred in nearly all the faster-flowing rivers of the Netherlands, Germany, Belgium, and France, throughout the Danube system, and in the Russian rivers flowing into the Azov and Black seas. They were in England too, although the species has never been known to occur in Scotland or Ireland. A century or so ago most of the barbel in England were confined to the Yorkshire river system, the Trent and its tributaries (all emptying into the Humber estuary),

and the Thames and its tributaries. All these waters flow east, in the direction of the long-extinct North Sea river.

The position now is very different, mainly as a result of man's intervention, for over the past century barbel have been widely re-distributed. In 1896, 100 fish were transferred from the Thames to the Dorset Stour. They rapidly spread to the Hampshire Avon, and these two rivers soon became premier barbel fisheries, as they are today. In the mid-fifties barbel were placed in the Bristol Avon, Severn, Welland, Nene, and Great Ouse. These stockings met with varying degrees of success. The Severn fish multiplied and spread rapidly and the Bristol Avon fish spread slowly but successfully, while in the other waters they made no impact at all. The other major river, the Trent, suffered greatly through industrial pollution but over the past ten years it has made a remarkable recovery and is once again a good barbel river.

Today's angler has a better choice of waters than for many years. He can hope to catch barbel in the Ouse, Nidd, Derwent, Swale, Ure (all in Yorkshire), the Trent and its tributary the Dove, the Severn, the Lee, the Thames and its tributary the Kennet, the Hampshire Avon, and the Stour in Dorset. In other rivers the fish are spread very thinly or the best stretches are in private hands.

A fish of 10 lb is the goal of every keen barbel angler, but it is possible to go many years without ever seeing such a fish. On the other hand, specimens of 11, 12, and even 13 lb are taken each season, but these fish are exceptional. The current official British record is 13 lb 12 oz, yet there is no doubt that many larger fish have been caught. Salmon anglers have accounted for no fewer than six huge fish, between 14 lb 4 oz and 17 lb 4 oz, none of which counted for record purposes as they were taken during the coarse fish close season.

During the 1930s a string of 13- and 14-pounders were recorded, most of them from the Hampshire Avon. Even earlier the Trent, Thames, and Lee each produced at least one fish in excess of 14 lb. My favourite story concerns a monster barbel of 16 lb 10 oz taken from the Trent towards the end of last century. It was caught on a stout line, baited with a slice of lamprey, the whole lot being staked out overnight in the hope of eels. Imagine the shock on the captor's face when he saw what he had. To cap even this, fish estimated at 20 lb were seen in the Avon in the late 1950s, but none were ever known to take a bait.

This is heady stuff, but the prospects for the casual angler are somewhat different, dependent on which river he chooses. The Hampshire Avon, although it has declined in recent years, is still the best prospect for a big fish. Average weight is high, with the general run of fish around 4 to 7 lb, but it is not easy fishing. One barbel a trip is about the norm, and it is not unusual to catch nothing. On the other hand, a good day could make your dreams come true.

The Thames can be hit and miss, and local knowledge of the barbels' whereabouts is necess-

A typical barbel from the Hampshire Avon — most famous of all the barbel rivers

A weedy swim on a Hampshire chalk stream

ary, but the quality of the fishing is sometimes good with fish of 5 to 7 lb being caught each season. A better bet would be the Yorkshire river system. Waters like the Swale and the Nidd hold large numbers of barbel of 1 to 3 lb, and good chances of better. The Trent holds numbers of fish in that size class, but they are much more numerous upstream of Nottingham. Rivers like the Dove and the Kennet are specialist waters; it needs time and application to get the best from them.

The Severn is perhaps the best all-round barbel water in the country. Since the original introduction, the barbel have spread up and down the river to give many miles of first-class fishing. Most of the fish run between 1 and 4 lb, with a good chance of a 6- or 7-pounder. Another important fact is that much of the river is available on a day-ticket basis, or with a reasonably priced season ticket.

Having selected a water, the angler should know something of the habits and life-style of his quarry before he sets out to catch it. The most important thing to understand is that barbel move about the river a great deal, particularly if water levels fluctuate. I have many times heard a passing angler complain to his companion, 'Can't understand it. Last week I had a dozen good barbel from that swim; this week, not a bite.'

What our angler has failed to take into account is that it rained between his visits, the river level came up a few inches, and the speed of the current increased. The barbel did not like it, so they dropped downstream 100 yards to where the river deepened slightly and the current slowed a little. Or perhaps it had been a dry, hot week when the level had fallen and the water slowed a little. In that case the fish may have gone upstream to where the river shallowed and flowed a bit quicker. Had there been a flood, they could have moved a mile. The right current speed is the most important factor in locating barbel.

The next important point is bottom make-up. Except in unusual circumstances, barbel will not be found over a muddy riverbed; neither do they care for a rocky bottom, such as is often found on the Trent. Their preference is always for gravel, of the finer sort and closely packed, but not too dense. If you can *just* force a pole into the bottom, it is about right. Cover helps. A half-submerged tree stuck in the river is best. Failing that, beds of trailing weeds

are good. Anything the barbel can hide under will do, even the steep slope of the bank itself, provided the water is a fair depth at that spot. If none of these conditions exist, the fish will lie up in the deepest water available to them, even if that water is only 6 inches deeper than the surrounding area.

Another major factor is the actual fishing time. If possible, fish the evening – say, from 7 pm until an hour after dark. On the vast majority of rivers this is the fish's chosen feeding time. I have sometimes stayed all night, but it has not improved my catches. Early morning sessions have given only brief feeding spells.

A swim on the Dove that I used to fish was a 9 feet deep pool on a bend, with the current pushing hard down my near bank, leaving a slack the other side which was shallower. Upstream the river shal-

lowed to 3 feet, with a good pace and plenty of waving streamer weed. The whole area was gravel. After marking these fish with a harmless dye I was able to conclude that this swim held a resident population of 16 fish, two of more than 6 lb, one of more than 5 lb, the rest between 2 lb and just over 4 lb.

At normal levels they spent most of the day at the bottom of the hole, not really feeding at all. Some time after 6 pm they began to feed, but still remaining in the pool. By the time the sun had gone they were working slowly upstream, arriving in the 3 foot shallows as darkness fell. They worked up the shallows for about 50 yards, then dropped back into the pool about 1½ hours after dark. Feeding virtually ceased until dawn, when again they got their heads down for about the first 2 hours of daylight. At this time they did not leave the pool.

If the river came up a few inches the fish tended to move towards the slacker side of the pool, but

Landing a lively barbel on Yorkshire's river Nidd

kept to roughly the same pattern. If the water came up a foot or more, all the fish moved 300 yards upstream to another larger pool until the level dropped. Virtually all the barbel in the river had regular movement patterns, and once these were understood the angler could catch fish regularly by moving swims as the fish moved.

By now the newcomer is probably thinking all this is far too complicated, and he will probably never catch such fish. I hope to show that it is not difficult once you have a grasp of the barbel's habits.

Before describing the actual fishing, a word about baits. In the natural state, barbel use their four barbules to detect small creatures in the gravel and are capable of picking up stones to get at the creatures underneath. They will also spend time cleaning algae and filamentous weed from a patch of gravel, leaving an area about 2 feet square all clean and shining.

On stretches of rivers that do not get much angling pressure the fish never become accustomed to eating anglers' baits and as a result can be extremely difficult to catch. When such a situation faced me on the stretch of the Dove I mentioned earlier, I overcame it by drastic measures. Over a period of several months I threw in hundreds of pounds of luncheon meat, in bait-size pieces. My aim was to brainwash the fish into believing that meat grew in the river, to persuade them to eat it in preference to their natural diet. It worked. During the two years that I fished that area I probably caught every barbel in it on luncheon meat, and the time came when I was catching the same fish over and over again.

It was a very interesting, but expensive, experiment and it went a long way towards answering the questions I had asked myself nearly twenty years earlier. It formed the basis of my current approach: to persuade the fish to eat what I want them to eat, and to some extent when I want them to eat it. Let me describe a situation that many anglers face, and suggest the best way to tackle it.

You have arrived at the water at midday, which you know is not really the best time. Earlier anglers have taken what seem to be the best swims, and you are left with a featureless even-flowing piece of water. Still, there seems to be a slight increase of pace about 20 yards out. You quickly set up a through-actioned rod with a fixed-spool reel loaded with 5 lb line, and tie on a small bomb. You cast to the head of the swim. The lead rolls round a

little and snags up – rocks on the bottom, it seems. A cast to the downstream end of the run sees the lead swinging round in the current, vibrating gently. That is good; it means a gravel bottom.

You now put on the business end of the tackle: first a safety-pin type of link swivel, for a quick change of lead or feeder; then a $\frac{1}{4}$ inch piece of valve-rubber to act as a shock-absorber during casting; a plastic leger-stop; and finally the hook. The finished end tackle is shown below. The stop is positioned about 18 inches from the hook, but be prepared to vary this if bites are slow in coming.

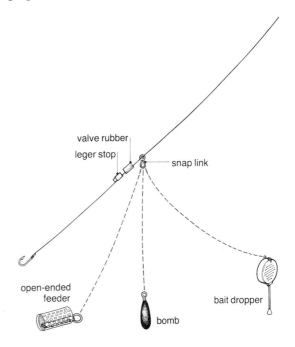

The really important constituent is hempseed. This has the power both to attract barbel and to stimulate them into feeding. The previous night you stewed two pints of hemp until the white kernels were just showing, then rinsed them in cold water. Your aim was to get a good carpet on the bottom before you start to fish. If the swim had been nearer to the bank you would have used a bait-dropper, clipping it on the line with the link swivel. As this swim is further out you will use an open-ended feeder to deposit the hemp. Six feeders full, six casts later, there is a good spread of the seed at the tail end of the swim. You can leave the feeder on the line, but my practice is to change it for a bomb once the groundbaiting is done. The bomb is easier to cast, and far more accurate.

105

Opposite: A double figure barbel from the river Wensum

Almost any bait can be used, but two grains of sweetcorn on a number 10 hook is a good bet. It is wise to have alternative baits in case the corn fails. Luncheon meat, cheese, bunches of maggots, lobworm, and bread have all worked for me at various times. Try a change of bait if the fish appear to stop feeding. This can often bring an extra fish, or even start them feeding all over again.

This approach to barbel will work on waters large or small; I have used it successfully on several rivers. Your chances increase dramatically as the light fades. There are, of course, many other ways to catch these fish, such as trotting a float and rolling a leger, but these styles are more difficult to use and are best left until the angler has plenty of experience.

The barbel has tremendous fighting power. Even fish of 2 or 3 lb will give you a scrap to remember, and a fish over 5 lb is almost unstoppable over a short distance. I well remember a swim with a sunken tree where I used to fish with 8 lb line. I caught barbel to about 4¾ lb, but I regularly lost better fish which forged powerfully under the tree and snagged me up. Finally, I set up a powerful rod, 10 lb line, and a strong hook. I used a dead minnow for bait, as this will often sort out a bigger than average fish.

The first barbel I hooked headed strongly downstream about 15 feet away from the snag. 'Great,' I thought, nipping quickly down the bank to stay level with the fish, 'there's no way you'll ever make it back to that tree now.' Almost as if the fish had heard me, it turned and started to move ponderously back upstream. I clamped down hard, determined not to give an inch of line. The barbel ignored me, and carried on at the same slow pace. The rod bent to an impossible angle, the corks curving under my hands. The line was making tinny noises, and even my elbow joints were making cracking sounds. The fish ploughed into the snag and the line broke like a pistol shot.

I end this piece with a solemn warning. Should you experience such a battle with a barbel, your dreams will be full of plans to win the next fight. In short, you will become a barbel addict – for life.

Match fishing for the barbel on the Derbyshire Derwent

South-West
Water Authority

THE SOUTH-WEST WATER AUTHORITY area has much more to offer than cream teas, topless beaches, and traffic jams. It has always been a happy hunting ground for sea anglers, and the tumbling rivers are a game fisher's dream. But what is there for the coarse fisherman? Compared with most other areas, not a lot. Devon and Cornwall are simply not built for coarse fishing, but where it can be created it has been, and some of it is very good indeed.

The Exe is the only big river offering coarse fishing, but in the short lengths which are available the sport can be quite superb. The salmon which run to spawn in the majestic upper reaches have to bump their way through enormous bream shoals in the Exeter section controlled by Exeter and District AA, and with fish of 6–7 lb common, the quality matches the quantity.

Bream can be caught among the mullet in the tidal river, but the first mile above the tidal, the Port Royal section, is the key area. It was here, from the Ballast Quay, that the 51 lb 4 oz match catch record was taken. There was another bream catch of 46 lb 8 oz in the same match, and an early pleasure catch in the 1984 season weighed over 90 lb. There is also a good head of dace and roach. Above the weirs enclosing the Ballast Quay the fishing was equally impressive for another 1½ miles, but it declined badly following a flood prevention scheme, and Tiverton & District AC is still waiting for it to return to form.

There is further coarse fishing, for dace and roach, at Cowley and Thorverton Bridge, but the rest is for game fishing. Exeter & District AA has a number of short sections of the river Culm, a tributary of the Exe, which can offer good roach,

dace, and grayling fishing. The roach have been known to go to 3 lb, but the fishing is best when there is a bit of extra water coming down. The same club has Abrook pond, near Newton Abbot, which holds carp to 20 lb and outstanding tench to 7 lb, but apart from the Exe its most important fishery in the region – and certainly the trickiest – is the Exeter Canal.

Seven miles of fishing run from the Maritime Museum in the middle of Exeter to Turf lock at Topsham. Exeter & District AA controls five miles; the other two belong to Exeter City Council, which issues free permits to local anglers. It is by no means the standard type of narrow-boat canal, extending 30 to 35 yards wide in most places, and up to 80 yards in some. It is 10 to 11 feet deep, on average, and the locals have a sort of love–hate relationship with the fishery. Nobody has ever mastered it, they reckon. It can reward expert anglers one day and kick them in the teeth the next.

The water can pull quite strongly, which makes it hard to float-fish effectively; swingtip and quivertip legering are usually the effective alternatives. The rewards for getting it right can be tremendous – superb roach catches on hemp and tares early in the season, when the float is effective,

Trotting a glide on the Dorset Stour

and bream to 5 lb turning up in catches to 80 lb most summers. Match catches are not quite so spectacular, the record being a bit deceptive at 33 lb. That was set in the 1970s and was entirely rudd, which had just been transferred from another fishery. Rudd catches to 100 lb were made for a short time, before they spread themselves much more thinly over the whole length. Pike fishing is a difficult proposition in most of the South West, but they are quite numerous in this canal.

Apart from the somewhat limited river and canal fishing, the main coarse fishing strength lies in the lake and reservoir fishing. Much of it is of relatively recent development, the guiding principle being that angling families are more likely to be attracted to Devon and Cornwall if coarse fishing is available alongside the game and sea fishing. It is now available from the far west – Boscathnoe reservoir near Penzance – to the Wessex border,

and some of it is very good indeed. It also helps that there is no close season, at least not a statutorily imposed break from 15 March to 16 June, which is common in most other parts of the country.

Coarse fishing hereabouts was of little or no importance when close seasons were imposed elsewhere, and while a few fishery owners have imposed their own breaks there seems to be scant chance of a general change. There is little or no scientific evidence that close seasons are beneficial to fish or fisheries; indeed, none was produced when the Anglian Water Authority tried to impose a close season on the landlocked waters of Lincolnshire after 50 years of continual fishing. It had the impossible task of proving that some of the best coarse fisheries in Lincolnshire were suffering from the lack of a close season. It lost so badly that even

Right: A quiet corner of the Exeter Canal

the anglers who opposed it were embarrassed by its performance at a two-day public inquiry.

The condition of the coarse fisheries in the South West is good enough to deter a similar campaign. 'Am I going to hear any evidence?' was the testy question from the Ministry of Agriculture

Matchman launches bait for barbel

inspector on day two of the Lincolnshire inquiry, and it did more than sink the Anglian Authority. It warned fisheries departments everywhere that to achieve major change they would need more than mere opinion and pleas for administrative conformity. Few have since looked for evidence on what is clearly a very touchy subject, but where it has been done (Yorkshire in 1983) the results have been bad for the no-close-season lobby. Yorkshire found that the situations in Lincolnshire and South West were in many ways preferable.

Anyone wanting to do his own investigation has plenty to study in Devon and Cornwall. Would Marazion AC's Boscathnoe reservoir fish better if it was protected? It does pretty well at the moment, with evening match catches to 22 lb in three hours – carp, tench, bream, rudd, perch, and eels. Wheal Grey, Marazion's china claypit near Ashton, has carp to 30 lb, with plenty in the 10 to 15 lb bracket and many more between 2 and 6 lb. Wheal Grey is slightly bigger at 4 acres.

Little waters are perhaps not worth a mention in any other area, but small is beautiful in these parts. The South West has trouble keeping the taps running in peak holiday seasons simply because there are very few big expanses of water. By far the largest available to the coarse angler is Slapton Ley, 200 acres of pike, perch, rudd, roach, and eel fishing near Dartmouth. It is separated from the sea at Start Bay by a road and a spit of sand. Nowhere are top class sea and coarse fishing so close together. The coarse fishing is boat only, bookable in advance from the Slapton Ley Field Centre.

The South West Water Authority is proud of the development of its reservoir fisheries, and seems to go out of its way to ensure that the coarse angler is not forgotten. Where there are two reservoirs close together, one is developed as a coarse fishery. Upper Tamar, not far from Bude, is for trout; lower Tamar is a 40-acre coarse fishery offering excellent sport with carp, rudd, tench, bream and, curiously for a stillwater, dace. The same goes for Upper and Lower Slade reservoirs near Ilfracombe. Lower Slade is 6 acres of mixed fishing, liable to produce a trout or two among the roach, perch, bream, carp, and tench. Near both Falmouth and Penryn are the Argal and College reservoirs, similar in size. College is 38 acres and the coarse fishery. The official list of records for this water is indicative of the general standard – carp to 26 lb, perch to 4 lb 8 oz, bream to 8 lb, tench to 7 lb 8 oz; impressive by any standards.

Another SWWA fishery is Squabmoor, near Budleigh Salterton, 4.3 acres holding carp, roach, rudd, tench, and bream. Its Darracott fishery, 2.6 acres near Torrington, has carp, tench, bream, roach, perch, and rudd. Not all the major coastal or inland holiday centres offer nearby coarse fishing, mainly because there is nothing suitable for development.

Many do, however, and inquiries at local tackle or sports shops will lead the angler to coarse fishing at or near the following centres, none of which have been previously mentioned: Barnstaple,

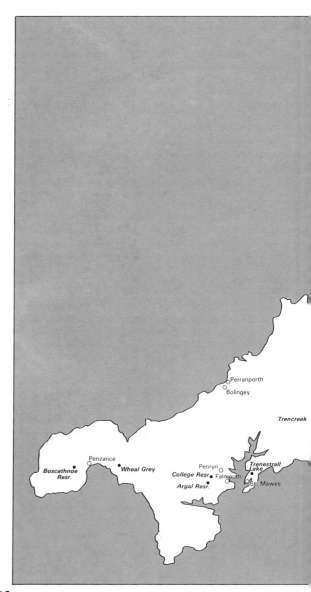

where Barnstaple and District AA has several pond fisheries; Bovey Tracey, where both Exeter and District AA and Newton Abbot FA have ponds; Bude, where the Bude Canal AA controls 1¼ miles of canal; Cullompton, a small carp and perch fishery at Billingsmoor Farm; Holsworthy, three small lakes holding mirror carp, tench and rudd; Kenton and Kingsteignton, where there is more Exeter AA pond fishing, and Newton Abbot Fly Fishing Association has four day ticket ponds at Kingsteignton too; Launceston, five lakes available; Looe, four lakes within six miles; Newton Abbot, five lakes controlled by Newton Abbot FA, plus Stover Lake in Stover Country Park; Perranporth, lake at Bolingey; St Austell, Trencreek Lakes; St Mawes, Trenestrall Lake; Saltash, Crafthole Reservoir and a Royal Albert Bridge AC lake at St Germans; Tiverton, the Grand Western canal and two ponds at Sampford Peverell and Stevenstone lake at Torrington.

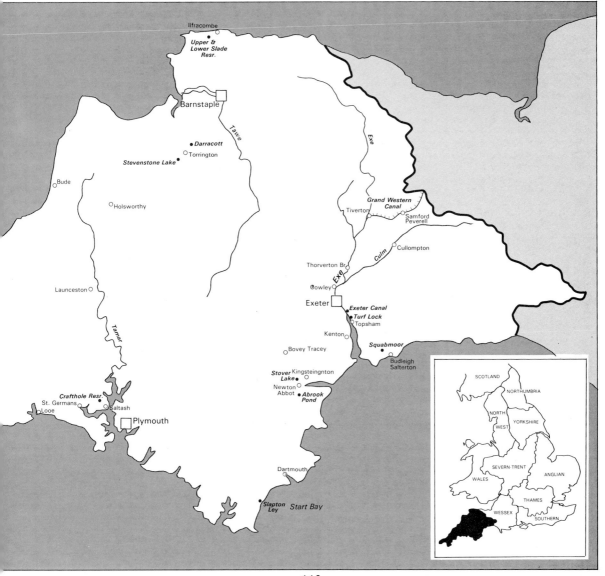

Weir fishing on the river Exe

Wessex
Water Authority

Few parts of the country can match the splendidly rich variety of fishing offered in the Wessex Water Authority area. It has the Bristol Avon to the north, the Hampshire Avon to the east, and the matchless drain fishing of the Somerset Levels in the south-west corner. The scenery is as varied and interesting as the fishing; timeless and unchanging beauty, at least to the casual observer. Angling history has been made here, and events of long ago are talked about wherever anglers gather.

Nowadays, however, not everything they say is entirely uncritical, certainly as far as the Hampshire Avon is concerned. There is no more famous river than this, as reference to this book's barbel and chub chapters will confirm. The vast majority of barbel over 13 lb have come from the Hampshire Avon, including the biggest caught on rod and line. No barbel angler can study the list without a feeling of awe and wonder, but that soon gives way to puzzlement. Why no monsters in the last decade? What happened (probably many years prior to 1975, when the last really big barbel was caught), to slow down and switch off a production line which had been turning them out at intervals since the 1930s?

Theories abound, and they are probably all wholly or partly correct. Disappearance of the water meadows, agricultural pollution, abstraction, severe weed cutting, disease and de-oxygenation from proliferating trout farms ... Whatever the reasons, the river is not what it was to those who know it best, and they are very worried men. We hope some means will be found to halt and reverse the decline, though we must not lose sight of the fact that the Avon remains an excellent fishery in comparison with many others. It still produces good chub and double-figure barbel, especially on the Royalty fishery above Christchurch, where many of the very big barbel have been taken in the past. Most of the accessible coarse fishing is between Salisbury and Christchurch, and it is noted for all the main river species, as well as chub and barbel.

Some of the fisheries are as famous as the river itself – the Longford Estate, Downton, Somerley (salmon only, but it was once thought to hold barbel well in excess of the record) and, of course, the Royalty. Clubs controlling good fishing include Christchurch AC, Salisbury & District AC, and the London AA, but it is worth pointing out that the Wessex authority is one of the few to produce a comprehensive guide to all the fishing in its area. It is available from the authority's offices in Poole, Bath, and Bridgwater, and is well worth the seeking.

Key Avon tributaries holding good coarse fish are the Wylye, which once held the dace record, and the Nadder. The Dorset Stour wanders from the east to find the sea in much the same place as the Avon, and it is almost as famous. It holds all the same species to much the same quality. The biggest fishery in the lower reaches is the Throop, which is bracketed with the Royalty in the hearts and minds of barbel and chub anglers. The biggest barbel from the Stour is thought to be 14 lb 12 oz taken in 1965; like some from the Avon, it was foulhooked by a salmon angler. Christchurch AC has plenty of fishing on the lower river, and there is free fishing at Longham and Red Hill, courtesy of Bournemouth Corporation.

Between Wimborne Minster and Blandford, the Stour is almost totally club controlled, mainly by Wimborne & District AC, Red Spinners AS, and the Southampton Piscatorial Society. Blandford is a noted centre for quality coarse fish, including roach over 2 lb, chub over 5 lb, and dace to the magic pound mark. Two other clubs have control here, Blandford & District AC and Durweston AS.

The smaller rivers in the Avon and Dorset area are not as accessible, but there is winter coarse fishing on the tidal section of the Piddle (Wareham & District AS) and limited fishing on the Frome (Dorchester AS and Wessex Water Authority). Christchurch AC has fishing on the Moors River,

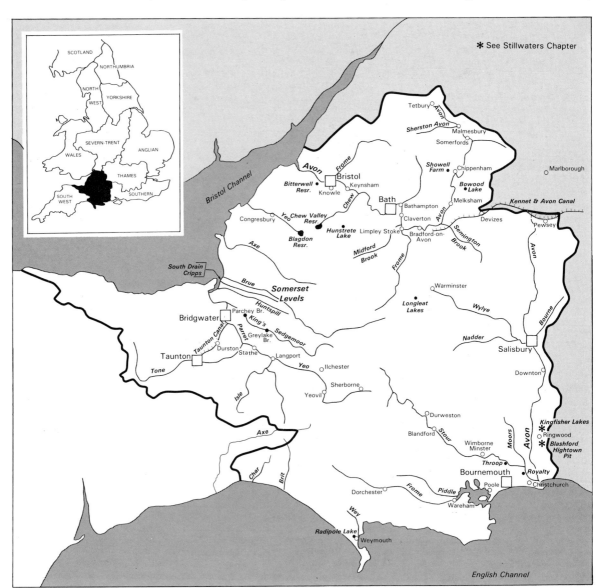

Match in progress on the King's Sedgemoor drain, near Bridgwater

but on other small rivers – the Wey, Bourne, Brit, and Char – it is a question of trying one's luck with an approach to farmers and riparian owners.

The many rivers in the Somerset division are very different to those in the east. The Congresbury Yeo, Axe, Brue, Yeo, Parret, and Isle tumble down the Mendips as fine trout waters, then they amble across the Somerset Levels to the sea as part of a very wide choice for coarse fishermen. They can all produce big fish. The Axe, for example, has a 6 lb 3 oz chub to its credit, and a 26 lb pike. It is mostly controlled by the North Somerset Association of Angling Clubs. The Yeo, also noted for quality fish, is mostly controlled by Yeovil & Sherborne AA and Ilchester & District AA.

Top roach from the Brue is 3 lb 14¾ oz, and it also holds quality tench, chub, and bream. Roach catches to 50 lb are quite possible, especially in winter, and chub weights often go to 70 lb. Control of this river is mostly with the Glaston Manor AA, North Somerset Association of Anglers, and Bristol & District AA. The Parret has a match catch record of 96 lb 3 oz of bream in six hours, which says enough. Control is with various' clubs, including Stoke sub Hamdon & District AA, Wessex Federation of Angling Clubs, and Langport & District AA.

The Tone through Taunton can offer big carp, with chub, bream and roach, and is one of the few West Country rivers holding grayling.

Remarkable though the river fishing can be, however, the waters which are best known to outsiders are the great land drains on the Levels – the King's Sedgemoor, the Huntspill, South drain, and Cripps river, which runs between the Huntspill and the Brue. This, undoubtedly, is because of the great national championships fished on these waters.

History books record the battle of Sedgemoor in 1695, when the Duke of Monmouth's rebels were routed by the forces of the King, but there were two more battles of Sedgemoor, in 1955 and 1965, on the very same spot. On both occasions the tramp of marching anglers' feet from Parchey bridge and Greylake bridge set the bream shoals moving, until they collided and stayed at the half-way point, right where the drain takes a bend. In 1955 every championship record was smashed, including the record team weight of 136 lb 15 oz by Sheffield Amalgamated. They were spearheaded by Jack Carr, drawn on that fateful bend, who

A placid day on the Bristol Avon

destroyed the individual catch record with 68 lb 2¼ oz of bream. In that one section, 99 anglers caught 1100 lb, and 12 had nearly 500 lb of that total.

The reputation of the Sedgemoor as a stand-out bream fishery was made, and it was reinforced by the repeat performance in 1965, when Rugby's Dave Burr demolished Carr's record with 76 lb 9 oz. On both occasions there were great catches from the Huntspill, South drain, and Cripps, and it has been much the same ever since. All the main drain species show in quality and quantity, but weed can be a problem in the summer months. Controlling clubs on these waters include Bridgwater AA, North Somerset Association of Anglers, and Glaston Manor AA.

Somerset anglers are certainly well served, but many of them would claim that the best fishery has not been mentioned yet. There are carp to 30 lb in Taunton AA's West Sedgemoor drain at Stathe, and vast numbers of smaller carp. The tench fishing is excellent, and fine roach show in catches which

Opposite: Chub fishing on the Hampshire Avon

commonly top 35 lb. More impressive still, however, is the Bridgwater and Taunton Canal, where Durston is the dividing line between Bridgwater AA and Taunton AA fisheries. This water teems with tench which sometimes top 6 lb, bream which go to 8 lb, and roach which have been recorded over 3 lb.

The remaining river division in Wessex is dominated by the Bristol Avon and its tributaries, and while the Stour and Hampshire Avon to the east can boast bigger fish there is no doubt which river has the edge for consistency. The Bristol Avon is regarded as one of the fairest competition rivers in the country – usually a euphemism for consistently mediocre, but that is far from the case here. No matter what weight an angler is sitting on, he knows he can be beaten; the celebrations begin only when all the weight cards are back at match HQ.

Big weights, occasional big fish, and superb surroundings – the Bristol Avon provides them all. The records show that the river has been fishing well for a long time, but it is still producing the goods. The five-hour match record, raised to 78 lb

9½ oz at Ladydown in 1975, fell at the beginning of the 1984 season when 79 lb 8 oz of bream were caught at Showell Farm, between Chippenham and Melksham. Shortly afterwards it could have gone again, this time at Bradford-on-Avon, where an angler with 73 lb 4½ oz lost four big bream.

These fish grow big, with 8 lb plus a possibility, but the river is by no means dominated by bream. It can produce all the main coarse fish species, including barbel, which were introduced at Bathampton, Claverton, and the dreamy-looking Limpley Stoke sections between 1955. They have thrived, multiplied and migrated, the record now being 10 lb 5¼ oz from Chippenham in 1982. The fishing starts right in the Bristol Docks, where tickets are obtainable from the Baltic Wharf Leisure Centre and the Bristol & West of England Federation of Anglers.

Beyond Bristol a considerable number of clubs have fishing rights, but those with the most extensive and important holdings are Bathampton AA, Bradford-on-Avon & District AA, Melksham & District AA, Chippenham AA, Isis AC, and Somerfords FA. At Malmesbury the river divides into two, the Sherston Avon and Tetbury Avon which, while holding coarse fish, are primarily trout waters. Of the tributaries holding coarse fish the most important is the Somerset Frome, where Frome & District AA, Bradford-on-Avon & District AA, and the Avon Tributaries AA have excellent fishing. The Blagdon and Chew Valley lakes are among the most noted trout waters in the country, but the river Chew is mainly coarse fishing, and the leading clubs

here are Keynsham AA and Knowle AA which, with the Avon Tributaries AA, also have fishing on Midford brook.

There is more coarse fishing on the Marden, which feeds the Avon upstream of Chippenham. The main club here is Calne AA, and the Bradford-on-Avon club has good coarse fishing on Semington brook, which enters the Avon below Melksham. The third Frome in the Wessex area, the once-polluted Bristol Frome, now holds coarse fish, but it is by no means as appealing as the Avon itself.

Another important waterway is the Kennet and Avon canal, 58 kilometres of which wanders across country from Bath to the Thames Water Authority border. It holds all the usual canal coarse fish, including rudd and crucian carp, and is capable of both big catches and large specimens. Six clubs control long lengths – Bathampton AA, Bristol & West of England AF, Bradford-on-Avon & District AA, Devizes AA, Pewsey AA, and Marlborough & District AA.

Throughout the Wessex WA area there are no really large expanses of stillwater devoted to coarse fishing, but there are many small ponds, lakes, and pits offering good sport. Many are controlled by clubs already mentioned and they often provide good carp fishing. Two of the biggest eels in angling history are credited to Hunstrete lake, near Chelwood (8 lb 10 oz) and Bitterwell reservoir, near Bristol (8 lb 8 oz). Other noted waters include Radipole lake, near Weymouth, Bowood lake on the Bowood Estate at Calne (Wiltshire), and the lakes at the famous Longleat Estate at Warminster.

Southern
Water Authority

In THE AGE of the computer it must be possible for someone to calculate what proportion of specimen fish are taken each year in the South, though it would be a depressing exercise for angling enthusiasts in other regions. It takes little research to uncover the fact that most of the country's important and prolific stillwaters are clustered within the boundaries of the Thames Water Authority in particular and those of the Southern Water Authority. The latter's area extends from the Medway and Stour systems of Kent in the east, through Sussex, and on to the famous but very exclusive chalk streams of Hampshire in the west. Because of the importance of the southern stillwaters it makes sense to give them a chapter of their own, dealing only with the rivers under the headings of the Southern and Thames water authorities.

There is not as much to say about some of the SWA rivers, simply because opportunities for the ordinary angler are limited. Virtually the whole of the Test, for example, is off limits for coarse fishing. We are left to dream about the lovely grayling which share the rich habitat with the game fish. Almost as exclusive is the Itchen, the second of four rivers running into Southampton water. The only access is to free fishing below the weir at Swaythling and between City Mill and Wharf Mill in Winchester. Public fishing is also allowed between Woodmill and Mansbridge in Southampton.

There is no coarse fishing on either the Hamble or the Meon. Indeed, Hampshire's only realistic river fishing is to the west, at the other side of the Wessex WA border.

Moving east into Sussex, we find coarse fishing on the Chichester Canal, four miles of water connecting Chichester with the harbour at Birdham. It holds most species, including tench and carp; tickets are sold at local tackle shops.

One of the most interesting rivers in Sussex is undoubtedly the Arun, which rises in the north of the county and flows into the Channel at Littlehampton. It has a lengthy estuary holding bass and mullet in the summer months, and the lower reaches of the river are also tidal. Fishing the top of the tide down gets the best results, which can be spectacular. The bream match catch record is 88 lb. There are pike running to 29 lb, chub to 7 lb, roach, and dace.

Most of the available ticket fishing is on the lower 15 miles or so from Wisborough Green (Crawley AS) through Pulborough (Pulborough AS, CALPAC, and Leisure Sport), Bury (local tackle shops), Amberley (café at Amberley bridge),

121

*Previous page: Chris Yates after chub on the
Sussex Rother*

Arundel (tackle shops; free fishing via Southern WA) and Littlehampton, where the five miles below Arundel bridge is free fishing. There is coarse fishing on the Sussex Rother, which runs into the Arun at Pulborough, but access is very limited. One ticket source, at Habin bridge, near Rogate, is Southern Anglers, Portsmouth.

Further east, the Adur, running into the sea at Shoreham, has nice summer estuary fishing for mullet and bass, but the coarse fishing is limited. It includes a short length at Tenchford, a three-mile length near Steyning (Pulborough & Steyning AS), a CALPAC fishery at Henfield, and a stretch at Bramber (Sussex County AA). The Sussex Ouse has no day ticket fishing, though Haywards Heath & District AA offers holiday weekly tickets.

Similarly the Cuckmere, which reaches the Channel west of Eastbourne, is too closely con-

trolled to interest the visitor, but there is some superb fishing in this area – Wallers Haven, near Hailsham. This is the biggest land drain in the south and, like similar waters in the fenlands, it offers excellent bream fishing. Catches sometimes top 50 lb. Other species include carp and tench, and the pike run to 20 lb. Hailsham AA controls most of it, and local tackle shops sell day tickets.

The next river system east is also a good bet – the Kentish Rother and the Royal Military Canal. There are several ticket sources on the Rother, but the main one is Rye & District AS. The society has five or six miles out of around nine miles of usable water in the lower reaches, where the best coarse fishing is. At its best it is exceptional, with a match catch record of 129 lb 8 oz of bream. The river once held the chub record with a 7-pounder, and there are still good fish in pockets. It is also credited with

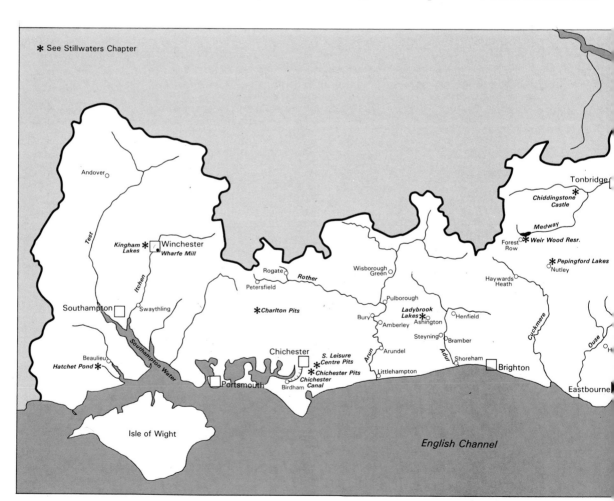

The Black Rabbit section of the Arun, near Arundel

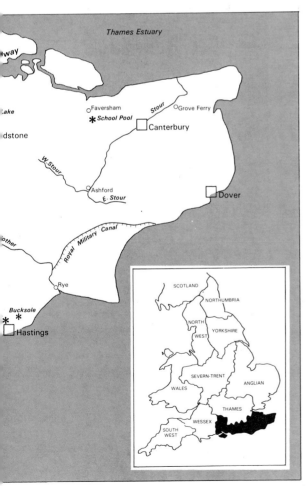

perch to 4 lb 7 oz and a roach of 3 lb 4½ oz.

The canal is a dreamy and vastly underrated fishery by those who do not know it well, with many lilies and no boats. It was built as a defence line during the Napoleonic wars; now it is part of the Romney Marsh drainage system, and a haven of peace. The match catch record is thought to be around 80 lb, and it grows exceptional carp and tench. Carp have been reported to 32 lb (1978) and tench to 8 lb 1 oz (1982). Biggest controlling club is the Ashford AS.

Such is the quality of the Rother and the canal that hundreds of miles of drains on the Romney Marsh are rarely fished. If you wish to get lost in the wilds, Rye & District and several other clubs will sell you a ticket. The waters hold most species, including wild carp, and tench which go to 7 lb.

The remaining main rivers are the Kentish Stour and, of course, the Medway. The Stour rises near Ashford, wending its way through the North Downs, but as a coarse fishery the area from Canterbury downstream is the best bet. There is a free stretch in Canterbury on the left bank, and Canterbury & District AA controls the famous section from Grove Ferry to Plucks Gutter. It is predominantly roach fishing these days, with pockets of bream. Good pike can be encountered in some areas, the best 28 lb; the match catch record is 78 lb 15 oz. The river here is tidal, with a big change in water height at times.

125

The Medway is a major coarse fishery from Tonbridge downstream, the two main controlling clubs being Tonbridge & District A&FPS and the Maidstone Victory & Medway PS. Both sell day tickets on the bank. It is mostly roach and bream fishing and, therefore, a popular match venue, with top weight around 60 lb.

There is a history of big fish of a variety of species, but it is beginning to look a little dated. An eel of 7 lb 6 oz is the only really big specimen reported in the 1980s, though in the previous decade chub to 7 lb 9 oz were taken and a perch of 5 lb 4 oz was reported, but for some reason did not achieve the record status such a weight should have earned. There have been roach to 3 lb 1 oz, and it can also produce carp over 20 lb.

Most of the Medway tributaries have little or no day ticket access – a particular pity in the case of the Beult, which is widely known to contain very large roach.

'THE KING of Island Rivers; if deficient in the grander features of landscape it is rich in pictorial beauty.' So starts *The Book of the Thames*, written by S C Hall in 1859. With a fascinating insight into the social history of the time, it covers the whole river from source to the estuary. It also carries some interesting if questionable references to fishing. 'Perch grow, however, to a much larger size, frequently weighing four or five pounds and occasionally so large as eight or nine pounds.' 'The pike is the largest and most ravenous, growing sometimes to enormous size – often fifty, sixty or even seventy pounds.' Few fish of even half those sizes are taken from the Thames today but the methods described by Hall have changed very little in 125 years.

Today, thanks to the efforts of Thames Water and its predecessors, the Thames is emerging as one of the premier river venues in the country. Its many tributaries – some chalk streams, others meandering lowland streams – offer the widest possible variety of fishing. Even salmon, after an absence of 150 years, are once more to be found in the Thames. The headwaters of the Thames above Cricklade, and some of the tributaries that swell its size, the Churn, Coln, Ray, and Colne, can all provide good fishing, but access is not always easy and some of the better swims can be remote. Most species can be caught, but roach and chub will make up the bulk of any catch.

Between Cricklade and Lechlade there is some good roach fishing with bread flake always sorting out the better specimens. Some chub and barbel show upstream of the road bridge, with the possibility of the odd large barbel, but down through St John's lock and Buscot it is mostly small roach and chub. In the Anchor section at Kelmscot the chub tend to be larger. Matches are often won with weights in excess of 50 lb, and two notable chub swims regularly produce in excess of 30 lb. Below this the fishing can be patchy; 20 lb is a good weight until the bream start to show at Radcot, where bags of 40 lb plus are quite on the cards. The bream tend to average 2 lb 8 oz to 3 lb 8 oz. Downstream of Radcot, where bream run rather smaller, 15 lb is a good day's fishing.

On the Clanfield waters, below Radcot, the chub fishing is excellent and chub can be taken all along this stretch. Catches of over 70 lb have been recorded and the current Upper Thames match record of 95 lb came from this area. In the Rushey lock section, chub run to around 5 lb and barbel of 7 lb plus are common. Around Tadpole bridge two noted barbel swims produce good fishing consistently; two in excess of 10 lb have been taken in one net. Match weights of 25 to 40 lb, mostly chub, are average. Good chub fishing continues through the Shifford reaches, with some big roach and perch, but barbel are less often taken along here, although the ones that are caught are often big.

The river Windrush enters the Thames at Newbridge. The lower part of the river is mainly coarse fishing – chub, roach, dace, and barbel; the higher reaches are trout fisheries. Between Newbridge and Bablock Hythe the most consistent weights are made up of chub and bream, but good roach and a few good perch will always turn up in the top part of the Pinkhill stretch, towards Bablock Hythe. Ten pounds is a good weight, but lower down 70 lb is possible if the bream shoals can be located and encouraged to feed.

From Eynsham, where the river Evenlode enters the Thames, to Oxford, the fishing is modest at best. Good bags will turn up; 30 lb roach catches have been taken where the Evenlode runs in, but such weights are not common. Chub, bream, and roach can all be found all along this stretch, but few notable specimen fish.

The area around Oxford is dominated by the famous Medley stretch where the river runs alongside the vast acreage of Port Meadow, one of the largest areas of common land in the country. Here the chub predominate, but some solitary barbel grow to double-figure size and the bream, if they can be contacted in this, the widest part of the Upper Thames, can often be match winners.

The river Cherwell flows into the Thames a mile or so downstream of Medley, and it is the peg opposite the Cherwell mouth that anglers like to draw when fishing downstream of the city centre. Weights of 50 lb to over 100 lb have been recorded here, along with several very notable chub. The Cherwell itself must be one of the least artificial rivers in the Thames Valley; its route and banks are entirely natural. Some good fishing is to be had in places on the Cherwell, but the sport does not always match the scenic beauty, and local knowledge is essential. A mile or two further downstream, between Iffley and Sandford locks, some very good bags of bream can be taken.

Below Oxford, through Abingdon to Wallingford, the river varies very little in character, being

River Thames weir pool at Mapledurham

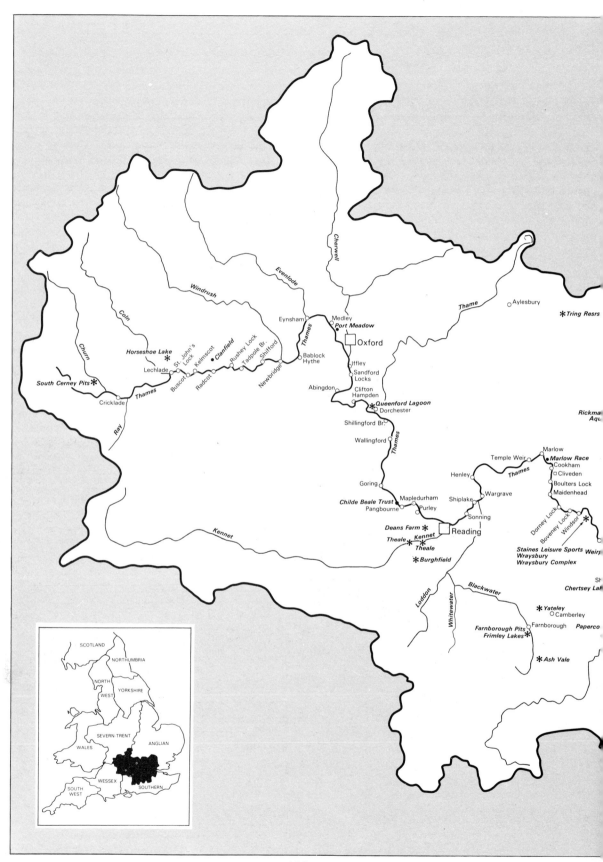

Aylesbury

Cherwell

Evenlode

Windrush

Coln

Churn

Thame

*Tring Resrs

Eynsham

Medley
Port Meadow

Thames

Oxford

Iffley

Sandford
Locks

Bablock
Hythe

Horseshoe Lake
*

St. John's
Lock

Clanfield

Kelmscot

Rushey Lock

Tadpole Br.

Shifford

Lechlade

Buscot

Radcot

Newbridge

South Cerney Pits *

Thames

Abingdon

Clifton
Hampden

Cricklade

Ray

*Queenford Lagoon
Dorchester

Shillingford Br.

Wallingford

Thames

*Rickma
Aqu*

Marlow

Temple Weir

Marlow Race
Cookham

□ Cliveden

Henley

Thames

Boulters Lock
Maidenhead

Goring

Childe Beale Trust
Pangbourne

Mapledurham

Purley

Shiplake

Wargrave

Dorney Lock

Windsor *

Deans Farm *

Theale *

Kennet
Theale

Reading

Boveney Lock

Sonning

*Staines Leisure Sports
Wraysbury
Wraysbury Complex*

Weir

Kennet

* *Burghfield*

Loddon

Whitewater

Blackwater

Sh
Chertsey La

* *Yateley*
○ Camberley

Farnborough Pits
Frimley Lakes *

Farnborough

Paperco

* *Ash Vale*

SCOTLAND

NORTHUMBRIA

NORTH
WEST

YORKSHIRE

SEVERN-TRENT

WALES

ANGLIAN

WESSEX

SOUTH
WEST

SOUTHERN

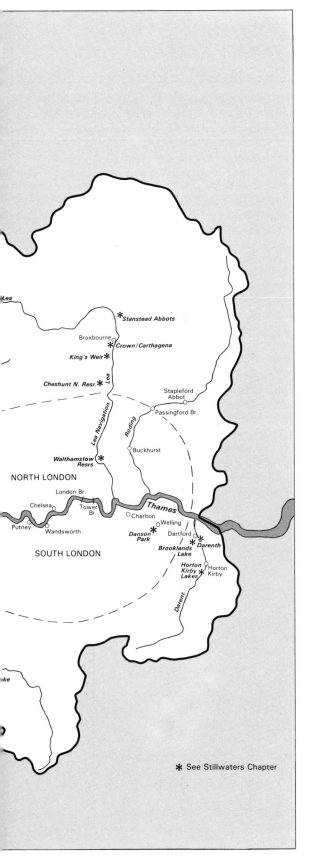

* See Stillwaters Chapter

fairly uniform in width and depth. At Clifton Hampden, on water belonging to the Oxford and District Association, some of the biggest Thames carp are to be caught in the area downstream of the bridge. Chub and barbel also abound in this stretch.

The river Thame joins the Thames at Dorchester, in the shadow of the great abbey church of St Peter and St Paul. The lower reaches of the Thames can provide good mixed fishing, but further upstream the growth of the town of Aylesbury has had a significant effect on the fishing for many miles.

Barbel are becoming quite prominent in the stretch downstream from Dorchester, although this is still very much a good mixed fishery for bream, roach, dace, and chub. Most of the Thames carp around this part of the river originated from stock introduced over 20 years ago in the Shillingford bridge area. Fish in the mid 20 lb class are quite frequently taken, not always by design.

Some of the best catches of Thames chub are taken from the Wallingford area, with individual fish to 5 lb and bags in excess of 100 lb not infrequent. Downstream of Wallingford, if the shoals can be located, similar bags of bream can be caught, with some fish up to 6 lb. Roach, dace, perch, and carp can be caught all the way through.

At Goring very large bags of chub can be taken during the early season, usually on the feeder near the far bank. Here, unfortunately, if the chub are not feeding, there is little else to go for. Downstream of Goring, just above Pangbourne, is the marvellous Childe Beale Trust water. Just why this bit of the Thames is so good for bream is difficult to see, but the world five-hour match record was once held by Mike Stratton of Reading with 174 lb of bream from this section. Day tickets are available and the water is bookable for matches. The bream predominate all the way in this area but good roach and chub can be taken if the bream do not show. In the Purley area, downstream of Pangbourne, the fishing is very patchy, but occasionally turns up good catches of bream and chub.

Getting down into the Reading area and the Reading & District water at Mapledurham, the Chazey Farm stretch turns up good bags of chub, bream, and roach. No records are likely to be broken but the fishing is consistent. On the Reading Promenade the fishing is free, though a peg fee is required if it is booked for a match through the Borough Council offices. Fish of all species can be caught along this part of the Thames. No really big bags have been recorded for some time, but the occasional big perch to 3 lb 8 oz can be a welcome bonus.

More free fishing is available below Reading bridge at Kings Meadow on the south bank, but below Kings Meadow to the Kennet is Reading & District water for members only.

The river Kennet, much of it controlled by Reading & District, must provide some of the best fishing anywhere in the Thames Valley. The barbel are plentiful and big, with 5 to 10 lb specimens likely to turn up almost anywhere. Some go up to 13 lb. Chub, roach, dace, and bream all give good sport in the fast flow. Tench to 8 lb have also been taken from the Kennet. On the main river, Reading & District again has the fishing below the Kennet down to Sonning, but on the Sonning-Shiplake-Wargrave stretch the fishing is patchy, with only occasional good bags of chub or bream.

At Henley, on waters controlled by Remenham AC, there is a ban on the use of lead shot. Anglers fishing the area should be warned that lead substitutes must be used. Heavy rowing activities along this reach tend to disturb the fish almost as much as the fisherman, and sport can be very patchy. Temple weir, just upstream of Marlow, holds some top quality barbel and chub, and in the winter months bream shoals settle in the deeper slack water.

Below Temple weir, on waters controlled by Marlow AS, barbel and chub are again the dominant species. During the summer the bream tend to lie just upstream of Marlow bridge. Favourite method for either species is hemp or caster, usually on the feeder. In Marlow weirpool, near the old Compleat Angler hotel, there are more big barbel and some big Thames trout. The old-fashioned method of drawing the hook up the weir apron and using the resulting bunch of silkweed as hookbait is still practised here, and it can be a very effective bait when properly presented.

The area known locally as Marlow Race – under the bypass bridge down to the old castle landmark – is again barbel country, with some chub and some big bream mixed in. Near Wooton's boathouse, chub tend to be the dominant species with 50 lb bags quite common.

Around Cookham, with the exception of the few pegs between the yacht club and the road bridge, the fishing is very patchy until you get to the Cliveden reach, with the magnificent beech woods on the far bank. Here the fishing is good and all species can be caught, the islands above Boulters lock being a favourite spot. The Sounding Arches at Maidenhead is another well known and well written about barbel hotspot but below this, down to Dorney & Boveney lock, the sport is once more patchy, though there are some good fish about.

A problem the Thames angler has to contend with is boat traffic. This far downstream and below there can often be more boats per mile than anglers.

Between Boveney lock and Windsor there is excellent dace fishing. A few big barbel are caught but most run to only around 3 to 4 lb. A few good perch of 1 lb plus are once more being taken in the Old Windsor area. Down to Staines, past Runnymede and Magna Carta Island, occasional very big roach are taken, but chub and modest sized barbel are the most likely to make up bags of 20 to 30 lb. In Staines weirpool there are barbel in excess of 5 lb.

Downstream of Staines it is all, or mostly all, free fishing. The towpath bank below Staines is generally believed to be all free fishing but there are one or two places where there are access rights only, to pass and repass along the bank. In these cases local knowledge is essential. From Staines all the way down to Teddington most species are to be found, but mostly small roach and dace. In the Hampton area bags of roach and dace of 7 to 10 lb are not uncommon, with dace probably the most predominant. A few bream to 2 lb are always possible, but big bags of bream are seldom taken. The closer the river gets to Teddington the more mediocre the fishing seems to become.

By far the best fishing anywhere in this area must be the weirpools, particularly at Shepperton weir, where night fishing sessions have produced some exceedingly good fish of all species, roach, chub, and barbel particularly. Barbel downstream of Staines are not too numerous, though the most likely spots are the weirpools. The same could generally be said of chub. They too seem to show their best in the weirpools. The rivers Loddon, Blackwater, Whitewater, and Colne run into the Thames between Reading and Teddington. The fishing on all of them varies enormously.

If any proof is still needed of the benefits of the tremendous clean-up of England's capital river you would need to look no further than the tidal reaches below Teddington lock. Here is the home of one of the Thames's oldest angling clubs, the Francis Francis Club, which to this day does its fishing from punts.

Most species can now be found in the tidal reaches, and in Teddington weirpool bags of bream in excess of 50 lb have been taken from the deeper holes, with individual fish to 4 lb. Breadflake is the preferred bait for sorting out the big roach and bream during the early season, while the huge dace shoals provide popular sport from September through to the end of the season. Chub are not noted for being numerous or big in the tidal Thames, but some very big pike are caught in the area immediately below Teddington.

Tackle should not be too light for any fishing. The father of the current Francis Francis secretary had an 18 lb 8 oz carp while fishing in 2½ feet of water for gudgeon. Well worth a visit if you are in the area is the Fisherman's Bar at the Fox public house in Twickenham, where photos provide a catalogue of the more notable catches.

Downstream of Putney bridge, best known to non-Londoners as the start of the annual Oxford and Cambridge Boat Race, dace is the quarry most anglers go for. The first two hours or so of the rising tide are probably the best for fishing all the way down the tidal reaches. Further downstream it is necessary to watch the tide very carefully. In the Wandsworth area it is possible to get on to the foreshore with the receding tide about three hours after high water, but you must not stray far from your access point; the tide comes in quickly when it turns, and you could be in trouble. Around Chelsea Flour Mill there are many carp to be caught, crucian and common, with some of 20 lb.

In the Kings Reach, between County Hall and the Royal Festival Hall, some huge bags of dace have been taken, mainly on maggot, but bread and redworm can often be very effective. There are two well known bream shoals around London bridge area. They can be clearly seen but they tend to stick to mid-stream and, in warm weather, very close to the surface. At Tower bridge there have been more than a hundred 2 lb plus roach taken from eel traps.

In addition to the clubs mentioned, many others control fishing on the Thames, including Oxford APS, Berks & Oxon AA, Oxford & District AA, Witney AS, Abingdon & Oxford AA, Marlow AC, and Old Windsor AC.

Paying due attention to the Thames has left little opportunity to consider other rivers, some of which offer the same standard of sport. The Lee is a superb coarse fishery between Hertford and Tottenham, and is mostly either free fishing or by tickets sold on the bank. The Roding offers quite

good sport for chub, roach, and dace in the Buckhurst, Passingford bridge, and Stapleford Abbot areas of Essex. There are several outstanding canals, too – the Grand Union , Basingstoke, Oxford, and the last few miles of the Kennet and Avon.

Stillwaters
(Thames and Southern WA areas)

IT WOULD be a daunting task to compile a comprehensive list of all the stillwaters in the Thames and Southern Water Authority areas, with information about the fish they contain. There are hundreds of lakes in the Thames area alone, and no angler could get to know them all in several lifetimes. The aim here will be to mention some of the most famous and to track the angler on to some good fishing in an area where the choice must seem bewildering.

In many parts of the country gravel pits are usually let off to clubs which may or may not offer day ticket facilities. In the south, gravel company fishing is more organised. Three companies in particular control an impressive amount of fishing, some of it truly outstanding. Many anglers, reading of some of the catches, get the impression that the waters must be highly exclusive; in fact they are often day or reasonably priced season ticket waters which anyone can fish, though in some cases there may be a limit on the number of permits.

Savay lake, at Harefield, near Denham, Middlesex, is probably the most famous carp water apart from the legendary Redmire. It is a Redlands Angling Scheme water which offers day tickets. Apart from giant carp, it holds specimen bream, tench, and pike. Redlands has a dozen lake complexes altogether, all day ticket and season ticket. Apart from Savay the best known are probably the Deans Farm fishery at Reading; the Crown/Carthagena fishery at Broxbourne, Hertfordshire (three lakes totalling 40 acres plus fishing on the river Lea and Lea Navigation Channel); King's Weir fishery at Wormley, Hertfordshire; and Old Bury Hill Lake at Dorking, Surrey.

The Amey Anglers Association sells an annual permit covering a variety of good waters, including the Theale complex between Theale and Reading, the Wraysbury complex near Windsor, the Linford lakes near Newport Pagnell, the Dorchester on Thames complex, and Queensford lagoon, off the

Dorchester bypass (which recently produced two unclaimed record bream, the biggest 15 lb 6 oz). The Amey Roadstone Corporation has other waters which are not yet incorporated into Amey AA. These include the famous Horseshoe Lake just north of Lechlade, for which day and season permits are available.

Leisure Sport Angling, set up by the Ready Mixed Concrete Group of Companies, is the biggest of the three, with most of its fishing in the Home Counties. There are 21 separate venues; separate permits are sold for each and one which covers all of them.

The selection includes Ash Vale, at Ash Vale, Surrey, three small lakes which nevertheless hold specimen fish, including tench over 8 lb; Broxbourne, four lakes holding pike to 31 lb, carp to 28 lb 12 oz, tench to 8 lb, bream to 10 lb 4 oz, and roach to 3 lb 2 oz; Burghfield, Berks, three lakes with big fish and a stretch of the river Kennet holding barbel to 9 lb plus; Chertsey lake near Chertsey, Surrey; Chigborough, at Maldon, Essex; Larkfield, near Maidstone (noted for carp to 29 lb, pike to 27 lb, and good fish of most other species); Stanstead Abbots, Hertfordshire, which has carp to 30 lb; Theale (not to be confused with the Amey AA water in the same area); Wraysbury (again not the same water as Amey's), which has a very impressive specimen list – carp 31 lb 5 oz, pike 27 lb 4 oz, bream 10 lb 2 oz, tench 9 lb 10 oz, roach 3 lb 6 oz, eel 4 lb 5 oz; and Darenth, near Dartford, Kent, which for carp is Leisure Sport's answer to Redlands' Savay. Here 20 lb plus carp are commonplace, and they run to 31 lb.

Waters holding even bigger fish include Yateley, near Camberley, Surrey, with a small group of huge carp running to 45 lb and pike to 30 lb, tench to 8 lb 3 oz, and bream to 13 lb 4 oz. Papercourt, near Ripley, Surrey, has carp to 25 lb, pike to 32 lb, and big tench. Leisure Sport's Staines water at Wraysbury has carp to 38 lb.

Catch information has been scattered through the list simply to indicate the possibilities, but if we err it will be on the modest side. The companies have to rely on what anglers tell them, and on some waters there is a conspiracy of silence which infuriates the fishery managers. To give just one example, Redlands' Deans Farm fishery at Reading has produced bigger bream than have ever been reported; local opinion is they could run to 20 lb. Even if the figures are on the low side, they still speak volumes of the potential of southern stillwaters.

Many other waters besides gravel pits offer the same superb sport. Kent is littered with good carp lakes, which often hold big tench as well. These include Brooklands Lake, Dartford; Horton Kirby lakes, Horton Kirby; School Pool at Faversham; Damson Park at Welling; and Johnson's Lake, Larkfield, which is better known for tench than carp. Chiddingstone Castle holds good bream. All sell day tickets on site.

In Hertfordshire are the famous Tring reservoirs, Marsworth, Startops, and Wilstone, which are noted for big bream. Wilstone holds the catfish record, 43 lb 8 oz in 1970. Other Hertfordshire waters not already mentioned include Cheshunt North reservoir and Rickmansworth Aquadrome. Seven of the big Walthamstow reservoirs offer good coarse fishing – Walthamstow Nos 1 to 3, East and West Warwick, and High and Low Maynard. Sadly, however, the Lambeth reservoirs, which once produced a record roach, are virtually fishless. That is the opinion of London AA, which controls the fishing, and we have to admire its honesty.

The LAA does have some fine fishing, however, though it rates its best stillwaters now as the lakes at Glansford, near Long Melford, and Bures lake – all in Suffolk. Bures lake holds big bream and tench. Sussex waters include the Bucksole, Ecclesbourne, and Clive Vale reservoirs in Hastings; Peppingford lakes at Nutley; Weir Wood reservoir at Forest Row; Chichester pits; Ladybrook lakes, Ashington; and the Southern Leisure Centre pits at Chichester.

In Hampshire some of the most noted stillwaters are just over the Wessex border, notably Kingfisher Lake at Ringwood and the Blashford and Hightown pits in the same area. Among those in the Southern or Thames area are the Charlton pits at Charlton, Farnborough pits and Frimley lakes at Farnborough, Hatchet pond at Beaulieu, and Kingham lakes at Winchester. The Thames WA area reaches into Gloucestershire, where there is not much stillwater fishing. Notable exceptions are the famous South Cerney pits controlled by a club of the same name. They are prolific ticket waters, especially for tench and bream.

Many names have been mentioned, but the surface has barely been scratched. It is hard to stand anywhere in the South without being pretty close to a good stillwater fishery. Local inquiries, especially at tackle shops, will invariably track them down.

Anglian
Water Authority

DETAILED SUMMARY of the fishing in the vast Anglian Water area is virtually impossible. It takes in the territory once administered by five different river authorities – Lincolnshire, Welland & Nene, Great Ouse, East Suffolk & Norfolk, Norfolk and Essex. In the main it is bream country, much of it the accidental by-product of the drainage systems created to protect the rich, flat farmland of Eastern England. The whole area is steeped in angling history. Place names leap from the map to remind anglers – those with a decade or two of experience, at any rate – of great deeds by legendary characters.

Many of the rivers and drains fish less well for bream than they did decades ago. They once attracted anglers to events in many hundreds, sometimes thousands, most of them travelling long distances. To rise above the pack required something special, in both the fishing and the angler. People like Billy Lane and Freddie Foster were legends in their lifetimes, triumphant in countless matches. We will never see their like again. The fishing has become much more inconsistent. The great fields have dwindled, and will never rise again.

Even if the fishing came all the way back to its former glory, the price of petrol now would hold back the masses, and rivers like the Trent, which have improved as many eastern waters have declined, serve now as formidable barriers between the Fens and many of their former customers. The great days are over, but that does not mean this huge Anglian area is a write-off. Far from it. The fishing varies from average to superb, as you will learn from what has to be a rapid-fire summary.

In Lincolnshire the key river is the Witham. It offers fine sport with chub, dace, roach, and bream in the non-navigable sections between Lincoln and Grantham. It is carved up by a lot of small clubs, but both Grantham AA and Sheffield & District AA control long stretches. From Lincoln to Boston it is almost exclusively controlled by the Witham & District Joint Anglers Federation, which is a conglomerate of clubs, easily joined. They include Lincoln AA, Boston AA, Sheffield Amalgamated, and Grimsby & District. The fishing here is mainly roach, which show best in the winter, and bream. Few years go by without a match weight over 50 lb at noted areas such as Kirkstead, Dogdyke, Langrick, and Boston West. Other fine waters controlled by the Federation include the Fossdyke, the Louth canal, and the Steeping river, a noted bream and roach water flowing into the Wash between Boston and Skegness.

To the north is the Ancholme, a 'bream or bust' river controlled by Scunthorpe AA. It is patchy, but regularly produces bream weights to 50 lb or more. Boston AA has miles of fishing on the patchwork of drains near the town. The South Forty Foot, Bargate Drain, Sibsey Trader, West Fen, and Upper and Lower Hobhole drains are household names to many anglers. They are all noted for good bream and roach fishing, and most hold big pike – especially the Forty Foot, which has 30-pounders to its credit.

The river Glen wends into the Wash near Spalding – an excellent roach water in the winter. It is the first of the rivers in the Welland & Nene area, which those two great rivers dominate. The Welland is really two vastly different rivers. The upper section is still natural river, with streamy glides packed with good chub and roach. While there are many, many miles of upper Welland, the river is best below Stamford, especially on the long lengths controlled by the Deeping St James club, which is ticket water.

By far the best known section is the lower river from Crowland to Spalding, venue for many famous matches and brewery sponsored galas, most of which are now defunct. There are times when anglers wonder where the bream have gone, but they showed in force on one amazing day in 1983, when every angler for about a mile was catching them, the biggest catches reaching almost 100 lb. It is rare for them all to feed at once, but when they do it is a sight to behold.

There are odd good chub in the lower Welland too, big pike, and some very good tench. The fishing is controlled by Peterborough & District AA, and Sheffield & District AA has the Coronation Channel in Spalding. This offers good roach and bream fishing, and is heavily match-booked on summer Sundays.

Pike fishing on Ormesby Broad

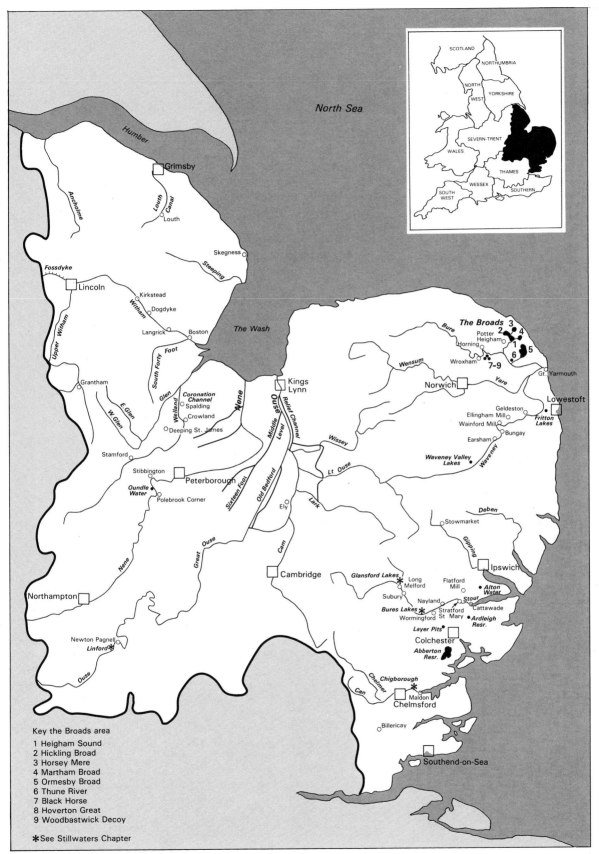

North Sea

Humber

Grimsby

Louth Canal

Louth

Ancholme

Fossdyke

Lincoln

Skegness

Steeping

Kirkstead

Dogdyke

Witham

Langrick

Boston

The Wash

South Forty Foot

Upper Witham

Glen

Grantham

E. Glen

W. Glen

Welland

Coronation Channel

Spalding

Crowland

Nene

Deeping St. James

Kings Lynn

Stamford

Middle Level

Relief Channel

Ouse

Stibbington

Peterborough

Oundle Water

Polebrook Corner

Sixteen Foot

Old Bedford

Ely

Wissey

Lt Ouse

Lark

Cam

Great Ouse

Nene

Northampton

Cambridge

Newton Pagnell

Linford✻

Ouse

The Broads

Bure

3 4
2
Potter Heigham
1 5
Horning
6
Wroxham
7-9

Gt. Yarmouth

Wensum

Norwich

Yare

Lowestoft

Geldeston

Ellingham Mill

Wainford Mill

Bungay

Fritton Lakes

Earsham

Waveney Valley Lakes

Waveney

Deben

Stowmarket

Gipping

Ipswich

Glansford Lakes✻

Long Melford

Flatford Mill

Alton Water

Subury

Nayland

Stratford St Mary

Stour

Cattawade

Bures Lakes✻

Wormingford

Ardleigh Resr.

Layer Pits

Colchester

Abberton Resr.

Chelmer

Chigborough✻

Can

Maldon

Chelmsford

Billericay

Southend-on-Sea

Key the Broads area
1 Heigham Sound
2 Hickling Broad
3 Horsey Mere
4 Martham Broad
5 Ormesby Broad
6 Thune River
7 Black Horse
8 Hoverton Great
9 Woodbastwick Decoy

✻See Stillwaters Chapter

Inset map:
SCOTLAND
NORTHUMBRIA
NORTH WEST
YORKSHIRE
SEVERN-TRENT
WALES
THAMES
SOUTH WEST
WESSEX
SOUTHERN

The river Nene is similar to the Welland in superficial character, but the lower end does not offer the same quality of roach and bream fishing. The north and south banks above the Dog in a Doublet are perhaps more consistent, but anglers seldom see the really big catches of former years. Above Peterborough there are pockets of outstanding chub fishing down willow-lined banks, good roach and the odd big bream shoal. The 1975 National Champion Michael Hoad-Reddick, from Rotherham, came up with a remarkable 63 lb 7 oz at Stibbington, for example. There are bream in the Oundle water at Polebrook Corner, and the Oundle area generally is good for roach.

Right up to and beyond Northampton there can be catches to gladden the heart, but it has to be said that many sections of this great river look a lot better than they fish. That is certainly true of much of the fishing in the Great Ouse area, once vital to anglers on the bream circuit. Water authority experts and anglers differ in their explanations for it, but there is no argument that in the 1970s every important water in the area lost form dramatically. Suddenly the once abundant cyprinids (roach and bream) were missing, and a massive cull of predators (pike and zander), was launched in a bid to correct the situation.

There are signs that it may be working. At the time of writing a number of big match weights of bream were being reported from the Great Ouse, notably in the London AA and King's Lynn AA fisheries. Who knows, it may develop to the point where local anglers stop travelling to the Trent – a telling reversal from the old days. The Trent represents a consistency which nothing in the Great Ouse area can yet match, though who, 20 years ago, would have believed it? How could anyone know what was to happen to such waters as the Relief Channel, Middle Level, Sixteen Foot, Popham's Eau, the Old Bedford and Delph and, of course, the Ouse itself, with its key tributaries such as the Wissey, Lark, and Cam?

The Ouse and Cam national championship in 1979 will go down as one of the most disastrous in angling history. Now some of these waters are capable of producing the occasional big catch, and possibly a brighter picture might emerge if more people fished them. There is a lot of good lake and gravel pit fishing in the area, including the 'catfish belt' waters in Bedfordshire and Buckinghamshire – Leighton Buzzard pits and Claydon lakes at Steeple Claydon (both season permit waters via

Leighton Buzzard AC) and the lakes at stately Woburn. Stillwaters have retained quality while rivers and drains have declined, but let us not be too gloomy about the prospects. Obituaries have been written for angling areas before, and they have proved premature.

This is true of the jewel in the Anglian crown – the Norfolk Broads and the rivers which connect them. The University of East Anglia was able to show that the Broads were on the brink of irreversible decline, principally as a result of too much boat traffic and various forms of pollution. Most of the problems have not and probably cannot be tackled. Experts say the habitat of aquatic birds, including the swan, is virtually destroyed, yet it is still politically convenient to blame anglers' lead for the whole of the swan problem.

Some of what remains of the unique broadland environment is now hostage to farming fortunes. It is, apparently, less important than a fractional increase in various EEC farm surpluses. It is difficult to be too optimistic about the long-term future of the Broads, especially for those who have watched the decline over the last 20 years or so. Fishing the rivers in summer is now only marginally more enjoyable than fishing the fast lane of the M1 on a bank holiday weekend and yet, in quieter areas and at more peaceful times of the year, some of the sport available can only be described as exceptional.

In the 1950s and 1960s the Upper Thurne area of the Broads, taking in Horsey Mere, Hickling, Heigham Sound, and Martham, offered such good pike fishing that few bothered to explore the vast potential of the rest of the area. The old stamping ground of the great Jim Vincent became the stage for other legendary characters such as Dennis Pye, Bill Giles, Reg Sandys, Len Spencer, Frank Wright, Edwin Vincent (son of Jim), and innovative newcomers such as Fred Wagstaffe and Bob Reynolds. An awesome number of big pike were taken, culminating in the 40-pounder by Peter Hancock from Horsey in 1967, which is now the record.

Soon after that, however, the fishing was wiped off the map. Horsey, Hickling, and Heigham were devastated by a de-oxygenating pollution, and opinions vary about the extent of the recovery which seems to be evident today. The area is producing giant pike once again, but beyond any doubt the majority of the fish reported were caught by anglers poaching the private Martham Broad, where there is now limited legal access by arrangement with the Norfolk Naturalists Trust.

One positive effect of the Upper Thurne disaster was to spread pike angling effort to other areas, and it soon became clear that Norfolk had plenty to offer. Areas which consistently produce very good pike include the river Bure from Wroxham to Horning; the broads leading off the Bure, including Wroxham, Woodbastwick Decoy, and the private Hoveton Great and Black Horse broads; the Thurne at Martham and Potter Heigham; and the Ormesby group of broads. In fact most of the patches of blue can offer pike sport which would be considered good to great in other parts of the country. It goes without saying that bream and roach populations have to be high to support the pike, but in summer the best opportunities are at night.

Some of the best and most peaceful fishing is on the Yare at and below Norwich and the city reaches of the Wensum. Local tackle shops will be only too pleased to guide the holiday angler towards the wealth of peaceful and productive lake fishing which is available in the Broads area. They might also be able to sort something out on the upper Wensum, increasingly carved up by little clubs and syndicates. This is well worth a little local research, for the river holds roach over 2 lb, chub over 5 lb, and pockets of big barbel, some in double figures.

The Waveney, most southerly of the Broads holiday rivers, is still a formidable fishery. It is mostly free fishing below Geldeston, the upper limit for boats, where the bream run 2 to 4 lb and the pike top 20 lb, with 30 lb a possibility. Ellingham Mill is where the chub start to show, among quality roach, nice dace, bream, and so on, and there is little change up to Wainford Mill, just below Bungay. This is Bungay Cherry Tree fishing, and Suffolk County AA has good fishing on Bungay Common.

Other popular areas include Earsham, where there is both free and Cherry Tree fishing – a good chub section. Waveney Valley lakes, which offer some of the best carp fishing in the country, once lost some fish into the river; Earsham is where they seem to have settled. Upper sections of the river still hold specimen fish, including roach over 2 lb and isolated big chub. There are not so many dace now, but the perch are making a comeback. Sadly, that does not seem to apply to Oulton Broad, once the premier water for the species. A better stillwater in the Lowestoft area is Fritton lake – good tench, bream and pike fishing, though the accessible area

Big bream catch from the Relief Channel

139

seems to be shrinking. Some of the best pike areas are now out of bounds.

Running south from Waveney, the next important water is the river Gipping, once the poor relation in East Anglia. Not any more, according to George Alderson who, as general manager of the Gipping Angling Preservation Society, is a rare bird – a full-time, paid angling official. And why not? It is a full-time job, and much of his time has been spent campaigning to improve the Gipping.

The change in the past 15 years has been tremendous. Bream catches now run to 50 lb at times. Roach over 2 lb and sometimes over 3 lb can show, along with chub to over 5 lb. Chub now predominate in some sections, and 4 lb fish are quite common. The tench fishing is good, sometimes even in winter when snow is on the ground, and carp show more and more often.

The key section is the 10 miles from Stowmarket to Ipswich. The preservation society controls most of it, offering day tickets on stretches near Ipswich and in places further upstream. The society also manages Alton Water for Anglian Water, more than 350 acres with 11 miles of bank and 415 permanent match pegs. Anyone can fish on day tickets, or book matches which commonly produce 50 to 70 lb top weights. The species include roach, bream, perch, hybrids, and pike which run to 30 lb. Another good fishery in the area is the river Deben, noted for quality fish, including a 28 lb 5 oz pike in 1975.

In the Colchester division of the AWA a key river is the Suffolk Stour. This river, much of which is controlled by Sudbury AA, Long Melford AC, and the London AA, has a big fish pedigree going way back to a 30 lb catfish at Flatford Mill in 1894. In more recent times it has produced roach to 3 lb 10 oz and dace over 1 lb, and good bream in many areas. Lower reaches at Wormingford, Nayland, and Stratford St Mary are controlled by the Colchester APS, and are noted for big bream. Six-pounders can show in match weights to 50 lb and more. Where the river widens and deepens towards Cattawade, approaching the sea, it is also good bream fishing.

Lots of little rivers wriggle like snakes all over Essex. One of the best is the Chelmer, and there is a very good free stretch in Chelmsford where the Can runs in. The bream here can reach 7 lb, and the roach quite often go over 2 lb. Most of the river is controlled by clubs, some of which, including Chelmsford AA, offer day tickets.

Notable stillwaters include Ardleigh reservoir, superb for specimen roach and perch when it is opened for coarse fishing at the end of the trout season; Abberton reservoir, noted for huge pike, big bream, and roach, for which day tickets must be obtained in advance from the Essex Water Company; and Layer pits at Colchester. These produce enormous catches of carp, but are open to outsiders only in occasional matches. Essex, however, is littered with many small stillwaters, usually offering good carp fishing. Tickets for some of them are available from clubs already mentioned, plus Billericay & District AC, SEGAB (a consortium of clubs), and Redbridge AA.

Severn-Trent
Water Authority

$\mathcal{A}$CCORDING TO biologists, the Trent has more fish for volume of water than any other river in England. It is probably the most important river for anglers in the Midlands and the North, and despite the enormous pressure it takes, it gets better all the time. We know from the old writings of people like J W Martin that the Trent was a superb river holding nearly all the common species, but Martin's river was unrecognisable to modern anglers until fairly recently. Polluted at the top end from the industrial Midlands, it held very few fish upstream of Nottingham. Below the city it held roach and gudgeon and precious little else, but the transformation in the past decade or so has been remarkable.

Pollution is now under control, and what were the filthiest tributaries are now capable of supporting fish life. The area which has come back from the dead extends almost into the heart of the Potteries. In the 1960s the river lost many of its roach to the UDN disease which was sweeping most of the country at the time. This probably helped to clear the way for the chub explosion which has taken place in the past 15 years. Chub are now predominant, but all the other species of coarse fish are increasing too.

Carp got into the river – almost certainly when it flooded into gravel pits. Once they would have died, but in the cleaner Trent they flourished, and were assisted to reproduce by the warm water from the many power stations. The Trent is now the premier carp river in England, capable of growing fish to more than 30 lb. Double-figure carp are commonplace. Bream got into the river by the same route as carp, and thrive for the same reasons. They can turn up almost anywhere, but bream sport in the tidal river below Cromwell Weir is particularly

impressive, with some of the fish now topping 7 lb, and 4-pounders not at all unusual.

The barbel of which Martin wrote so lovingly ceased to exist for many years, but they clung to existence in cleaner tributaries, the Dove and possibly the Derwent. A few years ago they came back. Anglers started catching what they called 'funny looking gudgeon', unable to believe that they were really tiny barbel. Now they are caught everywhere, including the tidal river, and they are reaching the point of predominance in some areas, especially between Nottingham and Burton upon Trent. Big shoals can also be encountered in many places downstream of Nottingham, including Burton Joyce and Caythorpe. The bigger barbel now are around 8 lb, and the first authentic 10-pounder in modern times is just around the corner.

Latest species to make a comeback is the perch, now common in many areas. In recent seasons perch over 3 lb have been taken in the Donnington area, and there is one reliable report of a 4-pounder. There is certainly plenty for the predatory perch to

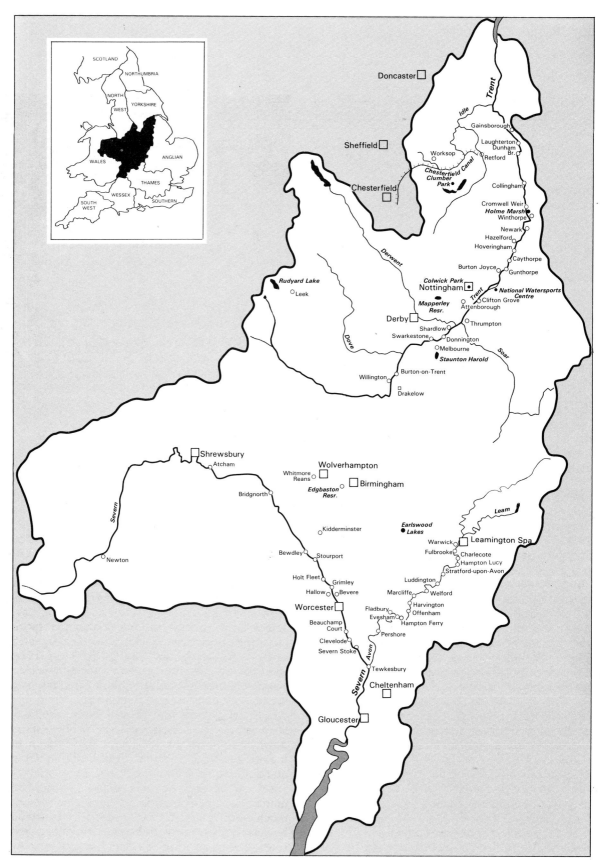

feed on, and the same goes for the pike, which can top 20 lb, especially in and near the various weir pools.

A detailed rundown of the fishing in each area is unnecessary, for everywhere fishes well. Undoubtedly the most attractive part of the river is upstream of Nottingham, where the river has never been made navigable. It has natural banks, fast shallows, glides, and deeps. Burton upon Trent now offers perhaps the best roach fishing on the river, and there are plenty of dace.

All points between Burton and Nottingham produce big catches of chub. There are big carp near Drakelow power station and the barbel show everywhere. They are particularly numerous at Willington, Swarkestone, and Shardlow, where catches commonly top 50 lb. Nottingham downstream is much less scenic, but the status of the fishing is uniformly magnificent. Clifton Grove, Gunthorpe, Burton Joyce, Hoveringham, Caythorpe, Hazelford, and Winthorpe are just a few of the venues with big catch potential.

Two areas which occasionally rise above the norm are the Coventry water at Thrumpton, which has produced chub catches over 100 lb in matches, and Holme Marsh, the downstream end of the non-tidal river. The swims just above Cromwell lock frequently produce enormous catches which can include chub, bream, and double-figure carp. The match catch record went over 100 lb in 1983.

Below the lock there are many miles of tidal water holding coarse fish, right down to Gainsborough. The most popular tidal fishing, though, is the top end between Laughterton through Dunham bridge to Collingham. There are vast shoals of big bream, and the chub are the biggest on the Trent, with 5-pounders turning up quite often in matches. The roach fishing is good, and the carp top 20 lb. It is a truly wonderful river once again; J W Martin would recognise it now.

The main tributaries are all good fisheries, especially the Soar, Dove, Derwent, and Idle. The chub fishing on the lower Derwent is exceptional, with a recent match catch record topping 100 lb. Clubs with impressive fishing include Doncaster AA, Sheffield & District AA, Rotherham UAF, Collingham AC, Worksop AAA, Newark PF, Nottingham AA, Nottingham Federation, and the Burton Joint Angling Association.

The Severn, a river of major importance to the angler, in some sections produces sport which is

Hazleford – a chub hot spot on the river Trent

virtually unrivalled. It rises in the mountainous grandeur of Montgomeryshire, and looks a lot better than it fishes along the 40 miles or so to Shrewsbury. Anglers and experts have diverging opinions as to why, but there seems little likelihood that the river record chub of 7 lb 14 oz will ever be beaten.

That fish was caught way back in 1948, at Newtown, and in those days the river received only one release of Welsh reservoir water each month. Now it gets around 26 million gallons every day, and anglers believe this has spoiled the sport. Nevertheless it can fish well at times, the top match catch upstream of Shrewsbury in 1983 being 28 lb. Through the town it begins to run slightly deeper, producing roach, good quality dace, chub, and barbel.

Barbel, introduced from the Kennet in 1956, are now the predominant species from Shrewsbury down to Bridgnorth and Bewdley. Top catch potential is virtually unlimited, as evidenced by the top match weight of 114 lb 11 oz. The fish can run very big too, with an 11½-pounder showing in a 1983 match. Local feeling is that the river now holds much bigger barbel than that, and nobody would be very surprised if the Severn produced the next record fish. Most of the monster barbel in angling

The river Soar at Abbey Park in Leicester

history have come from the Hampshire Avon, but that river has problems these days. On the Severn, however, they are going from strength to strength, and the top venues have tremendous pulling power – Stourport, Holt Fleet, Grimley, Bevere, Hallow … 8 to 10 feet of dreamy-looking water, steady flowing.

Below Worcester it is still big barbel. They win nearly all the matches at famous venues such as Beauchamp Court, Clevelode, and Severn Stoke, but every now and again there are signs of the return of bream. There was a 57 lb match catch of bream at Beauchamp Court in 1983, and 40 lb from the adjoining swim. At one time such catches were almost commonplace, and while nobody can be quite certain why the bream fishing declined, there is a theory that it happened gradually after the big oil tankers stopped going to Worcester.

Anglers' antipathy to power boats of any size is such that they applauded the disappearance of the ships. Now there are discussions about opening the river up once again to the large freight boats. If it comes off it will be interesting to see whether the restoration of the deep channel will create the right conditions for the return of the bream. There is already the basis of recovery. A 69 lb record catch at Grimley in the 1983 Severn championship was an even mixture of small bream and chub taken, inevitably, on the swimfeeder.

The really good fishing on the Severn is along these middle reaches. In the lower river, from Severn Stoke down through Tewkesbury to Gloucester, the fishing is very patchy these days, and the decline is currently the subject of investigation. In the 1950s and 1960s anyone with less than 20 lb in a match knew he had no chance at all, but now it seems to be the odd big weight with next to nothing behind it. One recent match for example, produced a 40 lb winning weight, but only three anglers caught.

It would seem, however, that the pike have a lot less trouble finding fish than the anglers do, for sport with these predators is outstanding near the Severn weirs, particularly at Tewkesbury. One small group of anglers took more than 100 double-figure pike in the winter of 1983, including several over 20 lb. The river record, however, is a 34-pounder taken at Atcham, just below Shrewsbury, some years ago.

The Severn is famous for its annual run of elvers, but it is by no means as impressive as it used to be. Secretive, shadowy figures once made fortunes netting elvers in the dead of night. Now they have to work much harder to make their money, and to keep it. The taxman has taken a sudden interest, and is unsportingly tracing them through the wholesalers. When the elvers were running in their teeming millions they were followed from the sea by shad, and it was common for anglers to catch them by the hundredweight in the lower river. The shad averaged about 1 lb and were sometimes caught at 4 lb. Now, however, they are seen but rarely.

The Birmingham Anglers Association controls much of the Severn, and its membership book is a real bargain. Other clubs and associations with excellent fishing include Gloucester DUAA, Tewkesbury AS, Kidderminster & District, Bridgnorth AA, Provincial AA, Shrewsbury AS, and Whitmore Reans.

In a region dominated by such great rivers as the Trent and Severn it is possible only to summarise the Warwickshire Avon very briefly. What a river it is: many anglers would never fish anywhere else. It has the lot – glorious scenery and an abundance of fish, with chub easily the most predominant.

Maybe the best way to sum it up is to dodge along the river, telling the story in headlines. The biggest barbel so far weighed 11 lb 8 oz. Hampton Ferry, dubbed the 'Wembley of match fishing' by the late Clive Smith because of the consistency of the sport available, has a match record of 41 lb of chub. At Offenham it is chub again, with a match record of 85 lb. At Harvington 30 to 40 lb match catches are common; at Marcliffe it is 30 to 50 lb, with a record of 57 lb.

Evesham, Welford, and Luddington to Stratford are much the same. About the only blot is the Luddington disaster in the world championships, when it came up in overnight flood to ruin what would have been a memorable match. Hampton Lucy, above Stratford, is where Shakespeare was caught poaching deer. Unfortunately there is no record of him fishing, but it was probably even better in his day than it is now. The modern angler cannot complain. Pleasure catches of dace below Hampton Lucy have gone to 70 lb; the best chub catches at Grove Farm, Charlecote, and Fulbrooke are around 40 lb most seasons.

The river can fish well at Warwick where the Leam runs in, but the Leam itself is a better bet. The best chub from this river weighed 6 lb 8 oz, the best

carp 17 lb, and the best roach 2 lb 14 oz. The Leam chub beats the Avon's best, a 6-pounder from Offenham, which also produced the 11 lb 8 oz barbel.

Bream predominated in the Avon before the chub took over, and it is still possible to find big fish. The best bream area is between Pershore and Fladbury; the best time is very early in the morning. One of the most impressive recent catches was 39 bream weighing 102 lb, best fish 8 lb 3 oz. It all happened between 6 and 9 in the morning. Another memorable catch was six bream, all of them over 8 lb. Curiously, the Avon is not noted for big pike, the record being 23 lb 8 oz from Fladbury.

Most of the fishing is easily available to the angler. Birmingham AA controls most of it, but there are 2½ miles of day ticket water (both banks) at Hampton Ferry. Other controlling clubs include Worcester DUAA, Cheltenham & District, Stratford AA, and Warwick AA.

Throughout the Severn–Trent area there is an enormous choice of stillwater fishing, and the advice here can be by no means comprehensive. Obvious choices include Clumber Park, near Worksop, one-time haunt of specimen roach and bream and now improving once again after a dewatering incident, and the extensive gravel pits at Attenborough, near Nottingham, which produce big pike and huge bream catches.

Other noted fisheries include Colwick Park, Nottingham; Earlswood lakes and Edgbaston reservoir, Birmingham; Mapperley reservoir at Derby, which once produced record carp; Rudyard lake, near Leek; Staunton Harold, near Melbourne, Derbyshire; and the rowing course lake at the National Watersports Centre, Holme Pierrepont, Nottinghamshire.

There is also a vast amount of canal fishing, probably more than in any other water authority area. Most offer good fishing, but the star turn without a doubt is the Chesterfield Canal, where Retford AA, Worksop & District AAA, and Sheffield & District AA have important holdings. Retford's water in particular produces huge weights of chub. Match weights have gone over 50 lb; no other canal can remotely match that.

Welsh
Water Authority

THERE IS a tendency to believe that coarse fishing is very scarce in Wales, perhaps because most of the rivers are noted salmon and sea trout waters. The reality, however, is that there are countless small lakes, too numerous to mention, which offer good coarse fishing. There are larger lakes like Bala, Trawsfynydd and Llangorse where the coarse fishing is good. Some of the rivers offer coarse fishing of a quality which is second to none, even if salmon and sea trout are the primary preoccupation of the ever practical Welsh. One potent lesson about game fisheries of which fishery managers elsewhere should perhaps take note is that efforts to control 'unwanted' species serve only to improve the quality of the coarse fish; examples of this are not hard to find in Wales.

There are three major coarse fishing rivers in the Principality. The Severn is dealt with under the Severn–Trent area; the other two are the Dee and the Wye. A fourth which is well worth a mention is the Usk, especially in the context of control measures producing big coarse fish. It would be wrong to pretend that the Usk is a coarse fishery. It is almost completely controlled by salmon and trout fishing clubs and syndicates, and the members deserve our envy.

The Usk, which runs into the Bristol Channel, is one of the most beautiful of all the rivers in Britain, wending its way through picturesque countryside in a series of shallow runs and slow deeps. The annual rod catch of salmon is around 800 a year, which explains why the Welsh are not too impressed with the coarse fish – but they are there. Chub are often caught in the 5 to 6 lb class; there are excellent grayling; and it is more than possible that one or two record dace have perished during the periodic culling campaigns carried out by the game fishing syndicates.

According to some of the game/coarse all-rounders, Usk dace are even bigger than they are on the Wye (of which more later). How to get at them, however, using methods which are not too offensive to the game fisheries, is something of a problem. One way is to make polite requests at farms along the river, when the salmon and trout seasons are over. Another would be to inquire at the many day ticket sources for game fishing on the river, which are listed in the Welsh National Water Development Authority's *Guide to Fresh Water Fishing in Wales*.

It may seem odd for one angling guide to promote another, but our aim is totally different from the WNWDA's. It simply provides a breakdown of the fishing in each catchment area, giving information of the type of fishing and where tickets and licences are available. It is an outstanding effort

Storm over Trawsfynydd

and an excellent buy for the angling tourist, game or coarse. The address for inquiries is Cambrian Way, Brecon, Powys (telephone Brecon [0874] 3181).

If the Usk is frustrating for the coarse fish specimen hunter, so is the Wye. Here again it is the salmon which influence the rules, though to nowhere near the same extent. The Wye rises on Plynlimmon; the same Welsh mountain sends the Severn on its journey into England. The two sources are just over the hill from one another, and it must be doubtful whether two such marvellous rivers arise so close together anywhere else.

The Wye is noted for the quality of its chub and dace. The latter run about three to the pound on good rivers elsewhere, but here it is more like two, and there is the possibility of catching that elusive pounder, which the vast majority of anglers never see throughout their careers; pound dace are more often spoken of than weighed. Fortunately, the coarse angler is not unwelcome on the Wye, providing he plays it strictly by the rule book. Maggots are not allowed until the salmon season ends in October, but bread proves a perfectly acceptable standby, especially for the chub. Dace are present well into the upper reaches at Builth Wells and Newbridge, but Hay-on-Wye is the first place where there is easy access to an abundance of fish.

It was here, just over a decade ago, that a group of anglers made numerous attempts to make dace catches of 100 lb, an unthinkable target for anglers on more normal rivers. The attempts failed – but

only just, for the anglers topped 90 lb several times. The Hay area can also produce the odd good catch of perch nowadays, fish of around the pound mark showing in catches to 30 lb. From Hay downstream the fishing is controlled by several large estates, and the owners will not entertain coarse fishing until the salmon fishing is over. Thereafter an inquiry at an estate office might well receive a positive response. One important ticket source is the Red Lion at Bredwardine.

Down at Hereford the fishing becomes more available again, the Hereford Angling Association controlling it from Belmont through the tennis courts to Bartonsham and Field Farm. Then it is the famous Carrots water (named after the Bunch of Carrots pub), which is a renowned salmon fishery. There are no day tickets at all here; the one chance to get on is when the Wye championship is fished in October, the first Sunday after the salmon fishing ends.

The last time this match was fished (at the time of writing), it produced the river's first 100 lb plus chub catch at Hereford. Just prior to that, over 90 lb was the record, replacing 87 lb 11 oz at Whitney, near Hay-on-Wye, which had stood for some years. All these were chub catches, taken on bread and maggot baits. Some of the chub run very big, with specimens to 7 lb on record, and roach can top 2 lb. Fine pike can be found where chub and dace abound, the biggest on record topping 37 lb.

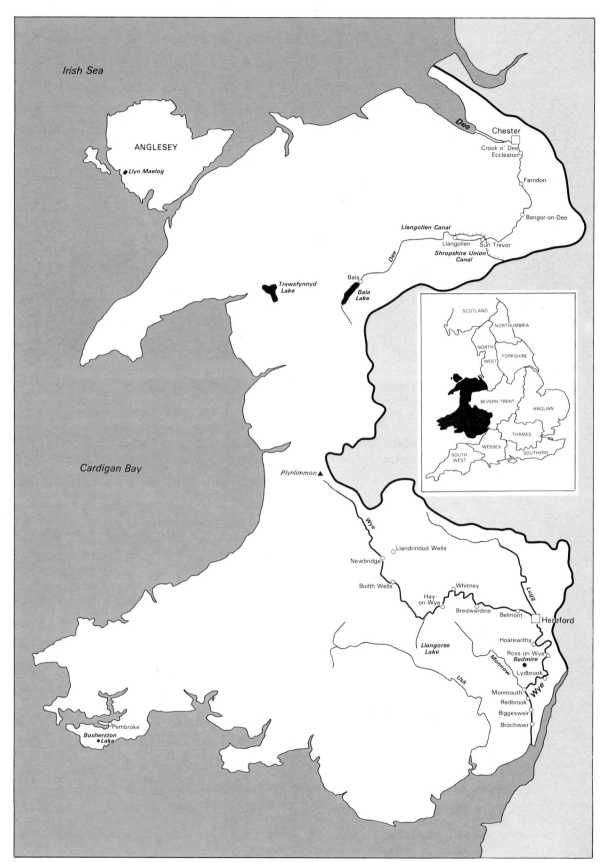

Irish Sea

ANGLESEY

● Llyn Maelog

Dee

Chester

Crook o' Dee
Eccleston

Farndon

Bangor-on-Dee

Llangollen Canal

Llangollen   Sun Trevor

Shropshire Union
Canal

Dee

Bala

Trawsfynnyd
Lake

Bala
Lake

SCOTLAND

NORTHUMBRIA

NORTH
WEST   YORKSHIRE

SEVERN TRENT   ANGLIAN

THAMES

WESSEX   SOUTHERN

SOUTH
WEST

Cardigan Bay

Plynlimmon ▲

Wye

Llandrindod Wells

Newbridge

Builth Wells

Whitney

Hay-
on-Wye

Bredwardine

Lugg

Belmont

Hereford

Hoarewithy

Llangorse
Lake

Ross on Wye
Redmire
●
Lydbrook

Monnow

Usk

Wye

Monmouth
Redbrook
Biggesweir
Brochweir

Pembroke

Bosherston
● Lake

Below the Hereford reaches there is good coarse fishing at Hoarwithy from autumn onwards, and down at Ross-on-Wye the local club controls a lengthy section which is available on day ticket. Below Ross there are the famous Monmouth sections, Redbrook and Lydbrook. Biggesweir and Brockweir mark the limit of the serious coarse fishing, though there are fish in the tidal section, including flounders. Sea fish other than salmon run the river, including big eels, and lampreys 2 feet long. In late May there can be a big run of Twaite shad, which fall readily to fly and spinner. The fish average about 1 lb 4 oz, and they have mouths so hard and bony that it is not uncommon to lose them. 'Catch 100 and you will have lost 200,' says one local expert. The shad are poor for eating, but they are killed for their roe, which is a delicacy.

Another alien is the barbel, illegally stocked, to the chagrin of both the salmon men and the Welsh Water Authority, but they are seldom seen. Quite recently large bleak have appeared, too, and winter matches have been won at Ross and Hereford with 7 to 8 lb of bleak.

Two important tributaries of the Wye are the Monnow, which enters at Monmouth, and the Lugg, which joins below Hereford. Both are renowned for their chub, dace, and grayling.

The river Dee is a coarse fishery through its entire scenic length, thanks to the huge lake at Bala, which is the source of the river. Opportunities for fishing are somewhat sparse, however, until it reaches Llangollen. Liverpool AS has a stretch here near the Chain Bridge hotel; it includes one of the best salmon pools on the river. The dace fishing is good, and so is grayling sport in the winter. Most of the fishing in the area is private, however, and the next point of easy access is the Monsanto pool below Sun Trevor. This is a day ticket length which produces dace and some big roach.

At Bangor-on-Dee the river really becomes an attractive proposition for coarse fishing. It twists and turns in a series of shallow glides and deeper pools, and is as good as it looks for both dace and chub, which have been known to go well over 6 lb. Day tickets are available at the local newsagent's shop, but there are many private club waters between Bangor and Farndon, another prolific centre. Access is easier here, and on down to Chester, than anywhere else. The Dee Angler's Association has plenty of fishing. It is an amalgamation of clubs with open membership – St Helens AA, Warrington AA, Liverpool & District, Chester AA, and Llay AA. The membership books for most of these clubs are available in local tackle shops.

Bream begin to show in this area, alongside dace, chub, and roach. There is free fishing on the English bank at Farndon from the bridge to the style. This is worth a try; top catches can be 60 to 70 lb, and 20 lb plus is fairly common.

The next centre of interest is Crook o' Dee to Dirty Lane (free fishing), and then Eccleston and Chester, where the chances of a big bream catch are very high. The match catch record for the river, taken at Eccleston in 1973, is 57 lb 6 oz. There is free fishing at Chester from Kissing Gate to the suspension bridge, but the best fishing in the area is controlled by Chester AA.

There is a seasonal pattern to the fishing on the Dee. Chester sections fish superbly well from Sep-

Fly fishing for grayling near Betws-y-Coed

tember to the end of the season, especially for dace and big roach. Bangor-on-Dee is good up to the turn of the year, and Farndon is particularly good from January to March, when the dace begin to mass together prior to spawning. Eccleston's usual peak period for bream is in the autumn.

It is difficult to travel far in Wales without tripping over legends. Two concern Llangorse lake, a free fishery of 400 acres which lies 10 miles west of Abergavenny. Only a true prince of the area can command the water birds to rise, they say. One angling writer was moved to observe that there must be many water skiers with royal blood.

The other Llangorse legend could be true. In November 1846 one Owen Owen is said to have hooked a mighty pike on spinner. Mentions of this fish, which weighed 68 lb, have recurred over the years and, if it was genuine, it was the biggest freshwater fish ever caught in Wales. True or false, it cannot be other than an inspiration for the anglers who still seek the big pike of Llangorse, which also offers good sport with roach, bream, carp, and perch.

Many other lakes in Wales deserve the coarse angler's attention, but it is possible here to mention only some of the more interesting ones. Bosherston lake, five miles south-west of Pembroke, offers roach, perch, and eels, but is best known for pike, which have been known to run to 32 lb, and tench, which are numerous in the 3 to 4 lb class, with a few running much bigger.

Few anglers can drive along Bala lake (Llyn Tegid) without wanting to fish it, and there are plenty of ticket sources (lake warden and in the town of Bala). Created, like so many of Britain's large lakes, in the Ice Age, it retains a unique species, the gwyniad. This fish is very similar in appearance to other Ice Age relics, the powan of Loch Lomond and the schelly, which inhabits some of the Lake District waters. Bala extends 4½ miles, and is up to a mile wide. Mountain lakes like this are not often noted for growing very large fish, but there are few complaints about the quality of the roach, perch, and pike fishing. Other species show too, including gudgeon and grayling.

At 1200 acres, Trawsfynydd (in Gwynedd) is as big as Bala. It was man-made more than 50 years ago as part of a hydro-electric scheme. In the 1960s it acquired a nuclear power station, and the warm water from that encouraged the growth of the perch and rudd populations. Huge catches of both would be possible, using standard coarse fishing tactics, but anglers are inhibited by rules designed to protect the trout. However, with the perch regularly topping 2 lb, it is well worth a visit.

Llandrindod Wells draws many summer visitors to mid-Wales, and anglers among them are happy to make the trip. The 14-acre lake in the town offers coarse fishing of a high standard, including carp to 20 lb. One of the best stillwater coarse fisheries in Wales is Llyn Maelog, on Anglesey. It grows perch and roach to 3 lb, and has recently been stocked with bream from Llangorse. Also worth investigation is the Llangollen arm of the Shropshire Union canal, which must be one of the few canals to produce quality dace fishing.

North-West
Water Authority

LIFELESS RIVERS, streams, and canals ... pollution, dereliction, and decay. That is the familiar image of the North-West in the mind of the outsider, but it is wrong. The change is so relatively recent, however, that most of the region's anglers still have vivid memories of hopelessness coupled with despair that anything would be done to remedy their plight. The late Tommy Blackledge, Wigan AA secretary and a vice president of the National Federation of Anglers, used to relieve the misery and frustration with a joke. 'We fish for bites, up here, not fish.'

Not any longer. While the North-West Water Authority still has more miles of polluted river than any other area of the country, the clean-up has been dramatic. That, with the heroic efforts of some forward-thinking angling clubs and associations, has created a great deal of fishing, much of it of a quality which would be envied even in areas with a much more burnished angling image.

Grayling now thrive in the once-polluted river Goyt, a Cheshire tributary of the Mersey, near Stockport. Even the occasional salmon now runs the Mersey itself, as far as Fiddler's Ferry, near Warrington. The government, local authorities and industry, with the water authority orchestrating the entire enterprise, are pledged to a 20-year clean-up of the Mersey and its tributaries costing a staggering £200 million. The ambitious plan, easily the biggest of its kind ever undertaken in this country, will create a vast new catchment to support coarse fish.

The river Douglas, once as badly polluted as the Mersey, can now support chub and roach in the lower reaches – definitely a water for the future for the anglers of Wigan and the surrounding area. It is capable of encouraging catches now, and dace and

chub are rapidly colonising the Yarrow, a Douglas tributary, where even a salmon has been caught. Significantly, the oxygen content of both rivers is high enough to support trout.

With the recovery of the formerly hopeless, anglers have seen great improvements in waters which have always been fishable. One indication is that five regional match catch records were established in the 1983/4 season and, since match catches usually point to even greater potential for the uncompetitive pleasure angler, it is worth listing those achievements: Dave Shaw (Wigan) 28 lb 10 oz, a new all-time best for the Liverpool DAA section of the Leeds/Liverpool Canal; John Croasdale (Izaak Walton, Preston), 19 lb 11 oz from the Bridgwater Canal at Leigh; Dave Brogden (England international from Preston), 17 lb 2 oz from the Lancaster Canal; Ged Rigby (Wigan) 20 lb 4½ oz in three hours from Carr Mill dam, St Helens; Kevin Ashurst (former world champion from Leigh), 13 lb 8 oz, the best in Wigan-organised matches on the lower sections of the Leeds/Liverpool Canal.

Two years earlier Wigan clubman George King made a name for himself by adding over 50 lb to the Carlisle record on the river Eden with an astonishing 98 lb of dace. Many say it will never be beaten.

National championships are now fished on the Leeds/Liverpool Canal in the suburbs of Liverpool, where nothing lived not too long ago. Tench are the predominant species here; they have thrived so well that they are now overstocked. The perch fishing, too, is excellent. The odd 3-pounder turns up every season, and the canal record for the species rose to 4 lb 2 oz in 1983. Small wonder it is regarded as the region's top canal, with fine roach and bream fishing as well – but will it remain so? It is fast being overtaken by the Trent & Mersey Canal, which has gone from fishless to a top rank water in only six years, thanks to the removal of discharges from salt workings.

Nowadays a stretch of 16 miles, from the confluence with the Bridgwater Canal at Preston Brook to Middlewich, is crawling with roach and a good head of perch. The basins around Northwich are alive with sporting carp to 8 lb. Top catch is 108 lb, taken on luncheon meat from a swim opposite one of the marinas.

A cleaner Trent & Mersey has influenced the return, after years in the doldrums, of the Bridgwater Canal. In the 1960s it was regarded as perhaps the best canal in Britain, and it could regain that status. At the moment it is rather dominated by small roach, perch, and little bream along the 16 miles of Warrington water and the five-mile Runcorn arm. Big fish sometimes make the headlines, usually in the area from Broadheath through to Trafford Park – an outstanding, if patchy fishery, for those who can shut their eyes to the grime.

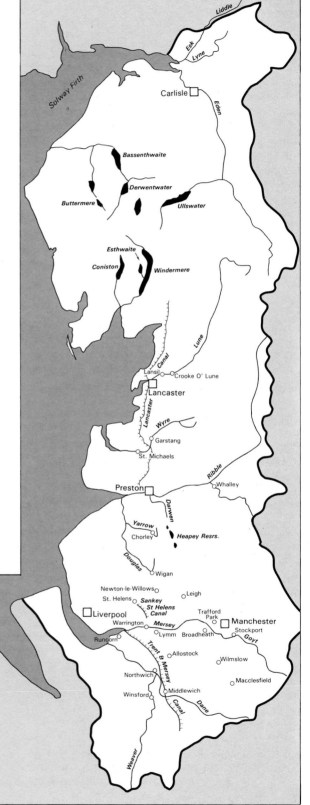

Improvement of the Trent & Mersey has encouraged some to try to work the miracle elsewhere. The busy and go-ahead Lymm AC has developed three miles of the Sankey–St Helens Canal at Warrington into a tremendous local fishery, providing doorstep fishing for thousands. The same function has been performed a few miles further north at Newton-le-Willows, where the fishing is more advanced and promising to join the region's best. Only a decade ago these areas were polluted and fishless. The fishing at Newton had to be rebuilt in 1977 after a sudden pollution wipeout.

Another recently developed fishery is the Leigh branch of the Leeds/Liverpool, which may ultimately rival the Liverpool end for the quality of its tench fishing. Sport with skimmer bream and roach is also coming along in leaps and bounds.

The energy and drive which go into the provision of new facilities is probably more marked in the North-West than anywhere else in Britain. Every drop of available water, particularly worked-out, water-filled excavations, is eagerly snapped up and developed, sometimes against formidable odds. Lynn AC, for example, bought an acidic quarry pool against the advice of water authority experts, who said turning it into a fishery was impossible. But the club neutralised and fertilised it, taking up countless hours of voluntary and back-breaking labour.

The end product is the fishery the club christened Lymmvale, a miracle water which has produced more record fish than any other. The golden orfe record has been topped so often that members have lost count, but they do remember 21 times in one day, the best being 5 lb 3 oz. Three grayling topped the record standard in one season, and in 1984 a tench of 9 lb 2 oz was taken by an angler who lost one even bigger. None of the records have been claimed: club rules say the fish must go straight back.

Lymm AC's sensible fishery management policies have produced an enviable collection of fisheries; their book is a bargain at any price. So is that of another North-West leader, Prince Albert AS, from Macclesfield, which has used both fishery management and a seemingly bottomless bank account to provide great fishing. It took on three Cheshire sandpits, Woodlands pool and Sand and Dove meres, all on the same site at Allostock, between Knutsford and Holmes Chapel, and turned them into five-star mixed fisheries. Another

of the society's many projects has been Rossmere, near Wilmslow, Cheshire. This is still being built up, but outstanding catches already include a hundredweight of tench.

Much of the North-West's fishing takes place in surroundings which are gloriously out of tune with the mental image of outsiders, but there is some remarkably good fishing in the grimmest surroundings. Ince Moss, for example, is situated amid Wigan's moonscape of dereliction. Shale excavation where the the water table is close to the surface has created some 50 acres of water offering fine tench fishing. During winter floods on one of the tench lakes, fish escaped to pastures new; without man lending a hand with stocking, the whole area is

Bream fishing on a Cheshire mere

Landing a chub on the river Ribble

thriving. One early season catch was reputedly around the ton.

Annual pollutions and severe fish kills were once commonplace on the river Ribble. They happen rarely now, and the presence of grayling below the mouth of the once troublesome Calder tributary indicates the improvement in quality. Ribble chub catches have been known to top 100 lb and dace weights can be enormous in winter.

Barbel are coming into prominence in the lower reaches around Preston, having been illegally stocked from the river Severn in 1970 and 1972. Biggest known barbel catch is 123 lb of fish to 6 lb, and the river record for the species is 11 lb 2 oz. With the Ribble a prolific river for breeding, a Severn-style population explosion of barbel is quite possible. Big roach to 2 lb plus can still be caught, though not as often as in the late 1970s, and the occasional bream to 6 lb is taken. There are a couple of resident shoals in the tidal water at Preston.

The Calder, responsible for so many Ribble pollutions, has improved beyond recognition. It is almost as good as the main river for 20 lb plus

catches of chub and dace, at least as far as the weir at Whalley, near Blackburn. It is easier to fish than the main river, and if improvement schemes go to plan it could be even better in the future.

Another Ribble tributary, the Darwen, enters at Walton-le-Dale, Preston, and it tends to fish well when the Ribble is up in flood. Partly polluted, it fishes well for chub, dace, and roach for the first half mile, and the fish population is gradually spreading further upstream. The neighbouring Wyre gets little publicity, but it can be outstanding for chub, the better day ticket fishing being from St Michael's to Churchtown, near Garstang. Roach to 2 lb can show, too, and there are quite a number between 1 and 1½ lb. There is sport to be had in the tidal section, too, usually for an hour or so either side of high tide.

Lancaster anglers have a nice variety of choice, with the river Lune and the Lancaster Canal. The Lune can be a very moody water, but on the better days it can produce bream to 8 lb, especially on the Lansil AC water by the M6 viaduct. The roach grow big, and one of the real delights is winter dace fishing in the picture postcard setting of the Crook O' Lune. Catch the river running off after flood, and catches of 30 lb of quality dace are not out of the ordinary. The Lancaster Canal has made a comeback as a very sound fishery, with ever-increasing numbers of roach supplementing good bream fishing in the basins. Tench, too, are on the increase.

The end of the trout fishing season in mid October sees greatly increased activity on the river Eden in and around Carlisle, though there is coarse fishing available in summer too. For some reason the chub show more often in summer than winter. One recent match result sums up the potential and the quality: 62 lb 8 oz of chub, with the best fish around 6 lb 8 oz. In winter many matches are won with 30 to 40 lb of top quality dace. They run 8 to 12 oz, with the odd fish over 1 lb, and the shoals are vast and densely packed. They will feed in bitterly cold weather, too.

The Eden's salmon fishing is not as impressive as it once was, but coarse fish are still removed in the interests of game fishing. It has the effect of improving the quality of the fish which remain, and some think the Eden could one day produce a record chub. The same is true of other rivers towards the Border. The Liddle, a tributary of the Border Esk, is said to have produced an 11 lb chub.

The Esk itself has some monsters, as does the river Lyne, again through under-population. A serious problem here, however, is poachers cyaniding the salmon pools. Access to the Esk is difficult, but it could be worth making local inquiries. The occasional match has been allowed, with ulterior motives. One club had a 55 lb top weight of dace and several weights over 40 lb, but it packed up early when it learned it was expected to throw the 'vermin' up the bank.

The Lake District, of course, offers a vast amount of stillwater fishing. It is impossible to mention it all, though the better waters include Bassenthwaite, which is capable of producing pike to 20 lb and perch over 2 lb; Buttermere, perch which sometimes top 3 lb; Coniston, pike, perch, and the increasingly rare char; Derwentwater, pike, perch, eels, and the unique vendace, which is seen very rarely now; Esthwaite, which has the usual Lakeland species plus roach and rudd; Ullswater, which also has a unique species, the schelly; Windermere, for pike, perch, and char.

To the south, the river Weaver, much of it looking like a Dutch barge canal, is improving very rapidly, with recently introduced carp spreading like wildfire. Roach, bream, and tench are also on the increase. Upstream of Winsford is very good in winter, when the roach and bream shoals gather prior to spawning. The river Dane is also a fine fishery now, with chub bags to 80 lb at Middlewich and barbel to 9 lb a possibility.

Wigan & District AA owns the Heapey reservoir chain near Chorley, six waters which offer excellent roach fishing. Catches to 60 lb on No 2 reservoir can include 2 lb fish, and the No 1 reservoir now has carp into double figures. The perch can go to 3 lb, especially in No 2. Much of the fishing in this big area is available on day ticket or controlled by clubs with open memberships. Of those mentioned, Prince Albert has a waiting list, but anyone can join the others. The main ones are Northern AA, Warrington AA, Wigan & District AA, St Helens AA, Liverpool & District AA, Lymm AC, and Northwich AA.

Yorkshire
Water Authority

THERE MAY be money where there is muck, but there is not much else. The industrial revolution finished off the rivers of South Yorkshire where once steelworks apprentices went on strike in protest at the regularity with which river Don salmon appeared on the menu. If only they had known what the dark age was to bring.

It is an age from which we are only now emerging. Modernised sewage plants and tighter regulations are paying dividends in terms of fish life. So too, sadly, is the decline of the great industries which choked the life out of the Rother and Dearne, and from the lower reaches of the Don, Calder, and Aire.

It is increasingly possible to pan a little gold. The river Don, even in the heart of Sheffield, can now produce a few roach and little bream, and trout are sometimes swept down from cleaner waters upstream of the city, where dedicated men have battled hard to defeat nature. One day, perhaps, these tragic rivers will come fully back to life, but until they do the real fishing is in the 'other Yorkshire', which nobody sees except natives and enlightened travellers.

It is up there in James Herriot territory. Swale, Ure, Nidd, Aire . . . the children learn to chant the river names, in descending order from the north, in their early geography lessons. Then they probably forget – except the anglers, who come to learn that they are more than just meandering blue lines on maps. Each one has a character all of its own.

Without exception, they all offer fine trout fishing in the upper reaches. Grayling provide the only competition until, at often indefinable points downstream, pockets of chub and barbel take up residence. Their presence is often unsuspected by those who seek the trout, but eventually the dividing line becomes clear.

On the river Swale it is at Richmond where coarse fish begin to predominate. There are large shoals of barbel, chub, and dace, and it is streamy water where the skilled float fishermen have the edge. Down through Catterick it remains much the same, but as the river edges its way towards its confluence with the Ure the character begins to change. It keeps the chub, barbel, and dace, but in the slower and deeper sections good roach can show, with possibilities of 2-pounders.

Pike, too, become more and more numerous, with some of them growing well upwards of 20 lb, but it is the chub and barbel which draw most of the anglers. Methods vary from float-fished maggot and caster to big bait legering with luncheon meat, cheese, wasp grub, crust, and bread. The dream is a 10 lb plus barbel, but it is rarely accomplished. Yorkshire barbel do not achieve quite the same proportions as their cousins in the south.

In modern times the Swale has become a patchy river, especially for the competitive angler. The biggest catches come when somebody competent finds himself on a big shoal of chub. One of the biggest catches in five hours was 82 lb 6 oz at Helperby in 1977, but Topcliffe, Cundall, Myton, and

most other well-known centres can offer huge weights in the right conditions.

The Swale can colour up very rapidly when it rains on the fells, but the Ure is even more volatile. It can rise several feet in a very short time, and can rearrange its own geography in awesome manner. Some of the upper sections change dramatically in winter floods, but the fishing is simply glorious.

The Ure becomes a coarse fishery of note some miles upstream of Ripon, though the fish start to show many miles higher up than that. Grayling, dace, chub, and barbel abound, and pike over 20 lb have an easy living. There the river is mostly fast flowing, with very few deeps, but the character changes below Ripon. Not far below Hewick bridge it drops deep, and mostly stays that way for the rest of the journey. It is hard to read; areas

157

which produce a lot of fish appear much the same as those which do not, but when the Ure hits form, almost anything is possible.

Big barbel and chub can show up the whole of the way, but so can big roach, and massive shoals of bream. The bream show in numbers from upstream of Boroughbridge, but the biggest catches come from the Dunsforth area, close to where the river officially becomes the Ouse. Match catches have topped 100 lb, with most of the fish around the 6 lb mark. Chub over 5 lb commonly show in this section, along with quality barbel.

The picture changes very little as the Ouse takes over and trundles down to York, with chub, bream, and barbel hotspots occurring all the way, especially where the river Nidd flows in. Roach become more abundant closer to York, and they offer excellent sport below the city, as do bream, barbel and even carp.

The river Nidd is the smallest of the main Yorkshire rivers, offering trout and grayling fishing from where it flows out of Gouthwaite reservoir. It begins to offer good coarse fishing around Knaresborough, but is best known in the lower reaches, where Bradford No 1 AA and Leeds Amalgamated control outstanding stretches, including Cowthorpe and Hammerton.

Catches nearing 70 lb have been taken in matches – chub, barbel or both – and while the river was once known for producing large quantities of

Barbel fishing on the Derwent at Stamford Bridge

smallish fish, there are signs that this is changing. The biggest barbel reported weighed 12 lb 11 oz – a rarity – but there are many more reports these days of fish over 8 lb. Roach over 2 lb can also show.

The river Wharfe is trout water for most of its picturesque length, with coarse fish becoming increasingly predominant from Ilkley downstream. It has the usual quota of good barbel and chub, and some very useful roach fishing, especially at Wetherby. This area has reportedly produced several roach over the 3 lb mark, which is exceptional, though in fish of those proportions there is always the possibility of hybridity, unless they are subject to close and expert examination.

Boston Spa is probably the leading day ticket centre on the Wharfe, offering good sport with all species, but the river gets really interesting in the tidal section below Tadcaster, a brewery town of considerable importance to all true Yorkshiremen. The tidal river has produced some outstanding catches over the years despite the problems of brewery effluent, but millions of pounds worth of expenditure on a new treatment works should soon begin to pay dividends.

Dace, chub, barbel, bream ... Yorkshire anglers have sharpened their considerable skills on them all in the tidal Wharfe. Even the odd carp can show up, and there is an extraordinarily prolific run of good-sized eels – so many that some matchmen have developed highly specialised techniques for catching them. Catches over 20 lb are commonplace.

If there has been a poor relation among the Yorkshire rivers, it is probably the Aire, especially in the areas touched by the heavy woollen industry, but in the past decade there has been a marked improvement. It is a much cleaner river now, upstream of Bradford, and chub catches over 20 lb no longer excite comment. The match catch record went over 30 lb in 1983.

Unlike other Yorkshire rivers, the Aire has coarse fish down the whole length, with plenty of chub, dace, and grayling in the trouty-looking water between Gargrave and Skipton. Below Skipton railway bridge, through Snaygill to Connonley, it runs deeper and steadier. At one time Connonley could produce roach weights of 40 lb or more, but these fish were lost in the 1960s when the whole country had disease problems with this species. They have never re-established themselves, perhaps because chub gained the ascendancy.

Pockets of good roach fishing still exist, how-

ever, and a 40 lb catch from the Keighley AC water at Uttley caused some excitement in 1983. It is quality rather than quantity which makes the Aire an attractive proposition, though. The records show dace at 1 lb 1¼ oz, chub over 5 lb, perch to nearly 3 lb, and pike to 20 lb.

Local anglers call the Aire 'the river of the future', but it can be difficult when it runs low, a state it seems to achieve too often. The huge sewage works at Esholt used to be the boundary marker denoting the end of the fishing, but improvement there has seen a gradual return of life to the river between Bradford and Leeds. It is possible now to catch coarse fish in the middle of Leeds.

The river Calder lives mostly on the knife edge of pollution, but somehow it clings not only to life but the good life in the Brighouse area. The surroundings may be grim, but consistently good roach and bream fishing make it an important match water. Warmed water from a power station has undoubtedly assisted rapid recovery from frequent pollution problems. Anglers have lost count of the times the Calder has been written off, only to emerge as good as ever the following season. Power station output is now at a much lower level. There could be more problems ahead, but the Calder usually makes fools of pessimists.

A vast area of eastern Yorkshire is drained by a lacework of little rivers and streams which feed another Yorkshire Ouse tributary, the Derwent. The Rye, Ricall, Dove, Seven, Costa beck, and Pickering beck are excellent trout water, also holding grayling, some of them big.

The main river has a chequered and often glorious history, and is probably better at producing the odd big fish than big catches. Rightly or wrongly, the upper reaches have the reputation for not fishing as well as they once did. Yedingham, at the top end, offers some good grayling fishing. Rillington and Scagglethorpe are lightly fished nowadays, but can produce good chub.

Old Malton, Hutton's Ambo, and Malton itself were terrific roach venues, but not so much is heard of them today. The best fishing now starts at Stamford Bridge, where legering tactics take the odd good chub above the weir. There is good chub fishing below the weir, and the York association's fishing downstream shows very good form. There are recent reports of barbel over 8 lb, including one of 10 lb, and the match record rose to 35 lb in 1983, the catch being mostly good-sized bream, with one barbel of 8 lb 4 oz.

Roach from the Ouse in the middle of York

Below Elvington weir, where it was tidal before the building of Barmby sluice, there are chub and plenty of bream. Giant pike are a possibility in this river, especially around Thorganby; the biggest reported was 34 lb 1 oz in 1980. The tidal fishing, especially that controlled by the Goole Association at Breighton, is very highly rated nowadays, with catches to 40 lb not uncommon.

The last of the important Yorkshire rivers is the Hull, which rises from chalk springs and empties into the Humber, 23 miles away. It is an unusual river which runs, with some pace, above the level of surrounding land and is fed from drains along the way.

One important tributary is the Driffield canal, which has big trout to 10 lb or more and the potential for a record grayling in the Yorkshire Water Authority fishing above Snakeholme lock. Grayling over 3 lb have been introduced from trout waters, including the top end of the Hull, which is private above Frodingham bridge.

Roach fishing can be good at Frodingham, where the Old Howe beck comes in, and winter roach sport is also useful between Tickton bridge and Beverley boatyard. The fish are hard to find in summer, when the river is weedy, but the roach are certainly worth looking for. The biggest is thought to be 2 lb 10 oz, weighed in a match.

Weed cutting in the upstream trout waters causes problems lower down in summer. When it reaches the tidal section below Hempholme weir it ebbs and flows with the tide for weeks on end, but the tidal fishing is good – plenty of bream, good quality chub which have been known to top 7 lb, and the occasional barbel. Below the confluence with West beck, a private trout water, the whole of the Hull is free fishing.

For a county with so many good rivers, Yorkshire is oddly short of notable stillwaters. Hornsea Mere has an amazing history of big roach and good pike sport, but that was mostly in the past. The Brandesburton series of gravel pits, controlled by the Hull association, are quite good fisheries, and one produced the impossible – a 40 lb Yorkshire carp, in a netting operation.

Castle Howard lake, near Malton, offers reasonable bream fishing and some big eels. Leeds ASA's Knotford Nook gravel pit between Pool and Otley is one of not very many Yorkshire waters which produce carp over 20 lb on rod and line. Perhaps the best stillwaters, though, are the Nostell Priory lakes near Wakefield. Recently stocked carp are now well into double figures. The best pike are nearly 30 lb, and the odd perch over 3 lb has been taken. The tench fishing is very good, and there is useful sport with roach and bream.

Much of Yorkshire's fishing is available from clubs with open memberships at modest prices. The major associations include Leeds ASA, Bradford City, Bradford No 1, York ASA, Hull & District, Castleford AA, Goole & District, and Ripon AC. The books are usually available in tackle shops in and around the towns of origin.

Northumbrian
Water Authority

DEPRESSION ... The word seems to have become as synonymous with the North East as it once was with the 1930s, or Steinbeck's *The Grapes of Wrath*. It is beaten into our minds by the seemingly endless TV reports from the shipyards, steelworks, pits, and railyards. We half expect it to apply to coarse fishing too, and to some extent it does. Wherever game fishing predominates – and it certainly does in Northumbria – it is easy to find coarse fishermen who believe their sport is not getting a fair crack of the whip. That feeling persists in this part of the world, perhaps unfairly. It would be as wrong to sacrifice good trout fishing for coarse as to ruin first class coarse fishing to create third rate trout fishing – a not unknown activity in areas such as Norfolk, in the not too distant past.

The main grumble in Northumbria, however, is that not enough seems to have been done to restore the coarse fish lost because of serious pollution in the once-magnificent Tees, the southernmost river in this area. To the far north, where Scotland's Tweed meanders down to touch a little bit of England, they mourn the loss of outstanding roach fishing, a consequence of ruthless control measures carried out for the benefit of game fishing.

Coarse fishermen the length and breadth of England still talk about the roach sport which used to be available in places such as Coldstream. Catches over 100 lb were commonplace; half a dozen fish over the 2 lb mark was nothing unusual. Given the attitude of river Tweed landowners, however, it could not last. They saw the roach, and even some of the people who came to catch them, as unwanted nuisances. The fish were netted and killed by the ton, though many were transferred

into England by clubs which could not resist the appeal of free stock fish. Their progeny live on in a surprising number of places, but the Tweed is now but a shadow of its former self – as a roach fishery, at any rate.

As for the Tees, it was devastated by a severe pollution in 1968 and has been hit several times since, culminating in a very bad oil pollution in 1983. 'Pretty as a picture, and like a picture in other ways as well. There is nothing below the surface.' That drastic description came from a Middlesbrough match angler who, before 1968, had lost count of his chub, dace, and roach catches over 20 lb from both the tidal and non-tidal river. Now he seldom fishes it, even though it is still capable of producing the odd catch or two around 20 lb.

The anglers claim that millions of fish have died in polluted waters, to be replaced by token

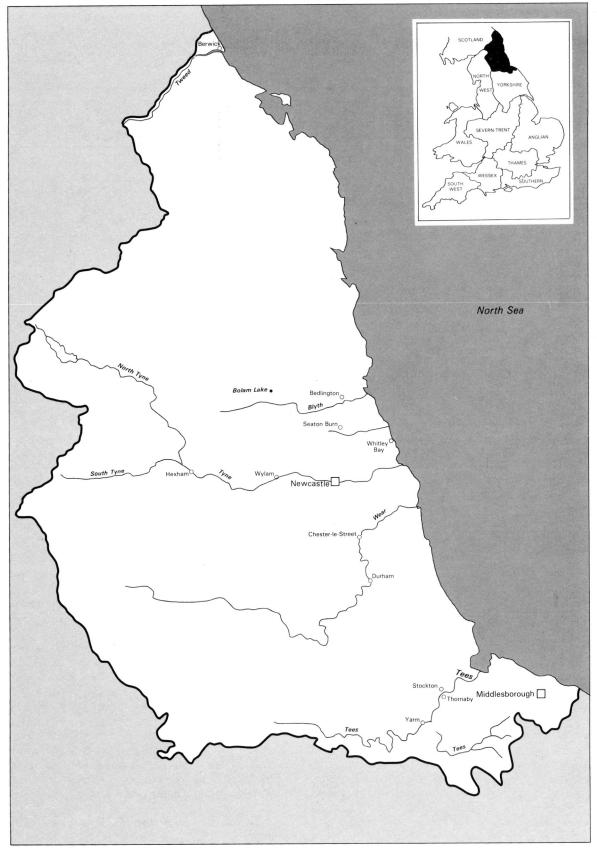

Berwick

Tweed

North Sea

North Tyne

Bolam Lake •   Bedlington

Blyth

Seaton Burn

Whitley
Bay

South Tyne   Hexham   Tyne   Wylam

Newcastle □

Wear

Chester-le-Street

Durham

Tees

Stockton

Thornaby   Middlesborough □

Yarm

Tees

Tees

SCOTLAND

NORTH
WEST   YORKSHIRE

SEVERN-TRENT

WALES   ANGLIAN

THAMES

SOUTH
WEST   WESSEX   SOUTHERN

Barbel – a species which is now establishing itself in the river Wear

thousands. There is much empty water and the odd good swim full of fish. Pollution permitting, they may one day repopulate the river to its former standards. Meanwhile those odd swims which do hold fish are well worth looking for, and the main sources for access and information are Stockton

A quality dace from the river Tees

AA, Thornaby AA, Yarm AC, Middlesbrough AC, and local tackle shops.

Between the Tweed and the Tees there is an enormous amount of game fishing and a little coarse fishing here and there. The lower reaches of the Tyne, for example, offer much better coarse fishing than outsiders might imagine. Principally a game river, of course, it holds good stocks of dace, roach, perch, and gudgeon in the tidal section below Wylam. Match catches run to 20 lb or so most seasons on sections controlled by a number of

small clubs – University of Newcastle Employees AC, Four in One AC, Ferryhill & District AC, Big Waters AC, and Middlesbrough AC.

There are other stretches of tidal water, but at the time of writing their future – notably who was to manage and administer the fishing – was in the process of being decided. The betting was that the local council would take charge. In the non-tidal section above Wylam, sport is much more game oriented, but the same species of coarse fish are quite abundant in the 14 miles or so of river running up to Hexham. Wylam AC, the Northumberland Anglers Federation, and the Tynedale Council at Hexham control some of it, and the sport is good. The rivers to the north of the Tyne are mostly game fisheries; even where coarse fish are present, access is often difficult, sometimes impossible.

The river Blyth is rated an excellent coarse fishery for grayling, perch, and roach, but the local council at Bedlington is the only source of day tickets. Apart from a variety of little streams holding grayling, the only other important venue for river coarse fishing is the Wear between Durham and Chester-le-Street. The only ticket source is Chester-le-Street & District AC at £1 a day, but there is some free fishing in Durham for roach and chub. The ticket fishing is for dace and roach, with some chub and odd barbel, which are beginning to establish themselves. Sport is more even in summer, but the biggest catches are in winter, when fish tend to congregate in the weir section. Match catches of 50 lb have been known, and they can include chub over 5 lb.

Not surprisingly in an area so dominated by game fishing on the rivers, there has been a considerable amount of stillwater development by coarse fishing organisations. It consists mostly of small lakes but, small though they may be, much loving enthusiasm has been devoted to them. Big Waters AC, for example, has the fishing on one-third of the fishery that gives it its name, Big Waters at Seaton Burn, and the club has – confusingly – a connected water called Little Big Waters. The other two-thirds of Big Waters is kept as a nature reserve, but the club is happy with its lot.

There are most of the usual lake species, including crucian, mirror, and common carp. There are quite a few double-figure carp up to about 16 lb – the equivalent of 30-pounders in the lusher pastures of Kent. Bream to 9 lb 8 oz have been stocked, too, and they are big fish by almost any standards.

The club has other waters, including five ponds near Berwick, holding roach, perch, pike, and some tench, and Marden quarry, near Whitley Bay, developed into a nice fishery from nothing in only four years. The club does not sell day tickets but anyone can join for a modest fee. Northumberland County Council controls Bolam lake on the outskirts.

Without these, and many other small stillwaters, the coarse angler really would be depressed in Northumbria, but it will be a very much happier place when the Tees returns from its 'death from the black stuff,' as one heartbroken writer put it in *Coarse Angler* magazine in March 1984.

Scotland

IT WILL NOT be possible to summarise Scotland's coarse fishing in quite the same way as that of the rest of Britain, for there are great differences to take into account. Coarse fishing, which can be outstandingly good in places, is nevertheless a minority interest. The abundance of game fishing means that it could be no other way, though in the past decade or so there has been a considerable increase in local – as opposed to visiting – interest in coarse fishing.

Anglers who have travelled in Scotland have soon discovered that it really is a different world. No licence is required for coarse fishing, for as yet there is no body which looks after coarse fishing to such an extent that it has to be financed. What money is spent is mostly devoted to eradicating alien species, and not even the Scots would try to charge for that. It is possible, however, that Scotland may one day have a coarse fishing set-up similar to England's.

The Scottish Federation for Coarse Angling was formed in 1975, with the specific aim of developing the fishing, and after five years of consolidation was accepted by the Scottish Sports Council as a representative body for angling. Grant money became available for administration, training, and competition. Now it has an international team competing in home internationals and in the world championships, and an ever-expanding match programme. The SFCA has no water of its own, but is actively seeking one with legal and financial help from the Sports Council.

Overall its progress has been impressive, and has undoubtedly had some bearing on the steady change in Scottish attitudes to coarse fishing. At the moment, though, many differences remain. In the absence of the insatiable demand for coarse fishing which has gobbled up almost every available yard of river in England, most Scottish rivers remain in private hands. Game fishing is highly organised, and often horrendously expensive, but many riparian owners think so little of their coarse fish that they will often allow free access to those who bother to ask.

That is a golden rule in Scotland. Always bother to ask, for some fishery owners can take deep exception to being taken for granted. On waters holding salmon and trout, in particular, the bailiffs have considerable powers of confiscation.

There is no official close season for coarse fish. Why protect species which are often regarded as some sort of dirty trick by Mother Nature? However, there can be rules which the visitor may find either unusual or unacceptable. No Sunday fishing applies to a considerable number of waters, and on others coarse fishing may be allowed only on condition that all the fish are either killed or taken away. Many enthusiasts, unwilling to comply, will go elsewhere, but it is doubtful whether this noble gesture has ever been of much benefit to the fish. Where that rule applies, there are usually intensive netting campaigns to reduce populations of unwanted fish, an exercise which often improves quality at the expense of numbers. In places, however, the netting has been relentless enough to destroy coarse fishing.

All this may sound rather unpromising, even depressing, but Scotland still has plenty to offer the coarse fishing enthusiast. Roughly speaking, almost all the coarse fishing is in the southern half of the country, below a line drawn from the river Tay system in the east to Loch Lomond in the west. North of that line there are lochs holding pike and perch, and the odd river which has grayling, but all the key areas are to the south.

The premier water is Lomond. Suffice to say here that it has all the known qualifications for

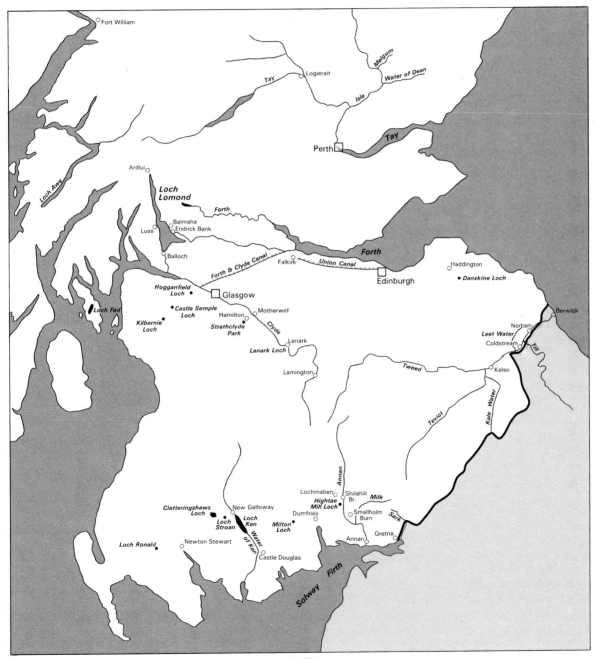

A typical catch of bream and roach from Lochmaben's Castle Loch

producing a new record pike, and therefore draws hundreds of pike enthusiasts, mostly in the English close season. There is some concern about the pike being hammered on the spawning shallows in April and May, but from June onwards there are relatively few anglers to enjoy a water which extends for some 30 miles from Ardlui on the northern tip of Balloch at the extreme southern end.

Big pike have been taken from all parts of the loch, belying the original assumption that the highly popular Balmaha, and the nearby Endrick Bank, are the key areas. Tommy Morgan's legendary 47 lb 11 oz monster was taken from the island area more or less due west of Balmaha, near the

western bank, but plenty of big fish have been taken out from Luss, and from the relative narrows to the north.

Angling visitors are well catered for by big hotels right down to bed and breakfast accommodation and camp sites. There are good boats for hire at the main centres, but be warned – never take Lomond lightly. It is virtually an inland sea, and all seas are treacherous. In her time Lomond has claimed even some of her own experienced boatmen; it is not a place to take foolish risks, no matter how great the potential rewards.

The fishing, which includes excellent roach sport and the offchance of the unique powan, is controlled by the Lomond Angling Improvement Association, which sells day and weekly tickets which do not entitle holders to fish the rivers running into the loch.

To the east of the northern limit is the Tay, a majestic and famous salmon river, and a tantalising prospect for the coarse angler. In the lower reaches in particular it has long been noted for roach, in both numbers and quality, though these fish have been available mostly in the tidal reaches of Perth, where the fishing is free. Some monstrous catches have been reported, though this is one of the rivers where netting is employed to keep the numbers down. Current word is that 100 lb plus roach catches are still being taken from the Perth Harbour area, and that nice grayling are also showing. A more prolific section for better quality fish is Logierait to Tummell mouth (permission from Logierait hotel).

The problem in dealing with the coarse fishing south of Lomond and the Tay is to choose whether to be comprehensive, or to concentrate on areas which have emerged as the most popular because the fishing is good and coarse fishermen are welcome. The latter is perhaps the best approach, but first here is a little generalised advice for those who do not like to follow the crowd.

With a few exceptions, to be mentioned later, the main coarse fish species available in Scotland are pike, roach, perch, and grayling. Pike and perch are present in most lochs and rivers, and while Lomond, by common consent, offers the best prospects, some of the others can provide good sport. The potential of many is little known to anyone except the locals.

Ask some of the more travelled English pike enthusiasts for alternatives to Lomond and they will usually mention Loch Ken, which has produced pike to 40 lb and has probably held much bigger than that; Loch Awe, which is noted for big pike; and Loch Fad on the Isle of Bute, which has plenty of 20-pounders and is reputed to have produced a 38-pounder. More adventurous souls have gone north of Awe to some of the impressive looking patches of blue above Fort William. They have had some good fish, but have convinced themselves that the potential is greater in the Lowlands.

For the dedicated grayling enthusiast Scotland offers a fascinating challenge. Some of the biggest grayling ever caught have come from Tay tributaries such as the Isla. The Melgum, an Isla tributary, once held the record with a 7 lb 2 oz fish, about which there are now grave doubts. Water of Dean, another Isla tributary, holds good grayling, as do the Greenock, the Tweed and its tributaries, the Teviot and Till, and many other rivers. The problem, often, is that they tend to reside in good game fisheries.

Asking permission to fish for grayling sometimes works. The only alternative is to pay for trout fishing and pursue the grayling under whatever limitations may be imposed by the rules for trout. Some of the better grayling in recent years have been taken by anglers taking a break from salmon fishing.

Most of the popular roach waters have been mentioned already, or soon will be, but as with grayling and pike there is the chance to do a little pioneering. The Forth is full of roach, and they run to 2 lb plus in the Tweed tributaries Kale Water and Leet Water. The lower end of the Water of Ken, before it runs into the loch, holds plenty of roach, and Loch Ken itself teems with them. The loch is very popular in the English coarse fish close season, when matches commonly produce roach catches over 30 lb. The west bank of Ken is free fishing, and there are day ticket sections elsewhere. Main sources are the New Galloway AA and the sports shop in Castle Douglas.

While roach are the main species there are also rudd and perch for the pike to feed on. The recent pattern here is for the bigger catches to show early in the English close season, perhaps because the roach are in the shallows to spawn.

Loch Ken is, of course, in the heart of the Dumfries and Galloway area, which has long been on the coarse angler's touring map. The area is more English in the character of its fishing than any other part of Scotland, thanks to the presence of bream, chub, carp, and tench. Castle Loch at

Lochmaben is one of the best bream fisheries in Britain, and with Ken is easily the best known of a series of lochs offering good coarse fishing. Bream weights often top 100 lb, but there are roach, carp, tench, and quality pike as well.

The nearby Hightae Mill Loch (limited boat fishing only) holds the same species to good quality too. Address for advance bookings: J Wildman, Moss Side, Hightae, Dumfries and Galloway. Other coarse fishing lochs include Clatteringshaws Loch, New Galloway (big trout and pike) for which tickets are available at local shops and from Newton Stewart AA, Loch Stroan, in the same area, Loch Ronald at Kirkowan, and Milton Loch west of Dumfries (big pike again).

The most famous river here is the Annan, thanks partly to a one-time record 10 lb 8 oz chub which is no longer believed, but it put the river on the chub fisher's map. It can still produce large specimens, though much of it is closely controlled game fishing. Some owners respond to polite requests, but the most accessible section is the 4½ miles from Shilahill bridge to Smallholm burn. Tickets are available from the RFT Commissioners, Gleneagle, Hightae, Dumfries and Galloway. The Milk, an Annan tributary, has big chub, but here it is a matter of polite requests to owners.

Another river capable of producing big chub is the Sark, which joins the Solway Firth east of the Annan near Gretna. Control here is with the Gretna Green AA.

Further north, the Glasgow area is quite well blessed with coarse fishing. Slicing across from Grangemouth to Glasgow is the Forth and Clyde canal, owned by the British Waterways Board. The key sections are Wyndford, run by the Central Match Angling Club (prolific tench area with fish to 4 lb and plenty of roach); Castlecarry, run by Edinburgh Coarse Anglers (predominantly perch, with roach, pike, and tench); Kelvinhead/Banknock/Dullatur, a BWB ticket water (good roach and tench area); Bowling and Dalmuir, also BWB ticket water (weedy but popular, producing roach, perch, eels, carp, tench and even goldfish). Another good canal for roach and perch is the Union, between Edinburgh and Falkirk.

The main river for Glaswegian anglers is, of course, the Clyde, nearly 50 miles of fishing which begins in the Lowther Hills. It offers both trout and coarse fishing, with no bait or method restrictions. It holds good perch, roach to 2 lb plus, big grayling, and the occasional chub; it is usually considered

best upstream of Motherwell. It is controlled by the United Clyde Angling Protection Association, Lanark & District AC, and the Lamington & District Angling Improvement Association.

There is fishing on the Clyde and on stillwater at Strathclyde Park, on the M74 at Hamilton. The stillwater, where the English close season is observed, offers bream, carp, roach, perch, and tench, and is a fast improving fishery. Two miles of the Clyde here are highly rated too, for roach, dace, grayling, and the odd chub.

Other stillwater fishing in this region includes Castle Semple Loch, about 20 miles south west of Glasgow; there, as at Strathclyde Park, permits are available on site. This too is becoming a prime fishery, with nets of roach and perch commonly topping 20 lb. Pike top the 20 lb mark. Kilbernie Loch, a few miles away, is one of the best stillwater fisheries in Britain. To give one example: it produced 880 lb of roach between 40 anglers in a home international match in 1983. Kilbernie AC sells tickets, but the water is closed between 7 October and 14 March.

Hogganfield Loch, in the Millerston area of Glasgow, is unusual in that it has been developed as

Grayling fishing on the river Tay

a coarse fishery. It has been stocked with carp, tench, bream, roach, and perch, but is difficult after the early morning because the water is very clear and pleasure boats abound. The fishing is free here, as it is at Lanark Loch, which is a better proposition. There are tench and perch, plus mirror carp in excess of 20 lb which, say the locals, are growing in spectacular fashion. There are smaller, wild carp in Danskine Loch on the East coast, 5 miles southeast of Haddington, which is leased by Edinburgh Coarse Anglers.

The eastern border area is dominated by the Tweed system, once a focus for visiting roach anglers, but severe control measures have had a drastic effect here. Anglers keep going, however, to check whether it has recovered some of its old form. The key areas are Kelso, Coldstream, and Norham. Between Berwick and the island upstream of the village the fishing is tidal and free, and at the moment it is showing signs of great improvement, especially for dace. There are abundant sources for tickets at the other main centres.

Notable Catches

Most anglers dream of catching notable fish, and some make special efforts to do so. Angling history is full of such attempts, a few of which have been successful. There can be no doubt that luck plays some part in the proceedings, though one needs plenty of skill to make the best of one's luck. We must always take account of those two factors, though many great events have resulted from anglers being in the right place at the right time.

Undeniably there have been periods in angling history when certain waters have produced outstanding examples of fish of particular species. Those who were there, and had the skill to guide their luck, made themselves virtually immortal. Their achievements will always be remembered. Many examples spring to mind – barbel and chub from the Royalty Fishery on the Hampshire Avon, bream from Tring reservoirs, perch from both Oulton Broad and Arlesey lake, roach from Hornsea Mere and the London reservoirs, rudd from Slapton Ley and Ringmere, and, of course, carp from Redmire Pool.

Angling's greatest catches would make a book on their own, but I can summarise some of the events which have most impressed and influenced me. Reference is made elsewhere to the great era on the Royalty in the 1930s and 1940s, and to a lesser extent in the 1950s and 1960s, but some of the details still seem astonishing.

During September 1933 the legendary F W K Wallis landed over 60 barbel, including fish of 14 lb 8 oz, 13 lb 8 oz, two of 11 lb 8 oz, three others over 11 lb, and three over 10 lb. In 1937 Claude Taylor and Wallis shared, in two days, a catch of 17 barbel weighing between 9 and 14 lb, with four in the 12 to 13 lb range. A fabulous brace was taken in March 1934, when Tom Keeber landed a 14 lb fish and his brother, two days later, topped that by 3 oz. Both fish were mounted in the same glass case. Then there was a tremendous run of big barbel, taken in a four-month period in the late 1950s by Bill Warren. He had 21 fish over 10 lb, the best 13 lb 4 oz, 12 lb 10 oz, and 12 lb 8 oz.

The Royalty's domination throughout this period can be seen from entries in the old *Anglers' News* Notable Fish competitions. In 1950, for example, there were 30 barbel over 10 lb, all of them from the Royalty.

It would be wrong to give the impression that no big barbel have been caught from other waters. The Trent and Thames have both produced large barbel in the past. Indeed, the Thames came up with a large number in the 1960s, several falling to the team of John Ginifer and Gwyn Williams, up to a weight of 13 lb 8 oz. In more recent years we have seen the Middle Avon, Wensum, and Kennet come into prominence, with such anglers as Tony Hart, Dave Plummer, and Peter Cranstoun taking numbers of double-figure barbel to 13 lb.

In my view, however, the greatest ever barbel catch belongs to the Trent. Not even the Hampshire

Avon can match it. It is best told in the words of J W Martin, the 'Trent Otter'.

'There used to be an old tackle dealer who lived in Catergate, Newark-on-Trent; Owen was his name. It is more than 30 years since I made his acquaintance, and then he was too old and feeble to go out fishing; but his enthusiasm was not dimmed by time, and he loved to fight his old battles over again.

'He showed me the barbel tackle he used 30 years before then, tackle that is never seen nowadays, and scarcely dreamed about; bottoms of double-twisted copper wire, a rod of solid timber weighing as much as three or more pounds, a line of hempen cord, and a leger that would brain the first barbel it dropped on. "Ah," said the old man, "I nearly had it all my own way those days; never hardly saw a barbel fisherman at work. But look here," he added, as he turned back the page of a well-thumbed notebook, "that was the only big catch of barbel I ever had in my life; six and eight fish, and even ten fish at a sitting I don't count as a big catch."

'That old notebook said 32 barbel had been slain that day; they weighed two hundredweight, largest nearly 15 lb, five of which weighed over 12 lb and the smallest of all a little over 3 lb, an average of nearly 7 lb per fish. I never heard before or since of such an average for barbel, and I never doubted the old man's word or his carefully preserved notebook, which added the information that the fish were caught in the park at East Stoke, on the Trent.'

In much the same way as the Royalty dominated barbel catches for almost 40 years, so it did with chub as well. From about the turn of the century, when E J Parker of the Piscatorial Society is said to have discovered the large Royalty chub, it produced numbers of fish over 5 lb almost every year until the 1960s. Then the numbers gradually petered out, the last really big chub probably being Jack Hilton's 7 lb 1 oz fish in January 1967.

Again, the Royalty's dominance can be seen from the *Anglers' News* competition. The qualifying weight for chub was 5 lb; in 1950 there were 25 entries, 23 of them from the Royalty. The following year there were 32 entries, 26 from this Christchurch water.

This period in the fishery's history almost certainly produced the most prolific chub catcher ever known, Bill Warren. He fished the Royalty for 13 years, amassing an astounding total of big fish.

During a nine-year period he caught 235 chub over 5 lb, 26 over 6 lb, and one of 7 lb 3 oz. Even that monster was not his biggest, for he added one of 7 lb 6 oz in January 1957.

No other river has ever been capable of that sort of sport, even for exceptional anglers. The nearby Stour has a fine reputation, however, particularly the Throop fishery. Even in recent years, while the Avon has paled into insignificance, the Stour has produced as many 5 lb plus chub as any other river.

The Great Ouse, particularly the Upper Ouse, was renowned for big chub. J W Martin writes of seeing a 7 lb 12 oz fish, and during the 1950s and 1960s Dick Walker and his friends caught some superb chub. Alas, this river, like so many others, has become the victim of progress. While the overall drop in the size and numbers of specimen fish in our rivers reflects continuous serious deterioration, the picture on many stillwaters is the opposite. More of the larger specimens are caught every year – particularly carp, tench, and bream.

Only in the case of bream, in fact, have past catches matched the present. For a period between 1930 and 1940 a considerable number of very large bream were caught from the Marsworth and Startops reservoirs at Tring. The highlight was a fantastic catch by Frank Bench, on 31 July 1939. Fishing with legered worm on a size 10 hook to 3 lb line, he landed bream of 6 lb 12 oz, 7 lb 7 oz, 8 lb 4 oz, 10 lb 8 oz, 11 lb 1 oz, 12 lb, 12 lb 8 oz, and 12 lb 15 oz.

After 1945 the big Tring bream disappeared, and it was not until the mid-1970s that they showed again. In June 1976 Ian Howcroft and Rod Lane made the largest catch of bream ever. They had 46 weighing an amazing 377 lb 8 oz, with an average weight of 8 lb. That leaves all the other big bream catches standing. The smallest weighed 6 lb and the largest 10 lb 8 oz.

Tring apart, the only other waters to produce big bream were the London reservoirs in the 1950s and 1960s. These included a number of double-figure fish to 11 lb 4 oz. During the past few years the number of 10 lb plus bream has increased dramatically. Tring has continued to produce them to over 12 lb. Several of the never-named Cheshire/Shropshire/Staffordshire meres have turned up huge bream, but for sheer numbers of 12 lb plus fish the Oxfordshire gravel pits must take the plaudits.

The history of carp and tench fishing follows a similar pattern, with dramatic increases in both numbers and size. It is sobering to realise that before 1950 only two tench over 7 lb and 16 carp over 20 lb had been recorded. Between 1950 and 1976 fewer than 30 tench over 7 lb were caught – on average about one each year. Now the tally must be several hundred each season. Similarly with carp. Not so long ago someone who caught 20 to 30 double-figure fish in a season had done remarkably well. Today it is not unusual for someone to have caught that many 20-pounders.

There have been so many great tench catches it is difficult to single out any particular one, but I will settle for the results of Len Head. In the mid-1970s he caught six tench between 7 lb and 8 lb 2 oz from Bures Lake in Suffolk – momentous results at the time. It signalled the start of the tench boom.

The list of carp-fishing achievements is also lengthy, but any list must include Jack Hilton's tally of three over 30 lb by 1971; Bob Morris taking a hundred doubles in a season; Bruce Ashby, in September 1978, becoming the first angler to catch 100 carp over 20 lb; Peter Springate and Ritchie MacDonald's catch of 13 carp over 20 lb in three days; Clive Diedrich's 1981/82 season's tally of 48 carp over 20 lb, including 11 over 30 lb; Peter Springate's capture of two carp of 36 lb 8 oz and 38 lb 8 oz on the same night; the capture of a 39 lb carp and a 34-pounder in one night on a Shropshire mere; Kevin Maddocks taking 20 carp over 20 lb, including four 30-pounders, from four different waters, in one season ... and so it goes on.

With roach, the first water to dominate the angling scene was Hornsea Mere, starting in 1915 and continuing into the 1940s. During this period there were a great many large catches of roach over 2 lb. Jim Bazley, the famous Leeds angler, caught 53 in one month. In 1915 E Kempsey had 19 for 44 lb 8 oz. Two years later Wilfred Cutting had 18 fish for 43 lb. In 1920 Herbert Field and G Tether shared a catch of 61 roach for 126 lb. About the time Hornsea began to decline, the London reservoirs began to produce large roach in numbers. In 1938 Bill Penney took Wilf Cutting's 3 lb 10 oz record away with a roach weighing 3 lb 14 oz from Lambeth reservoir. He had another the same day of 3 lb 1 oz.

The London reservoir roach run lasted until the early 1960s, and Bill Penney averaged about 50 fish over 2 lb each year in that period, though many other tremendous catches were made. In August 1958, for example, members of the Ultra Radio AC in Acton had, over three weekends, 140 roach over 2 lb at one of the Walton-on-Thames reservoirs, plus a further 12 over 3 lb. One member, in a single session, had 10 over 2 lb, best 3 lb 3 oz.

Several Hertfordshire rivers, particularly in the 1950s, produced excellent catches of big roach. Dick Walker made several from the tiny river Hiz at Hitchin Priory. He remembers having 50 to 60 lb in a keepnet which burst. He started again, ending up with 56 lb, including 14 roach over 2 lb. Before its sad decline the Hampshire Avon was wonderful for roach. Captain Len Parker, host for many years at the Bull Hotel at Downton, caught more than 200 fish over 2 lb from the Avon.

Big roach waters come and go all the time. In the early to mid 1970s three East Anglian waters, the Wensum, Waveney, and Bure, offered magnificent roach fishing. Hundreds of 2 lb to 2 lb 8 oz roach were caught each season, with some over 3 lb. The Wensum's form was amazing; we may never see the like again.

In recent years only the catches of massive roach by Mark McKeown, from a large gravel pit outside Reading, have equalled or maybe surpassed the remarkable catches of the past. In 1978 and 1979 Mark reported eight roach over 3 lb, the largest weighing 3 lb 8½ oz, plus a number of fish over 2 lb.

As for perch, recent events suggest that nobody can predict where a monster may turn up next, but who will ever forget Arlesey Lake, in Bedfordshire, or Oulton Broad? Arlesey was a freak water which no longer produces, but around 1951 it was headline news. Once again Richard Walker was in the thick of it, topping a string of memorable perch with a fish of 4 lb 13 oz. Walker devised a streamlined lead for the long range casting of lobworm baits into deep water, and it will be forever known as the Arlesey bomb.

A long and memorable run of big fish on Oulton petered out in the 1960s, never to return. The biggest substantiated fish was Syd Baker's one-time record of 4 lb 12 oz in 1962. There were other reports of 4-pounders, and at one time 3-pounders were quite easy. Colin Dyson remembers taking two to 3 lb 7 oz and a string of 2 lb plus fish in a day when he was barely out of the novice class.

Sadly, Oulton is nothing more than a powerboat track these days, but it is no use looking back. Look, instead, for waters where the great deeds of the past may be emulated or surpassed. Despite all the problems facing angling, that goal is not impossible.

Species Records

Top 25 Pike

72–0–0[1]	John Murray	Livebait	Loch Ken	1774
68–0–0	Owen Owen	Spinner	Llangorse lake	Nov 1846
65–0–0	Fred Johnston	Trailing	Lower Lough Erne	April 1880
61–0–0	Not known	–	River Bann	March 1884
52–0–0	Thomas Kenny	Spinner	Lough Macnean	Aug 1898
49–14–0	Col Thornton	Livebait	Loch Alva	June 1784
47–11–0[2]	Tommy Morgan	Livebait	Loch Lomond	July 1945
46–0–0	C F Giffard	–	Chillington pool	June 1822
42–0–0[3]	John Nudd	Livebait	Wroxham Broad	1901
40–6–0[4]	M Hopwood (Chatham)	Livebait	Kent water	Nov 1979
40–4–0	K Vogel (Essen, West Germany)	Spinner	Loch Ken	March 1972
40–3–8[5]	M H Waby (Ruskington)	–	Billinghay Skerth	unknown
40–0–0	Not known	–	Totteridge pond	July 1797
40–0–0	John Young	–	River Don	1866
40–0–0	R S Fennings	–	Suffolk	About 1880
40–0–0[6]	P Hancock (South Creake)	Deadbait	Horsey Mere	Feb 1967
39–8–0	D Leary	Deadbait	Lyng Pit	Jan 1984
39–7–0	G F Parrott	–	Dorset Stour	March 1909
39–0–0	C Loveland	Livebait	Knipton reservoir	Feb 1967
38–8–0	T Cottis (Colchester)	Livebait	Abberton reservoir	March 1980
38–4–0	P Emmings (London)	Livebait	Abberton reservoir	Dec 1969
38–0–0	Capt C Yarde	Livebait	Overstone Park lake	March 1941
38–0–0[7]	Not known	–	Frogmore pits	Oct 1972
38–0–0	R Stone (Bath)	Livebait	Norfolk Broads	Oct 1979
37–12–0	J R J	Spun deadbait	Private Warks lake	March 1882

[1] *This fish and some of the other very large pike have been mentioned in old books.*
[2] *The record until rejected in 1968.*
[3] *Colin Dyson has seen this fish in a glass case, but doubts whether it could have weighed 42 lb.*
[4] *Record not claimed, but a photograph appeared in* Angler's Mail.
[5] *Returned unverified; considered dubious.*
[6] *The official record.*
[7] *Never verified and must be considered doubtful.*

Top 25 Carp

51–8–0[1]	C Yates (Epsom)	Sweetcorn	Redmire	June 1980
45–12–0	R McDonald	Special	Yateley	Oct 1984
44–6–0	R Greenwood	Trout pellet paste	Beds pit	June 1984
44–0–0[2]	R Walker (Hitchin)	Paste/crust	Redmire	Sept 1952
43–13–8	C Yates (Epsom)	Sweetcorn	Redmire	Aug 1972
43–12–0[3]	Not known	–	Yateley	Aug 1984
43–8–0	K O'Connor	Special	Herts lake	Oct 1984
43–4–0[3]	A Tilbury	–	Yateley	July 1984
43–0–0	G Mountain	–	Tri-Lakes	July 1983
42–12–0	M Symonds (Fishers Green)	Special	Essex lake	1976

42–0–0	R Clay (Northampton)	Honey paste	Billing Aquadrome	Sept 1966
42–0–0	K Hodder	–	Yateley	Oct 1979
41–10–0	J Wenczka (Woodleigh)	–	Yateley	Aug 1981
41–5–0	C Riddington (Beckenham)	Protein	Yateley	Oct 1980
40–8–0	E G Price	Paste/crust	Redmire	Sept 1959
48–8–0	C Swaden	–	Longfield	1980
40–8–0[4]	C Clifford	Crust	Stockpond	Sept 1983
40–4–0[5]	L Jackson	–	Harrow	July 1982
40–4–0	P Harper	–	Silver End pit	Dec 1983
40–3–0	J Hilton (Hertford)	Sweetcorn	Redmire	Aug 1972
40–3–0	C Swaden	–	Longfield	1980
40–0–8	R Groombridge (Hemel Hempstead)	–	Boxmoor	July 1966
40–0–0	J McLeod (Birmingham)	Sweetcorn	Redmire	July 1972
40–0–0[6]	Not known	–	East Peckham	July 1972
39–10–0[5]	Not known	–	Colne Valley	1984

[1] National Association of Specialist Anglers record.
[2] BRFC record, though captor recognises Yates's fish.
[3] Same fish.
[4] Biggest carp known in Yorkshire. It was netted from a lake at Brandesburton and placed in captor's stockpond.
[5] Same fish.
[6] Reported from a water where rules said 'no publicity'.

Note: Not all very large carp are reported. Even some of those in the list have been culled from the secretive carp world's grapevine.

Top 25 Roach

4–2–0[1]	R Smith (Hillingdon)	Maggot	Ranworth Broad	June 1982
4–1–0[2]	R G Jones (Nottingham)	Lobworm	Notts gravel pit	June 1975
4–0–0[3]	T Fright (Hanworth)	–	Hampton reservoir	Sept 1961
4–0–0	T Charlesworth (Leighton Buzzard)	–	River Ouzel	Nov 1980
4–0–0	C Tolhurst (Dewsbury)	–	Yorks lake	Sept 1982
3–15–0	Malcolm Morris	Breadflake	Rading gravel pit	1983
3–14–12	J Hope (Bristol)	Flake	River Bure	March 1976
3–14–0[4]	W Penney (London)	Bread	Molesey reservoir	Sept 1938
3–14–0	Nigel Witham	Breadcrust	River Beult	1984
3–14–0[5]	A Brown (Stamford)	Caster	Tallington, Lincs, gravel pit	Aug 1964
3–14–0[6]	F I Hodgson	Fly	Lancs pond	May 1960
3–13–0	D de Bois (Nottingham)	Maggot	Private Notts lake	March 1982
3–12–12	–	Netted	Becontree AS at Dagenham	1934
3–12–0	Nigel Witham	Worm	River Beult	1983
3–12–0	D Walters	Maggot	River Sowe	March 1981
3–11–8	J Harriman (Nottingham)	–	Mapperley reservoir	1917
3–10–8	–	Found	When Barry Gurney reservoir (near Bristol) was emptied	Nov 1904
3–10–0[7]	W Cutting (Leeds)	Bread	Hornsea Mere (Yorkshire)	Aug 1917
3–10–0	A Whittock	–	Hants Avon	Jan 1935
3–10–0	J Scott (Hartford)	Maggot	Billings Pool (Cheshire)	July 1975
3–10–0	P Crozier (Havant)	Maggot	W Sussex gravel pit	Aug 1980
3–10–0	D Ling (Colchester)	Flake	Suffolk Stour	July 1975
3–9–12	T G Player	–	Thames	June 1949

175

Roach continued

3–9–8	N R Howard (Shifnal)	Maggot	Shropshire pool	July 1956
3–9–4	S Warren (Romford)	Worm	Essex lake	Oct 1963

[1] *Not claimed as a record; scales examined by BRFC were secondary, and could not be read. Probably a hybrid.*
[2] *Official BRFC record.*
[3] *Record size at time of capture, but was returned immediately.*
[4] *Record fish for 26 years until equalled by A Brown.*
[5] *Controversial; some experts say it was a roach/rudd hybrid.*
[6] *Out of season; biggest roach on a fly.*
[7] *Record fish for 21 years.*

Top 25 Perch

10–0–0[1]	Captor unknown	–	Bala Lake	unknown
8–0–0[1]	Caught on a night line	–	Wilts Avon	unknown
8–0–0	Mr Zerfall (London)	Flake	Hants Avon	1928
6–3–0[2]	W Griggs (Hounslow)	–	River Waveney	Before 1930
5–15–6[3]	P Clarke (Ipswich)	–	Suffolk Stour	Jan 1950
5–14–8	D Florey	Livebait	Farlow's Lake (Bucks)	Dec 1953
5–12–0[4]	E V Hodd (London)	Lob	Diana Pond (Hampton Court)	Aug 1957
5–4–12[5]	H Green (King's Lynn)	–	Stradsett Lake (W Norfolk)	Nov 1936
5–4–0	W Leach	–	Sandford Mill (Berks)	1873
5–4–0	K Gardner (Martham)	Lob	Norfolk lake	July 1970
5–4–0	R Dudley (West Malling)	Lob	River Medway	Dec 1975
5–3–4	P Mulgrew (Colchester)	–	Colchester pit	Oct 1968
5–2–0	L Gordon	–	River Waveney	1886
5–2–0[6]	Not known	–	River Waveney	1889
5–2–0	R Brown (Worcester)	Lob	Worcester lake	July 1966
5–2–0	M Lawrence (Thetford)	Livebait	Suffolk lake	Nov 1968
5–1–0	P Hall (Hullbridge)	Spinner	Rochford pit (Essex)	Jan 1972
5–0–0	Not known	–	Daventry reservoir	1908
4–15–2	J Sidley (Birmingham)	Lob	Birmingham pool	March 1976
4–15–0	F Steel	–	Chertsey	1941
4–14–12[7]	Mrs E Owen (Romsey)	Floating crust	King's Lake	March 1984
4–14–0[8]	W Weatherhead (Coventry)	Maggot	Jubilee pool	March 1984
4–14–0	C Croasdale	–	River Lune	Feb 1972
4–13–4	R Graham	–	Derbyshire pond	1911
4–13–0	R Walker (Flitwick)	Lobworm	Arlesey Lake	1951

[1] *Mentioned in Tate Regan's book* British Freshwater Fishes.
[2] *Reported seen in a glass case by angler Maurice Kausman.*
[3] *Record until rejected in 1968.*
[4] *Considered very doubtful; same angler reported a 9 lb Thames chub which turned out to be a trout.*
[5] *Record fish until 1950.*
[6] *Thought to have been netted.*
[7] *Official record.*
[8] *Caught same day as current record fish.*

Top 25 Bream

15–6–0	A Bromley (Stoke-on-Trent)	Maggot	Cheshire mere	July 1984
15–6–0	A Nicholson (Oxford)	Worm	Queenford lagoon	Aug 1984
14–14–0	A Nicholson (Oxford)	Worm	Queenford lagoon	Sept 1984
14–12–0[1]	A Nicholson (Oxford)	Worm	Queenford lagoon	Sept 1984
13–14–0	A Nicholson (Oxford)	Worm	Queenford lagoon	Aug 1984
13–14–0	C Dean	Worm	TC pit (Oxon)	Aug 1983
13–13–0	A Wilson (Blackpool)	Worm	TC pit	Sept 1983
13–12–0[2]	A Smith	Paste	TC pit	Aug 1983
13–9–0	M Davison (N Walsham)	Sweetcorn	Beeston Hall Lake	July 1982
13–8–0[3]	E G Costin	–	Chiddingston Castle	1945
13–8–0	A Wilson (Blackpool)	Lobworm	TC pit	Sept 1983
13–8–0	A R Heslop (Newport)	Maggot	Cop mere	Sept 1977
13–6–0	I Gibbs (Little Lever)	Worm	Radcliffe pond	Aug 1977
13–6–0	A Charlett (Oxford)	Maggot	TC pit	July 1982
13–6–0	A Wilson (Blackpool)	Lobworm	TC pit	Sept 1983
13–5–0	D South	Worm/caster	TC pit	July 1983
13–4–0	J Fisher (London)	Flake	Littleton lakes	June 1975
13–4–0	P Clarke (London)	Breadflake	Leisure Sports	Sept 1981
13–4–0	A Barker (Coventry)	Maggot	TC pit	Oct 1981
13–2–8	Not known	–	Startops reservoir	July 1931
13–2–0	D Ankers (Crewe)	Bradling	Cheshire mere	June 1976
13–2–0	C Bowman (Bagshot)	Maggot	Yateley	July 1980
13–2–0	A Wilson (Blackpool)	Lobworm	TC pit	Sept 1983
13–0–0	R Wells	–	Duchess Lake	Sept 1949
13–0–0	W Hardcastle (York)	Maggot	Pond at Fulford (Yorkshire)	Sept 1979
13–0–0	P McMurray (Worcester)	Maggot	TC pit	June 1981

[1] None claimed as British records, for various reasons.
[2] The official BRFC record.
[3] The record until rejected in 1968. Thought now to have been a wild carp.

Top 25 Tench

10–10–0[1]	D Kelly (Stoke-on-Trent)	Maggot	Cheshire mere	June 1981
10–4–0[2]	R Francis (Pinner)	Lobworm	Wilstone	June 1981
10–2–0[3]	E Edwards (St Helens)	Sweetcorn	Oxfordshire	June 1983
10–1–4[4]	A J Chester (Melton Mowbray)	Lobworm	Wilstone	June 1981
10–1–0	L Brown (Peterborough)	Worm	Peterborough pit	Aug 1975
9–11–0	R Seal (Farnborough)	Sweetcorn	Frimley L Sport	June 1978
9–11–0	B Blower (Manchester)	Maggot	Pickmere	Sept 1979
9–8–4	R Taylor (Rugby)	Sweetcorn	Lake at Newbould	June 1980
9–8–0	R Fisher (East Malling)	Bread	Johnson's Lake	June 1981
9–8–0	D Sharp (Whitchurch)	Maggot	Shropshire lake	July 1981
9–8–0	P Springate (London)	HNV paste	Wraysbury	June 1983
9–7–8	R Ecob (Melton Mowbray)	Lobworm	Wilstone	June 1980
9–7–0	A Rawden (Nottingham)	–	Oxfordshire	July 1983
9–6–0	P Lambert (S Harrow)	Sweetcorn	Harefield Lake	June 1978
9–6–0	A Wilson (Blackpool)	Worm	Wilstone	July 1984
9–6–0	F Guttfield (High Wicken)	Swan mussel	Whitbread's lake	July 1981
9–4–0	P Goddard (Hitchin)	Swan mussel	Whitbread's lake	June 1980
9–4–0	B Casey	Maggot	Oxfordshire	June 1983

Tench continued

9–3–4[5]	P Martin (Chertsey)	Paste	Chertsey lake	Aug 1960
9–3–0	L Strudwick (Cuffley)	Lobworm	Wilstone	June 1981
9–3–0	P Clements (Bradenall)	Sweetcorn	Yateley	June 1982
9–2–0	S Clarke (Hatch End)	Worm	Stocker's Lake	Sept 1982
9–2–0	S Plumb (Banbury)	Maggot	Oxfordshire	July 1981
9–2–0	J Parker (Kenley)	–	Wiremill Lake	Oct 1959
9–2–0[6]	B Wiseman (Kelvedon)	Bread	Rivenhall Lake	Sept 1963
9–2–0[7]	P Davidson (Bridgend)	Paste	Kenfig pool	June 1976
9–2–0	A Burton (Luton)	Crust	Bedfordshire	June 1980
9–2–0	P Snepp (Dartford)	HNV paste	Kent pit	1982

[1] Not claimed as a record; fish full of spawn and was returned.
[2] This fish was foulhooked.
[3] National Association of Specialist Anglers record.
[4] BRFC record.
[5] Record size at time of capture, but fishery rules demanded immediate return.
[6] Reportedly slipped back into the water after being weighed.
[7] The biggest Welsh fish.

Many other big tench would make this list if captors chose to report them.

Top 25 Eels

11–2–0[1]	S Terry (West Wittering)	Lob	Kingfisher Lake (Hants)	June 1978
10–3–0[2]	C Bone	Lob	River Lea	1984
8–13–0	N Taylor	Luncheon meat	Wem pool	1984
8–10–0[3]	A Dart (Bristol)	Deadbait	Hunstrete Lake (Bristol)	Aug 1979
8–10–0	J Harrison	Lob	Calfheath reservoir (Staffs)	1983
8–9–0	C Taylor (Wem)	Luncheon meat	Three Gate pit (Wem)	June 1981
8–8–0[4]	C W Mitchell	Livebait	Bitterwell reservoir (Bristol)	1922
8–8–0	Mr Ward	Deadbait	Fritton decoy	1948
8–7–0	N Frostwick (Barton Seagrave)	Lob	Grand Union Canal	May 1975
8–4–0	J Taylor (Hitchin)	Worm	Pond at Arlesey (Beds)	Aug 1978
8–4–0	J MacFarlane (Darlington)	Worm	River Tees	1964
8–3–0	J Sidley (Birmingham)	Lob	Earlswood lakes (Birmingham)	Sept 1978
8–2–0	B Leak (Burgess Hill)	Cheese	Burgess Hill Lake	Aug 1974
8–0–0[5]	R Jones (Newport)	Worm	Greystone Lake (Mon)	May 1968
8–8–0	A Cook (Hereford)	Sweetcorn	Savay Lake (Bucks)	Aug 1978
7–15–0	P Climo (Newport)	Lob	Greystone Lake (Mon)	May 1969
7–14–0	J Sidley (Birmingham)	Worm	Westwood Park Lake (Droitwich)	July 1980
7–13–0	M Hill (Hitchin)	Worm	Arlesey Lake (Beds)	Aug 1970
7–12–8	D Bennett (Wem)	Deadbait	Hawk Lake (Salop)	July 1979
7–12–0	I Mann (Redditch)	Livebait	Earlswood lakes (Birmingham)	Oct 1975
7–10–0	M Waters (Beverley)	Worm	Brandesburton ponds	June 1980
7–8–0	Mr Bond	Deadbait	Belvoir Bottom Lake	1932
7–8–0	A J Dewsnap	Livebait	Oulton Broad	1953
7–8–0	G Moss (London)	Deadbait	Thames (Romney lock)	1964
7–8–0	G Moss (London)	Deadbait	Thames (Windsor)	1964
7–8–0	R Jones (Newport)	Worm	Greystone Lake (Mon)	May 1968

[1] The BRFC record. Angler was fishing for carp at the time.
[2] Not properly substantiated.
[3] The previous record; this fish is now in a glass case at Veall's tackle shop in Bristol.
[4] The record until thrown out by the BRFC in 1968.
[5] Biggest Welsh eel; name of water was invented to conceal real location.

Top 25 Zander

17–4–0[1]	D Litton (St Germans)	Deadbait	Relief Channel	Oct 1977
16–6–0[2]	S Smith (Daventry)	Deadbait	Cut-off Channel	Oct 1976
15–12–0	L Strudwick (Cuffley)	Deadbait	Relief Channel	July 1978
15–8–0	D Litton (St Germans)	Deadbait	Relief Channel	Aug 1978
15–6–4	R Younge (Setchwell)	Deadbait	Relief Channel	Sept 1977
15–5–0	W Chillingworth (St Neots)	Livebait	Relief Channel	Feb 1971
15–2–0	M Leonard (Cambridge)	Livebait	Roswell Pit	March 1977
15–2–0	S Wilan (Cheshunt)	Deadbait	Cut-off Channel	Sept 1977
14–13–0	B Culley (Quorn)	Deadbait	Relief Channel	Dec 1978
14–11–0	M Barge (Coventry)	Livebait	Cut-off Channel	March 1977
14–10–0	A Newcombe (Grantham)	Deadbait	Relief Channel	Oct 1978
14–9–0	T West (Coventry)	Deadbait	Relief Channel	Oct 1978
14–8–0	A Chalcunowicz (Nuneaton)	Livebait	Relief Channel	Oct 1977
14–8–0	R Harker (Liverpool)	Livebait	Great Ouse	Nov 1979
14–7–0	P Williams (Dudley)	Deadbait	Relief Channel	Sept 1978
14–6–0	K Broughton (Sheffield)	Livebait	Relief Channel	Nov 1977
14–6–0	A Newcombe (Grantham)	Deadbait	Relief Channel	Sept 1978
14–5–0	M Rodwell (Wisbech)	Deadbait	Old Bedford	March 1976
14–5–0	R Woollard (Potter's Bar)	Deadbait	Relief Channel	Sept 1978
14–4–0	G Mayle (Ely)	Deadbait	Roswell Pit	Aug 1976
14–2–0	G Brown (Downham Market)	Deadbait	Relief Channel	July 1974
14–0–0[3]	Netted in AWA survey and released	–	Relief Channel	1979
14–0–0[4]	P Smith (Coventry)	Livebait	Cut-off Channel	March 1977
13–13–0	T Wells (Enfield)	Deadbait	Relief Channel	July 1979
13–11–0	S Harper (Peterborough)	Deadbait	Relief Channel	Aug 1979

[1] *Official record. Recognised by the National Association of Specialist Anglers at the weight the captor originally claimed, 17 lb 12 oz.*

[2] *Not claimed as a record, but there were good photographs and seven witnesses.*

[3] *An easily recognised fish which was caught the following year by G Whiley (Cheshunt), when it weighed only 12 lb 5 oz.*

[4] *Angler caught a 13 lb fish the same day, believed to make the best ever brace on a single outing. He also had a 12½ lb fish the same month.*

Top 25 Chub

13–4–0[1]	Unknown teenager	Liddle	March 1972
10–13–0[2]	P Morgan (Abergavenny)	Wye	Nov 1981
10–8–0	W Cockburn	Crane	1875
10–8–0[3]	Dr J A Cameron (Dumfries)	Annan	July 1955
8–12–0	J Lewis (London)	Mole	Oct 1964
8–8–8[4]	A Smith (Birmingham)	Blythe (Staffs)	Aug 1980
8–8–0	D Deeks	Sussex Rother	1951
8–4–8	A Johnson (Christchurch)	Hants Avon	Sept 1972
8–4–0[5]	G F Smith (Putney)	Hants Avon	Dec 1913
8–4–0	J Roberts (King's Lynn)	Wissey	1960
8–4–0	C Smith (Wortlington)	Thames	July 1975
8–3–4	R Thompson (Coventry)	Nene	Feb 1972
8–2–0	H Smith (London)	Hants Avon	July 1957
8–1–0[6]	M Townsend (Oxford)	Thames	Feb 1982
8–0–0	S Harmel (London)	Hants Avon	Aug 1964
8–0–0	Not known	Olway Brook (S Wales)	1973
8–0–0	S Tyrer (Liverpool)	Ribble	Jan 1976

Chub continued

8–0–0[7]	A Sargeant (Castle Bromwich)	Blythe (Staffs)	May 1976
8–0–8	D Grady (Pershore)	Wye	June 1976
7–15–0	P Minton (York)	Yorks Ouse	Oct 1964
7–14–8	Mrs H M Jones	Dorset Stour	Sept 1937
7–14–0	G Worth (Birmingham)	Severn	Dec 1948
7–11–8	P W Hunt	Great Ouse	Dec 1938
7–10–0	D Jones (Rhymney)	S Wales pond	March 1976
7–9–8	W Campbell (Hull)	Barmston Drain (Yorkshire)	Aug 1965

[1] *Reported in* Angler's Mail *but never verified.*
[2] *Not claimed as a record and not verified.*
[3] *Record until thrown out in 1968, but was disbelieved long before then.*
[4] *Not claimed as a record; fishery rules demanded immediate return.*
[5] *Recognised as the record by National Association of Specialist Anglers on glass case and other evidence. BRFC record is 7 lb 6 oz by Bill Warren (Hampshire Avon, 1957).*
[6] *Not claimed as record; captor did not wish to damage the fish.*
[7] *Not eligible for record; reported in close season.*

The Biggest Grayling

7–2–0[1]	J Stewart	River Melgum	1949
5–0–0	Found dead	River Camlet	unknown
4–8–0[2]	Dr T Sanctuary	River Wylye	1885
4–4–0	G Bryant	Itchen	unknown
4–0–0[3]	(Three) H J Mordaunt and M Headlam	Test	Dec 1905
4–0–0[4]	E Chambers (Hendon)	Chess	Jan 1965
3–14–0[5]	E J Stanton (Benfleet)	Driffield canal	Sept 1967
3–13–0[4]	E Chambers (Hendon)	Chess	Jan 1965
3–12–0	J Wigram	Test	1873
3–12–0	J Gieve	Test	1917
3–10–6	T Hall (Redditch)	Wye	Nov 1964
3–8–0	K Hall (Driffield)	Driffield canal	Oct 1964
3–4–12	E Vines (Sturminster Newton)	Frome (Dorset)	March 1966
3–4–0	J Whitcombe (North Newton)	Hants Avon	1970

[1] *Former record; no longer believed.*
[2] *The record before the Stewart fish.*
[3] *These three fish, caught by the two anglers on Boxing Day, were reported at the time to be a fraction over 4 lb.*
[4] *These fish were hailed as the best brace for 50 years – possibly an erroneous reference to the brace 60 years before.*
[5] *The Yorkshire record.*

Top 25 Rudd

4–8–0[1]	Revd E C Alston (Thetford)	Bread	Ringmere (Thetford)	June 1933
4–4–0	J F Green	–	Blackheath	1888
4–4–0[1]	Revd E C Alston (Thetford)	Bread	Ringmere (Thetford)	June 1933
4–3–6	A A Beardsley (Birmingham)	–	Slapton Ley	Sept 1952
4–3–2[2]	R Thomas (Sheffield)	–	Old Bedford River	July 1972
4–2–0	K Wood (Colchester)	Flake	Colchester lake	Sept 1979
4–1–0	A Crow (Braintree)	Caster	Essex lake	Oct 1974
3–15–0	Revd E C Alston (Thetford)	Bread	Ringmere	July 1933
3–15–0	W Clews	–	Moor Lane fishery (Staines)	1957

3–13–0	A Oldfield (Bollington)	Bread	Pool at Bollington	March 1960
3–13–0	W Tucker (Chertsey)	–	Thames	Jan 1962
3–13–0	J Simpson	Maggot	Private Peterborough pit	1963
3–13–0[3]	Unknown Rotherham angler	Maggot	Sixteen Foot Drain	1969
3–12–0	D A Fisher (Edgware)	–	Pond at Stanmore	July 1959
3–12–0	L Lindsay (Sawston)	–	Landbeach Lake	1962
3–12–0	K Palfrey (Taunton)	–	Bridgwater/Taunton Canal	1963
3–12–0	W Porter-Harris	Luncheon meat	Kempston Hardwick	Sept 1982
3–10–8	E G Costin (Crayford)	Sinking breadcrust	Home Pond, Swanley	Oct 1954
3–10–0	A Brogan	–	River Delph	July 1935
3–10–0	D Denham	Red worm	Shepperton Sand Pit	July 1954
3–10–0	J Leitch	Crust	Private Peterborough pit	June 1976
3–10–0	J Ellison	Flake	Bucks lake	June 1976
3–9–0	Mr Lambert	–	Brockett Hall (Herts)	1887
3–9–0	C F Russell	–	Slapton Ley	Aug 1934
3–9–0	A Anwyl (Blackpool)	–	Lake District water	July 1971

[1] *The bigger of these two fish is still recognised as the record.*
[2] *This huge fish for the water was not photographed, nor was any scale retained.*
[3] *This fish was taken in a match.*

Top 25 Barbel

17–4–0[1]	B Sheppard (Winchester)	Hants Avon	July 1971
17–0–0	Lady Rothes	Hants Avon (Avon Tyrrell)	unknown
16–10–0[2]	Caught on a night line	Trent (Carlton Mill)	unknown
16–4–0[3]	R Beddington	Hants Avon	1931
16–1–0[3]	C Cassey (Horndean)	Hants Avon	1960
15–12–0[3]	M W Hayter	Hants Avon	March 1943
14–12–0[3]	Dr D G Norton (Ferndown)	Dorset Stour	May 1965
14–6–0[4]	T Wheeler	Thames	1888
14–6–0[4]	A Tryon (Great Durnford)	Hants Avon	Sept 1934
14–6–0[4]	F W K Wallis (Nottingham)	Hants Avon	1937
14–4–0	R Jones (Swindon)	Thames	1909
14–4–0[3]	M W Hayter	Hants Avon	May 1929
14–4–0	F W K Wallis (Nottingham)	Hants Avon	Sept 1933
14–2–0	A Jessop (Hampton Wick)	Hants Avon	Dec 1968
14–0–12	E A Edwards (West Molesey)	Kennet	March 1954
14–0–0	S Hibbert	Trent	Before 1910
14–0–0	Not known	Lee	1880
14–0–0	Mr Simmons	Dorset Stour	Sept 1930
14–0–0[5]	E Leah (Bournemouth)	Dorset Stour	June 1972
13–14–0	C A Taylor	Hants Avon	Oct 1934
13–12–0[6]	J Day (Brierley Hill)	Hants Avon	Oct 1962
13–12–0	D Griffin (Shepperton)	Colne	Sept 1980
13–11–0	T Brown (London)	Kennet	Aug 1974
13–8–0	F W K Wallis (Nottingham)	Hants Avon	Oct 1934

Barbel continued

13–8–0	J Landau	Hants Avon	Nov 1948
13–8–0	P Mays (Charminster)	Dorset Stour	1964
13–8–0	J Ginifer (Huntingdon)	Thames tributary	Sept 1968

[1] *Fairly hooked by salmon angler.*
[2] *Mentioned in J W Martin's book,* Coarse Fish Angling.
[3] *All foulhooked, out of season, by salmon anglers.*
[4] *These three fish shared the record until the BRFC re-think in 1968. The National Association of Specialist Anglers recognises Tryon's fish as the record.*
[5] *Hooked 24 hours before the start of the season.*
[6] *The BRFC record.*

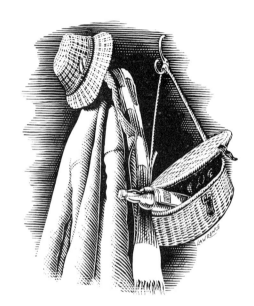

Water Authorities

ANGLIAN WATER
1 Ambury Road
Huntingdon
Cambridgeshire

Cambridge Division:
Great Ouse House
Clarendon Road
Cambridge

Colchester Division:
The Cowdray Centre
Cowdray Avenue
Colchester
Essex

Lincoln Division:
Waterside House
Waterside North
Lincoln

Norwich Division:
Yare House
62/64 Thorpe Road
Norwich

Oundle Division:
North Street
Oundle
Peterborough

**NORTHUMBRIAN
  WATER**
Northumbria House
Regent Centre
Gosforth
Newcastle upon Tyne

*Northumberland & Tyne
  Division:*
Northumbria House
Town Centre
Cramlington

*Tyne & Wear
Tees Division:*
Trenchard Avenue
Thornaby
Stockton
Cleveland

Wear Division:
Wear House
Abbey Road
Pity Mee
Durham

NORTH-WEST WATER
PO Box 12
New Town House
Buttermarket Street
Warrington

**SEVERN–TRENT
  WATER**
Abelson House
2297 Coventry Road
Sheldon
Birmingham

Severn Area:
64 Albert Road North
Malvern
Hereford and Worcester

Trent Area:
Meadow Lane
Nottingham

SOUTHERN WATER
Guildbourne House
Chatsworth Road
Worthing
West Sussex

*Hampshire & IOW
  Division:*
Guildbourne House
Worthing
West Sussex

Kent Division:
54 College Road
Maidstone
Kent

Sussex Division:
Falmer
Brighton

SOUTH-WEST
3–5 Bamfield Road
Exeter

East Area:
3–5 Bamfield Road
Exeter

West Area:
Victoria Square
Bodmin
Cornwall

THAMES WATER
Guildbourne House
Worthing
West Sussex

Metropolitan:
Rivers House
Crossness Sewage
  Treatment Works
Abbey Wood
London SE2

Mid Thames:
Ladymead By-Pass Road
Guildford
Surrey

Thames East:
Aspen House
The Grange
Crossbrook Street
Waltham Cross
Hertfordshire

Upper Thames:
Seacourt Tower
West Way
Botley
Oxford

WELSH WATER
Cambrian Way
Brecon
Powys

WESSEX WATER
Wessex House
Passage Street
Bristol

Avon & Dorset Division:
2 Nuffield Road
Poole
Dorset

Bristol Avon District:
PO Box 95
Broad Quay
Bath
Avon

Somerset Division:
PO Box 9
King Square
Bridgwater
Somerset

YORKSHIRE WATER
21 Park Square South
Leeds

Eastern Area:
Keld Head Hatchery
High Costa Mill
off Marton Lane
Pickering
North Yorkshire

Northern Area:
48 Skeldergate
York

Southern Area:
Branworth Road
Hexthorpe
Doncaster
South Yorkshire

Specialist Angling Organisations

Barbel Catchers Club
109 Eastfield Avenue
Haxby
York
Contact: *A Chrzanowski*

British Carp Study Group
Heywood House
Pill
Bristol
Contact: *P Mohan*

British Eel Anglers' Club
64 Granville Road
Gillingham
Kent
Contact: *M Bowles*

British Record (Rod Caught) Fish Committee
5 Cowgate
Peterborough
Contact: *P Tombleson*

Carp Anglers' Association
Heywood House
Pill
Bristol
Contact: *P Mohan*

Carp Society
217A Cemetery Road
Sheffield 11
Contact: *T Paisley*

Catfish Conservation Group
13 Bowyers Mews
Neath Hill
Milton Keynes
Buckinghamshire
Contact: *B Baldock*

Chub Study Group
17 Nutley Close
Ashford
Kent
Contact: *S Burke*

National Anglers Council
5 Cowgate
Peterborough
Cambridgeshire
Contact: *P Tombleson*

National Anguilla Club
20 The Greenway
Potters Bar
Hertfordshire
Contact: *D Walker*

National Association of Specialist Anglers
5 Delamere Road
Meadow Road
Bewdley
Hereford and Worcester
Contact: *D Taylor*

National Federation of Anglers
Halliday House
2 Wilson Street
Derby

Pike Anglers' Club
10 Britannia Road
Norwich
Norfolk
Contact: *M Page*

The Tenchfishers
New Hall
Gilden Way
Harlow
Essex
Contact: *T Marks*

Clubs and Fisheries

Abingdon & Oxford AA
19 Lower Radley
Radley
Abingdon
Oxfordshire
Contact: *G R Hook*

Amey AA
ARC HQ
The Ridge
Chipping Sodbury
Avon

Ashford AS
20 Musgrove Road
Ashford
Kent
Contact: *W Hodgkin*

Avon & Tributaries AA
17 Bath New Road
Radstock
Bath
Contact: *S Yates*

Barnstaple & District
6 Gribble Close
Barnstaple
Devon
Contact: *Mrs B Parkin*

Bath AA
23 Vineyards
Bath
Avon
Contact: *B Storey*

Bathampton AA
38 Beech Avenue
Combe Down
Shepton Mallet
Somerset
Contact: *A Adams*

Berks & Oxon AA
11 Reading Road
Cholsey
Berkshire
Contact: *R Simpson*

Big Waters AC
23 Weetwood Road
Collingwood Chase
Cranlington
Tyne and Wear
Contact: *I Woodley*

Billericay & District
159 Wood Street
Chelmsford
Essex
Contact: *E A Dyer*

Birmingham AA
100 Icknield Port Road
Birmingham 16

Blandford & District AC
29 Elizabeth Road
Blandford Forum
Dorset
Contact: *J Bell*

Boston AA
6 Churchill Drive
Boston
Lincolnshire
Contact: *D Maguire*

Bradford-on-Avon & District AA
6 Lyneham Way
Trowbridge
Wiltshire
Contact: *B Webster*

Bradford No 1 AA
44 Fleet Lane
Queensbury
Bradford
Yorkshire
Contact: *C W Smith*

Bridgnorth AS
23 Haughton Close
Tasley
Bridgnorth
Shropshire
Contact: *R Ball*

Bridgwater AA
6 Toll House Road
Cannington
Bridgwater
Somerset
Contact: *B Valentine
Slack*

**Bristol & District
Amalgamated Anglers**
16 Lansdown View
Kingswood
Bristol
BS15 4AW
Contact: *J S Parker*

**Bristol & West of England
Anglers Federation**
16 Falcon Close
Westbury-on-Trym
Bristol
Contact: *V Tyrrell*

**British Waterways Board,
Scotland**
(Forth & Clyde Canal
tickets)
Applecross Street
Glasgow

Bude Canal AA
86 Berries Avenue
Bude
Cornwall
Contact: *S Allen*

Bull Hotel
Downton
Salisbury
Wiltshire
Call or telephone:
Downton 20374

Bungay Cherry Tree AC
37 St Mary's Terrace
Flixton Road
Bungay
Suffolk
Contact: *I Gosling*

Burton Joint AA
Burton Joint AA Social
Club
30 Borough Road
Burton upon Trent
Staffordshire
Contact: *C Draper*

Burton Mutual AA
7 Denton Rise
Burton upon Trent
Staffordshire
Contact: *D J Clark*

Calne AA
16 Wessex Close
Calne
Wiltshire
Contact: *R J Reeves*

CALPAC
9 Kemble Road
West Croydon
Surrey
Contact: *J C Watts*

Canterbury & District AA
Riversdale
Mill Road
Sturry
Canterbury
Kent
Contact: *N S Stringer*

**Castleford & District S of
AC**
1 Hope Street East
Castleford
West Yorkshire
Contact: *G Hammill*

Central Match AC
93 Westergreens Avenue
Kirkintilloch
Strathclyde
Contact: *J Brown*

Chelmsford AA
8 Glebefield Road
Hatfield Peverel
Essex
Contact: *B Christopher*

Cheltenham AC
24 Spring Bank Grove
Cheltenham
Gloucestershire
Contact: *K Bulphin*

Cheltenham AS
2 Hollis Gardens
Hatherley
Cheltenham
Gloucestershire
Contact: *F Selley*

Chester A of A
40 Timberfield Road
Saughall
Chester
Cheshire
Contact: *P Massey*

Chester-le-Street AC
16 Gray Avenue
Chester-le-Street
Co Durham
Contact: *W Watson*

Childe Beale Trust
Pangbourne
Berkshire

Chippenham AC
23 Eastern Avenue
Monkton Park
Chippenham,
Wiltshire
Contact: *P A Greenaway*

Christchurch AC
32 Wycliffe Road
Winton
Bournemouth
Dorset
Contact: *Keith Hall*

Colchester APS
29 Lodge Road
Braintree
Essex
Contact: *M K Turner*

Collingham AC
93 Breamer Road
Collingham
Newark
Nottinghamshire
Contact: *Mrs J Wilson*

Crawley AS
41 Forester Road
Southgate
Crawley
West Sussex
Contact: *L P Waite*

Deeping St James AC
53 Castle Drive
Northborough
Market Deeping
Lincolnshire
Contact: *J Cran*

Devizes AA
Park View Cottage
Bath Road
Devizes
Wiltshire
Contact: *K Nisbeck*

Doncaster AA
134 Bentley Road
Bentley
Doncaster
South Yorkshire
Contact: *J Jepson*

Dorchester & District AS
10 Barrow Close
Castle Park
Dorchester
Dorset
Contact: *A J Trickey*

Durweston AS
Hethody
Durweston
Dorset
Contact: *J H Thatchell*

Edinburgh Coarse Anglers
3/3 Portland Place
Edinburgh
Contact: *G Glenn*

Essex Water Company
Hanningfield Works
South Hanningfield
Chelmsford
Essex

Exeter & District AA
46 Hatherleigh Road
Exeter
Devon
Contact: *D L Beaven*

Ferryhill & District AA
16 Conyers Terrace
Ferryhill
Co Durham
Contact: *N Davies*

Four in One AC
Woodside House
Low Westwood
Newcastle upon Tyne
Contact: *C Leedham*

Frome & District AA
103 The Butts
Frome
Somerset
Contact: *R J Lee*

Gipping APS
19 Clover Close
Ipswich
Suffolk
Contact: *G Alderson*

Glaston Manor AA
Crooksbury
Castlebrook
Compton Dundon
Somerton
Somerset
Contact: *P Daye*

Gloucester United AA
70 Robert Raikes Avenue
Tuffley
Gloucestershire
Contact: *J Gibby*

Goole & District AA
Barbican
Carr Lane
Goole
North Humberside
Contact: *P Cannon*

Grantham AA
28 Cottesmore Close
Grantham
Lincolnshire
Contact: *W J C Hutchins*

Gretna AA
Kirtleside Farm
Gretna Green *or*
Hunter's Lodge Hotel
Gretna
Dumfries and Galloway
Contact: *J Mills*

Grimsby & District ASA
62 Caistor Drive
Nunsthorpe
Grimsby
South Humberside
Contact: *J M Marshall*

Hailsham AA
Analan
Sandy Cross
Heathfield
East Sussex
Contact: *A Bates*

Haywards Heath & District AA
88a Noah's Ark Lane
Lindfield
East Sussex
Contact: *D Howard*

Hull & District AS
44 Barrington Avenue
Cottingham Road
Hull
North Humberside
Contact: *K Bone*

Ilchester & District AA
32 St Cleers Orchard
Somerton
Somerset
Contact: *R Hughes*

Isis AC
9 Noredown Way
Wootton Bassett
Wiltshire
Contact: *D A C Horsman*

Keynsham AA
7 Cedar Drive
Keynsham
Bristol
Contact: *G D Bingham*

Kidderminster & District AA
246 Marlpool Lane
Kidderminster
Hereford and Worcester
Contact: *M Millinchip*

Kilbernie AC
95 Dalry Road
Kilbernie
Strathclyde
Contact: *I Johnstone*

King's Lynn AA
1 Cock Drive
Downham Market
King's Lynn
Norfolk
Contact: *G T Bear*

Knowle AA
12 Lawford Avenue
Little Stoke
Bristol
Contact: *R M Roosevelt*

Lanark & District AC
137 St Leonards Street
Lanark
Strathclyde
Contact: *A C McLean*

Langport & District AA
2 Ducks Cottage
Thorney
Langport
Somerset
Contact: *Mrs E J Close*

Lansil AC
88 West End Road
Morecambe
Lancashire
Contact: *J E N Barnes*

Leeds & District ASA
Angler's Club
75 Stoney Rock Lane
Beckett Street
Leeds
Contact: *G Copley*

Leighton Buzzard AC
8 The Stile
Heath & Reach
Leighton Buzzard
Bedfordshire
Contact: *M G Holmes*

Leisure Sport Angling
RMC House
High Street
Feltham
Middlesex

Liverpool & District AA
97 Liverpool Road North
Maghull
Merseyside
Contact: *J Johnson*

Llay AC
9 Seventh Avenue
Llay
Wrexham
Clwyd
Contact: *V Dowling*

Loch Lomond Angling Improvement Association
224 Ingram Street
Glasgow

London AA
183 Hoe Street
Walthamstow
London E17
Contact: *The Secretary*

Longford & Trafalgar Estates
Waterways
Charlton All Saints
Salisbury
Telephone: Downton 21167

Longleat Estate
Longleat House
Warminster
Wiltshire
Contact: *The Agent*

Long Melford & District AA
6 Springfield Terrace
East Street
Sudbury
Suffolk
Contact: *N Mealham*

Lymm AC
15 Boswell Avenue
Warrington
Cheshire
Contact: *J Graham*

Maidstone Victory A&MPS
33 Hackney Road
Maidstone
Kent
Contact: *J Perkins*

Marazion AC
6 Chyandaunce Close
Gulval
Penzance
Cornwall
Contact: *B E Trevitt*

Marlborough & District AA
8 South View
Marlborough
Wiltshire
Contact: *M Ellis*

Marlow AC
15 Greenlands
Flackwell Heath
High Wycombe
Buckinghamshire
Contact: *G Hoing*

Melksham & District AA
1 Stirling Close
Bowerhill
Melksham
Wiltshire
Contact: *V Abbott*

Middlesbrough AC
5 Rutland Avenue
Marton
Middlesbrough
Cleveland
Contact: *B Watson*

Newark PF
58 Riverside Road
Newark
Nottinghamshire

New Galloway AA
Galloway View
Balmaclellan
Castle Douglas
Dumfries and Galloway
Contact: *N Birch*

Newton Abbott FA
21 Penn Meadows
Brixham
Torbay
Devon
Contact: *H Solomons*

Newton Stewart AA
c/o C McDowell
PO Telephone Garage
Newton Stewart
Dumfries and Galloway

Northern AA
11 Guildford Avenue
Chorley
Lancashire
Contact: *G Wilson*

North Somerset & West Wilts F of A
LCG
Marvic
Keyford Terrace
Frome
Somerset
Contact: *R Lee*

North Somerset Association of Angling Clubs
(Member clubs: **Clevedon, Highbridge,** and **Weston-super-Mare**)
St Martins
64 Clevedon Road
Tickenham
Clevedon
Avon
Contact: *R Newton*

Northumberland Anglers Federation
3 Ridley Place
Newcastle upon Tyne
Contact: *P Hall*

Northwich AA
Struma
Gadbrook Road
Rudheath
Northwich
Cheshire
Contact: *E Moore*

Nottingham AA
127B Digby Avenue
Mapperley
Nottinghamshire
Contact: *J Collin*

Nottingham & District FAS
17 Spring Green
Clifton
Nottingham
Contact: *W Belshaw*

Old Windsor AC
51 Bulkeley Avenue
Windsor
Berkshire
Contact: *D Meakes*

Oxford & District AA
18 Linden Road
Bicester
Oxfordshire
Contact: *P Weston*

Oxford APS
90 The Phelps
Kidlington
Oxford
Contact: *G Waddle*

Peterborough & District AA
75 Lawn Avenue
Dogsthorpe
Peterborough
Cambridgeshire
Contact: *W Yates*

Pewsey & District AA
11 Chisenbury Court
East Chisenbury
Pewsey
Wiltshire
Contact: *P Bewley*

Prince Albert AS
High Lodge
Upton
Macclesfield
Cheshire
Contact: *C Sparkes*

Provincial AA
11 Central Avenue
Bilston
Staffordshire
Contact: *W Hunt*

Pulborough, Steyning & District AS
5 South Lane
Houghton
Arundel
West Sussex
Contact: *M Booth*

Reading & District AA
8 Moats Crescent
Thame
Oxfordshire
Contact: *D Capon*

Redbridge AA
64 Primrose Avenue
Chadwell Heath
Essex
Contact: *C R Briscoe*

Redlands Angling Scheme
Lake View
Old Bury Hill
Dorking
Surrey

Red Spinners AS
33 Templewood
Welwyn Garden City
Hertfordshire
Contact: *C Kemp*

Retford AA
6 Orchard Leigh
Ordsall
Retford
Nottinghamshire
Contact: *H Oxby*

Ripon PA
3 Oak Road
Ripon
North Yorkshire
Contact: *P Goaden*

Rotherham UAF
4 Scarborough Road
Wickersley
Rotherham
South Yorkshire

Royal Albert Bridge AC
Tickets from:
Brokenshires, Newsagents
194 Saltash Road
Keyham
Plymouth
Devon

Royalty Fishery
West Hants Water Company
Mill Road
Christchurch
Hampshire

Rye & District AS Ltd
34 The Maltings
Peasmarsh
Rye
East Sussex
Contact: *A V Curd*

Salisbury & District
Inverleith
29 New Zealand Avenue
Salisbury
Wiltshire
Contact: *R W Hillier*

Scottish Federation for Coarse Angling
22 Roseburn Place
Edinburgh
Contact: *S McKenzie*

Scunthorpe & District AA
35 Merton Road
Bottesford
Scunthorpe
South Humberside
Contact: *I A Robertson*

SEGAB
46 Shortcrofts Road
Dagenham
Essex
Contact: *R Smith*

Sheffield & District AA
The Mission Hall
Clay Street
Attercliffe
Sheffield 9
Contact: *J Taylor*

Sheffield ASA
39 Sparken Hill
Worksop
Nottinghamshire
Contact: *A Baynes*

**Shrewsbury Piscatorial
Society**
14 Sycamore Close
Elm Park
Wellington
Telford
Shropshire
Contact: *M Kelley*

**Somerfords Fishing
Association**
The Old Orchard
Stanton St Quintin
Chippenham
Wiltshire
Contact: *M J Stoodley*

**Southampton Piscatorial
Society**
14 Furzedale Park
Hythe
Southampton
Hampshire
Contact: *B Blakey*

South Cerney AC
Sisters Farm
South Cerney
Cirencester
Gloucestershire
Contact: *H J Franklin*

Southern Anglers
7 Nelson Crescent
Horndean
Portsmouth
Hampshire
Contact: *T Irons*

St Helens AA
50 Laffack Road
St Helens Merseyside
Contact: *J Corkish*

Stockton AA
120 Station Road
Billingham
Middlesbrough
Cleveland
Contact: *R Corner*

**Stoke sub Hamdon &
District AA**
6 Hospital Lane
South Petherton Somerset
Contact: *A A C Gardner*

Stover Country Park
Estates Surveyors
Department
Devon County Council
County Hall
Exeter Devon

Stratford-upon-Avon AA
School House
Ullenhall Solihull
West Midlands
Contact: *D G Evason*

Sudbury & District AA
39 Pot Kiln Road
Great Cornward
Sudbury Suffolk
Contact: *T Fairless*

Suffolk County AAA
4 Merrifield Road
Lowestoft Suffolk
Contact: *G W Howard*

Sussex County AA
38 Limes Avenue
Horley Surrey
Contact: *Miss S
Colquhoun*

Taunton AA
30 Stoke Road
Taunton Somerset
Contact: *G Horrell*

Thornaby AA
10 Stainsby Gate
Thornaby
Cleveland
Contact: *D Speight*

Throop Fishery
School House
Holdenhurst
Bournemouth Dorset
Contact: *B Arnold*

Tiverton & District AC
21 Alstone Road
Tiverton Devon
Contact: *R Retallick*

**Tonbridge & District
AFPS**
59 Hunt Road
Tonbridge Kent
Contact: *A Wolfe*

United Clyde APS
39 Hillfoot Avenue
Wishaw Strathclyde
Contact: *J Quigley*

**University of Newcastle
Employers AC**
34 Hillhead Drive
West Denton
Newcastle upon Tyne
Contact: *B Watts*

Wareham & District AS
141 Wessex Oval
Wareham Dorset
Contact: *M Witter*

Warrington AA
22 Nora Street
Warrington Cheshire
Contact: *J S Jackson*

Warwick & District AA
218 Warwick Road
Kenilworth
Warwickshire
Contact: *L Sargeant* FSCA

**Wessex Federation of
Angling Clubs**
25 Ashwell Lane
Glastonbury
Somerset
Contact: *J J Mathrick*

Whitmore Reans CAA
Star Chambers
Princes Square
Wolverhampton
Contact: *R H Hughes*

Wigan & District AA
66 Balcarres Road
Aspull
Wigan
Lancashire
Contact: *W Gratton*

Wimborne & District AC
81 Leigh Lane
Wimborne
Dorset
Contact: *S A Card*

**Witham & District Joint
Anglers' Federation**
30 Gunby Avenue
Lincoln
Contact: *R Hobley*

Witney AS
49 Eastfield Road
Witney
Oxfordshire
Contact: *M Kirk*

**Worcester & District
UAA**
34 Bourne Avenue
Casthill
Bromsgrove
Hereford and
Worcestershire
Contact: *R Derrington*

Worksop & District AAA
31 Lincoln Street
Worksop
Nottinghamshire
Contact: *G D Rollinson*

Wylam AC
5 Jackson Road
Wylam
Tyne and Wear
Contact: *J Heaney*

Yarm AA
4 Blenavon Court
Yarm
Stockton on Tees
Cleveland
Contact: *A W Allen*

Yeovil & Sherborne AA
39 West Henford
Yeovil
Somerset
Contact: *N Garrett*

Index

Abberton reservoir, 65, 70, 140
Abergavenny, 150
Abingdon, 129
Abrook pond, 108
Adur, 124
Aire, 85, 156, 159
Allen, 35
Allostock, 153
Alton Water, 140
Amberley, 121
Ancholme, 135
Anchor, 128
Anglesey, 150
Anglian Water Authority, 109, 112, 135–140
Annan, 76, 81, 169
Ant, 19
Ardleigh reservoir, 35, 140
Ardlui, 168
Argal reservoir, 112
Arlesey Lake, 171, 173
Arun, 121, 124
Arundel, 124
Ashford, 125
Ashington, 134
Ashton, 112
Ash Vale, 134
Atcham, 144
Attenborough, 145
Avon (Bristol), 93, 97, 100, 115, 119, 120
Avon (Hampshire), 19, 35, 77, 81, 100, 101, 115, 116, 119, 144, 171, 172, 173
Avon (Warwickshire), 93, 95, 99, 145
Awe, Loch, 19, 169
Axe, 117
Aylesbury, 131
Aylsham, 87

Bablock Hythe, 129
Bala, 150
Bala Lake (Llyn Tegid), 146, 149, 150
Ballast Quay, 108
Balloch, 168
Balmaha, 168
Banbury, 49
Bangor-on-Dee, 149, 150
Banknock, 169
barbel, 13, **100–107**, 115, 116, 120, 128, 129, 131, 132, 134, 139, 141, 143, 144, 145, 149, 154, 155, 156, 157, 158, 159, 161, 165, 171, 172
Bargate Drain, 135
Barmston, 76
Barnstaple, 112
Bartonsham, 147
Bath, 115, 120
Bathampton, 120
Basingstoke Canal, 133
bass, 121
Bassenthwaite, 155
BB, 32

Beauchamp Court, 144
Beaulieu, 134
Bedlington, 165
Beeston Hall Lake, 49
Belmont, 147
Bernithan Pool, 23
Berwick, 165, 170
Beult, 126
Bevere, 144
Beverley, 161
Bevills Leam, 70
Bewdley, 143
Bigglesweir, 149
Big Waters, 165
Billingsmoor Farm, 113
Birdham, 121
Birmingham, 145
Bitterwell reservoir, 120
Blackburn, 154
Black Horse broad, 139
Blackwater, 132
Blagdon, 120
Blandford, 116
Blashford pit, 134
bleak, 43, 81, 149
Blyth, 165
Bolam Lake, 165
Bolingey, 113
Boscathnoe reservoir, 109, 112
Bosherston Lake, 150
Boston, 135
Boston Spa, 92, 95, 159
Boston West, 135
Border Esk, 155
Boroughbridge, 158
Boulters lock, 132
Bourne, 117
Boveney lock, 132
Bovey Tracey, 112
Bowling, 169
Bowood Estate, 120
Bradford, 159
Bradford-on-Avon, 120
Bramber, 124
Brandesburton, 161
bream, **49–55**, 69, 108, 109, 112, 117, 119, 120, 121, 124, 125, 126, 128, 129, 131, 132, 133, 134, 136, 138, 139, 140, 141, 143, 144, 145, 149, 150, 152, 153, 154, 155, 158, 159, 161, 165, 169, 170, 171, 172
Breighton, 161
Bridge Farm Lake, 87
Bridgnorth, 143
Bridgwater, 115
Bridgwater and Taunton Canal, 151, 152
Brighouse, 159
Bristol, 66, 120, 146
Brit, 117
Broadheath, 152
Brockweir, 149
Brooklands Lake, 134
Broxbourne, 133, 134
Brue, 117

Buckhurst, 133
Bucksole, 134
Bude, 112, 113
Budleigh Salterton, 112
Builth Wells, 147
Bungay, 139
Bure, 19, 34, 35, 139, 173
Bures Lake, 134, 173
Burghfield, 134
Burton upon Trent, 141, 143
Burton Joyce, 141, 143
Bury, 121
Bury St Edmunds, 69
Buscot, 128
Bute, Isle of, 169
Buttermere, 155

Calder, 153, 156, 159
Calne, 120
Cam, 138
Camberley, 134
Can, 140
Canterbury, 125
Carlisle, 151, 155
carp, 13, **23–32**, 33, 46, 52, 56, 58, 59, 62, 63, 66, 67, 73, 91, 112, 113, 117, 119, 120, 121, 124, 125, 126, 131, 133, 134, 139, 140, 141, 143, 145, 150, 152, 155, 158, 159, 161, 165, 169, 170, 171, 172, 173
Carr Mill dam, 151
Carrots Water, 147
Castlecarry, 169
Castle Douglas, 169
Castle Loch, 169
Castle Semple Loch, 170
Castle Howard lake, 161
catfish, 16, 138
Cattawade, 140
Catterick, 156
Caythorpe, 141, 143
Char, 117, 155
Charlecote, 145
Charlton, 134
Chazey Farm, 131
Chelmer, 140
Chelsea Flour Mill, 133
Chelwood, 120
Chertsey lake, 134
Cherwell, 35, 77, 129
Cheshunt North reservoir, 134
Chester, 149
Chester-le-Street, 165
Chew, 120
Chew Valley, 120
Chichester, 121, 134
Chichester Canal, 121
Chigborough, 134
Childe Beale Trust Water, 131
Chippenham, 120
Christchurch, 115, 172
Chorley, 155
chub, 13, 40, 43, 72, 73, **76–81**, 90, 91, 95, 99, 115, 116, 117, 121, 124, 126, 128,

129, 131, 132, 133, 136, 139, 140, 141, 143, 144, 145, 146, 147, 149, 151, 153, 154, 155, 156, 157, 158, 159, 161, 162, 165, 169, 170, 171, 172
Churchtown, 154
Churn, 128
City Mill, Winchester, 121
Clanfield, 128
Clatteringshaws Loch, 169
Claverton, 120
Claydon lakes, 138
Clevelode, 144
Clifton Grove, 143
Clifton Hampden, 131
Cliveden, 132
Clive Vale reservoirs, 134
Clumber Park, 145
Clyde, 169, 170
Colchester, 35, 65, 140
Coldstream, 162, 170
College reservoir, 112
Collingham, 143
Coln, 128
Colne, 128, 132
Colwick Park, 145
Coniston, 155
Connonley, 159
Cookham, 132
Coombe Abbey Lake, 71
Coronation Channel, 136
Costa beck, 159
County Hall, London, 133
Coventry, 71
Coventry and Oxford Canal, 71
Coventry water, Thrumpton, 143
Cowley, 108
Cowthorpe, 158
Crafthole reservoir, 113
Cricklade, 128
Cripps, 117, 119
Cromwell lock, 143
Cromwell weir, 141
Crook O'Dee, 149
Crook O'Lune, 154
Crowland, 136
Crown/Carthagena fishery, 133
Cuckmere, 124
Cullompton, 113
Culm, 108
Cundall, 156

dace, 43, 72, **91–99**, 108, 112, 116, 121, 129, 131, 132, 133, 139, 140, 143, 145, 146, 147, 149, 150, 151, 152, 153, 154, 155, 156, 157, 159, 162, 164, 165, 170
Dalmuir, 169
Damson Park, 134
Dane, 155
Danskine Loch, 170
Darenth, 134
Darracott, 112
Dartford, 134
Dartmouth, 112

Darwen, 154
Dean, Water of, 169
Deans Farm Fishery, 133, 134
Dearne, 156
Deben, 140
Dee (Welsh), 146, 149
Delph, 138
Denham, 133
Derby, 145
Derwent, 76, 141, 143
Derwent (Yorkshire), 19, 76, 100, 159
Derwentwater, 155
Dirty Lane, 149
Dogdyke, 135
Dog in a Doublet, 138
Don, 156
Donnington, 141
Dorchester on Thames, 131, 134
Dorking, 133
Dorney and Boveney lock, 132
Douglas, 151
Dove, 82, 85, 101, 102, 104, 105, 141, 143, 159
Dove mere, 153
Dowdeswell, 17
Downton, 115, 173
Drakelow, 143
Driffield Canal, 85, 161
Droitwich, 65
Dullatur, 169
Dumfries, 19, 169
Dunham, 143
Durham, 165
Durston, 119

Earlswood lakes, 145
Earsham, 139
Eastbourne, 124
East Carleton, 90
East Stoke, 172
East Warwick reservoir, 134
Ecclesbourne, 134
Eccleston, 149, 150
Eden, 92, 151, 155
Edgbaston reservoir, 145
Edinburgh, 169
eel, 13, 50, **64–68**, 72, 73, 101, 112, 120, 133, 144, 145, 149, 150, 155, 159, 169
Elvington weir, 161
Endrick Bank, 16, 17, 168
Esholt, 159
Esk, 155
Esthwaite, 155
Evenlode, 35, 129
Evesham, 145
Exe, 108
Exeter Canal, 108
Eye, 77
Eynsham, 129

Fad, Loch, 169
Falkirk, 169
Falmouth, 112
Farnborough, 134
Farndon, 149, 150
Faversham, 134
Fens, 69, 70, 135
Fiddler's Ferry, 151
Field Farm, 147
Fladbury, 145

Flatford Mill, 140
flounders, 149
Forest Row, 134
Forth, 169
Forth and Clyde Canal, 169
Fort William, 169
Forty Foot, 70
Fossdyke, 135
Frampton on Severn, 65
France, 100
Frimley lakes, 134
Fritton Lake, 139
Frodingham, 161
Frome (Bristol), 120
Frome (Dorset), 116
Frome (Somerset), 120
Fulbrooke, 145

Gainsborough, 143
Gargrave, 159
Garstang, 154
Geldeston, 139
Gipping, 140
Glansford, 134
Glasgow, 169, 170
Glen, 136
Gloucester, 76, 144
goldfish, 169
Goring, 131
Gouthwaite reservoir, 158
Goyt, 151
Grafham reservoir, 35
Grand Union Canal, 66, 133
Grangemouth, 169
Grantham, 135
grayling, **82–86**, 108, 117, 121, 146, 149, 150, 151, 153, 154, 156, 157, 158, 159, 161, 165, 167, 168, 169, 170
Great Ouse, 19, 35, 69, 70, 100, 138, 172
Greenock, 169
Gretna, 169
Greylake bridge, 117
Grimley, 144
Grove Farm, Charlecote, 145
Grove Ferry, 125
gudgeon, 43, 133, 141, 150, 164
Gunthorpe, 143
Gwynedd, 150
gwyniad, 150

Habin bridge, 124
Haddington, 170
Hailsham, 124
Hallow, 144
Hamble, 121
Hamilton, 170
Hammerton, 158
Hampton, 132
Hampton Ferry, 145
Hampton Lucy, 145
Hanningfield, 43
Harefield, 133
Hartington, 82
Harvington, 145
Hastings, 134
Hatchet pond, 134
Hay-on-Wye, 147
Hazelford, 143
Heapey reservoirs, 155
Heigham Sound, 138

Helperby, 156
Hemingford Grey, 56
Hempholme weir, 161
Henfield, 124
Hengrove Hall, 69
Henley, 132
Hereford, 147, 149
herring, 44, 72
Hertford, 133
Hewick bridge, 157
Hexham, 165
Hickling Broad, 88, 90, 138
High Maynard reservoir, 134
Hightae Mill Loch, 169
Hightown pit, 134
Hitchin Priory, 173
Hiz, 173
Hoarwithy, 149
Hogganfield Loch, 170
Holme Marsh, 143
Holme Pierrepont, 145
Holmes Chapel, 153
Holsworthy, 113
Holt Fleet, 144
Hornsea Mere, 34, 161, 171, 173
Horseshoe Lake, 134
Horsey Mere, 19, 138
Horton Kirby, 134
Hoveringham, 143
Hoveton Great broad, 139
Hull, 76, 161
Humber, 100, 161
Hunstrete Lake, 120
Huntingdon, 70
Huntspill, 117, 119
Hutton's Ambo, 159

Idle, 143
Iffley lock, 129
Ilfracombe, 112
Ilkley, 159
Ince Moss, 153
Ipswich, 140
Ise, 35
Isla, 85, 169
Isle, 117
Itchen, 121

Johnson's Lake, 134
Jubilee Pool, 41, 43

Kale Water, 169
Kelmscot, 128
Kelso, 170
Kelvinhead, 169
Ken, Loch, 17, 19, 168, 169
Kennet, 35, 101, 102, 132, 134, 143, 171
Kennet and Avon Canal, 120, 133
Kenton, 113
Kilbernie Loch, 170
Kingfisher Lake, 66, 134
Kingham lakes, 134
Kings Lake, 41, 43
King's Lynn, 41, 77
Kings Meadow, 132
King's Sedgemoor, 117
Kingsteignton, 113
Kings Reach, 133
Kings weir fishery, 133
Kirkowan, 169
Kirkstead, 135

Kissing Gate, 149
Knaresborough, 158
Knutsford, 153

Ladybrook lakes, 134
Ladydown, 120
Lake District, 88, 150, 155
Lambeth reservoir, 34, 134, 173
lamprey, 101, 149
Lanark Loch, 170
Lancaster Canal, 151, 154, 155
Lanesborough, 58
Langrick, 135
Lark, 138
Larkfield, 134
Laughterton, 143
Launceston, 113
Layer pits, 140
Lea, 58, 135
Leam, 77, 145
Lechlade, 128, 134
Lee, 101, 133
Leeds, 159, 173
Leeds/Liverpool Canal, 151, 152, 153
Leek, 145
Leet Water, 169
Leicester, 71
Leigh, 151, 153
Leighton Buzzard pits, 138
Lenwade, 87
Liddle, 155
Limpley Stoke, 120
Lincoln, 135
Linford, 133
Little Big Waters, 165
Littlehampton, 121, 124
Liverpool, 152, 153
Llandrindod Wells, 150
Llangollen, 149, 150
Llangorse Lake, 146, 150
Llyn Maelog, 150
Lochmaben, 19, 169
Loddon, 132
Logierait, 168
Lomond, Loch, 16, 19, 33, 150, 167, 168
London, 24, 71, 133
London reservoirs, 171, 172, 173
Longford Estate, 115
Longham, 116
Longleat Estate, 120
Long Melford, 134
Looe, 113
Louth canal, 135
Lower Hobhole, 135
Lower Slade reservoir, 112
Lower Tamar reservoir, 112
Lowestoft, 139
Low Maynard reservoir, 134
Lowther Hills, 169
Luddington, 95, 99, 145
Lugg, 149
Luss, 168
Lune, 154
Lydbrook, 149
Lymmvale, 85, 86, 153
Lyne, 155

Macclesfield, 153
mackerel, 44, 72
Magna Carta Island, 132

Maidenhead, 132
Maidstone, 134
Maldon, 134
Malmesbury, 120
Malton, 159, 161
Mansbridge, 121
Mapledurham, 131
Mapperley reservoir, 145
Marcliffe, 145
Marden, 120
Marden quarry, 165
Marlow, 132
Marsworth reservoir, 134, 172
Martham Broad, 19, 138, 139
Medley, 129
Medway, 35, 121, 125, 126
Melbourne, 145
Melgum, 85, 169
Melksham, 120
Meon, 121
Mersey, 151
Middle Avon, 171
Middle Level (Great Ouse), 138
Middle Level (Fens), 70
Middlesborough, 162
Middlewich, 152, 155
Midford brook, 120
Milk, 169
Millerston, 170
Milton Loch, 19, 169
minnow, 43, 81, 107
Monmouth, 149
Monnow, 149
Moors River, 116
Monsanto pool, 149
Motherwell, 170
mullet, 108, 121
Myton, 156

Nadder, 35, 115
Nar, 77
Nayland, 140
Nene, 24, 71, 100, 136, 138
Newbridge (Thames), 129
Newbridge (Welsh), 147
New Galloway, 169
Newport Pagnell, 133
Newton Abbot, 108, 113
Newton-le-Willows, 153
Newtown, 143
Nidd, 91, 92, 99, 100, 102, 156, 158
Norfolk Broads, 12, 19, 88, 138, 139
Norham, 170
Northampton, 138
North Bay, Oulton, 41
North Downs, 125
North Walsham, 49
Northumbrian Water Authority, 162–165
North-West Water Authority, 88, 151–155
Northwich, 152
Norwich, 41, 139
Nostell Priory, 161
Nottingham, 102, 141, 143, 145
Nutley, 134

Offenham, 145
Old Bedford, 138
Old Bury Hill, 70, 133

Old Howe beck, 161
Old Malton, 159
Old Windsor, 132
Ombersley, 41
orfe, 85, 153
Ormesby, 139
Otley, 161
Oulton Broad, 41, 139, 171, 173
Oundle Water, 138
Ouse (Norfolk), 138
Ouse (Sussex), 124
Ouse (Yorkshire), 19, 24, 76, 80, 100, 158, 159
Oxford, 76, 129
Oxford Canal, 133

Pangbourne, 131
Papercourt, 134
Parchey bridge, 117
Parret, 117
Parton Station, 17
Passingford bridge, 133
Pembroke, 150
Penryn, 112
Penzance, 109
Peppingford, 134
perch, 41–48, 50, 71, 112, 113, 125, 126, 128, 129, 131, 132, 139, 140, 141, 147, 150, 152, 155, 159, 161, 164, 165, 167, 168, 169, 171, 173
Pershore, 145
Perth, 168
Perranporth Lake, 113
Peterborough, 56, 138
Pickering beck, 159
Piddle, 116
pike, 13, 15–21, 33, 41, 43, 50, 66, 71, 73, 81, 91, 109, 112, 117, 121, 124, 125, 128, 133, 134, 136, 138, 139, 140, 143, 145, 147, 150, 155, 156, 157, 159, 161, 165, 167, 168, 169, 170
Pinkhill, 129
Plucks Gutter, 125
Plynlimmon, 147
Polebrook Corner, 138
Pool, 161
Poole, 115
Popham's Eau, 138
Port Meadow, 129
Port Royal, 108
Potter Heigham, 139
powan, 150
Preston, 151, 154
Preston Brook, 152
Pulborough, 121, 124
Putney bridge, 133

Queensford Lagoon, 49, 133

Radcot, 128
Radipole lake, 120
Ray, 128
Reading, 131, 132, 133, 134, 173
Redbrook, 149
Red Hill, 116
Redmire Pool, 23, 24, 133, 171
Ribble, 154
Ricall, 159

Richmond (Yorkshire), 156
Rickmansworth Aquadrome, 134
Rillington, 159
Ringmere, 87, 88, 171
Ringwood, 134
Ripley, 134
Ripon, 157
roach, 24, 33–40, 43, 44, 72, 90, 91, 108, 112, 116, 117, 119, 121, 125, 126, 128, 129, 131, 132, 133, 134, 135, 136, 138, 139, 140, 143, 145, 147, 149, 150, 151, 152, 153, 154, 155, 156, 158, 159, 161, 162, 164, 165, 168, 169, 170, 171, 173
Roding, 133
Rogate, 124
Romney Marsh, 125
Romsey, 41
Ronald, Loch, 169
Rossmere, 153
Ross-on-Wye, 23, 149
Rother (Kentish), 124, 125
Rother (Sussex), 124
Rother (Yorkshire), 156
Royal Military Canal, 124
Royalty fishery, 81, 115, 116, 171, 172
rudd, 43, 44, 72, 87–90, 91, 109, 112, 113, 120, 150, 155, 169, 171
Rudyard Lake, 145
Runcorn, 152
Runnymede, 132
Rushey lock, 128
Rye, 85, 159

Salisbury, 115
salmon, 33, 41, 87, 108, 115, 116, 128, 146, 147, 149, 151, 155, 156, 166, 168, 169
Saltash, 113
Sampford Peverell, 113
Sand mere, 153
Sandford lock, 129
Sankey–St Helens Canal, 153
sardine, 81
Sark, 169
Savay lake, 133, 134
Scagglethorpe, 159
schelly, 150, 155
School Pool, 134
Scotland, 19, 24, 43, 58, 85, 86, 100, 166–170
sea trout, 146
Seaton Burn, 165
Sedgemoor, 117, 119
Semington brook, 120
Seven, 159
Severn, 19, 65, 71, 77, 100, 101, 102, 143, 144, 145, 146, 147, 154
Severn–Trent Water Authority, 141–145
Severn Stoke, 144
shad, 145, 149
Shannon, 58
Shardlow, 143
Sheffield, 12, 13, 82, 85, 117, 156
Shepperton weir, 132
Sherston Avon, 120

Shifford, 128
Shilahill, 169
Shillingford bridge, 131
Shiplake, 132
Shoreham, 124
Showell Farm, 120
Shrewsbury, 143, 144
Shropshire Union Canal, 150
Sibsey Trader, 135
Sixteen Foot (Great Ouse), 138
Sixteen Foot (Fens), 70
Skegness, 135
Skipton, 159
Slapton Ley, 88, 112, 171
Smallholm, 169
smelt, 72
Snakeholme lock, 161
Snaygill, 159
Soar, 143
Solway Firth, 169
Somerley, 115
Somerset Levels, 115, 117
Sonning, 132
Sounding Arches, 132
South drain (Somerset Levels), 117, 119
Southampton, 121
South Cerney pits, 134
South Forty Foot (Boston), 135
South-West Water Authority, 88, 108–114
Southern Leisure Centre pits, 134
Southern Water Authority, 121–127, 133–134
Spalding, 136
sprat, 44, 72
Squabmoor, 112
St Austell, 113
St Germans, 113
St Helens, 151
St John's lock, 128
St Mawes, 113
St Michael's, 154
Staines, 132
Stamford, 136
Stamford Bridge, 159
Stanstead Abbots, 134
Stapleford Abbot, 133
Startops reservoir, 134, 172
Stathe, 119
Staunton Harold, 145
Steeping, 135
Steeple Claydon, 138
Stevenstone Lake, 113
Steyning, 124
Stibbington, 138
Stockport, 151
Stour (Dorset), 35, 77, 100, 101, 115, 116, 119, 172
Stour (Kentish), 35, 121, 125
Stour (Suffolk), 41, 70, 140
Stourport, 144
Stover Country Park, 113
Stover Lake, 113
Stow Bridge, 69
Stowmarket, 140
Stradsett Lake, 41
Stratford, 145
Stratford St Mary, 140
Strathclyde Park, 170
Stroan, Loch, 169
Sun Trevor, 149

Swale, 91, 100, 102, 156, 157
Swarkestone, 143
Swaythling, 121

Tadcaster, 95, 159
Tadpole bridge, 128
Taunton, 117
Tay, 33, 167, 168, 169
TC pit, 49
Teddington, 132, 133
Tees, 162, 164, 165
Temple weir, 132
tench, 12, 13, 56–63, 85, 112, 113, 117, 119, 121, 124, 125, 133, 134, 136, 139, 140, 150, 152, 153, 155, 161, 165, 169, 170, 172, 173
Tenchford, 124
Test, 121
Tetbury Avon, 120
Teviot, 169
Tewkesbury, 144
Thame, 131
Thames, 19, 24, 35, 77, 100, 101, 128, 129, 131, 132, 133, 171
Thames Valley, 129, 132
Thames Water Authority, 120, 121, 128–134
Theale, 133, 134
Thetford, 87
Thorganby, 159
Thorverton Bridge, 108
Throop fishery, 116, 172
Thrumpton, 143
Thurne, 19, 139
Tickton, 161
Till, 169
Tiverton, 113
Tone, 117
Tonbridge, 126
Topcliffe, 156
Topsham, 108

Torrington, 112, 113
Tottenham, 133
Tower bridge, 133
Trafford Park, 152
Trawsfynydd Lake, 146, 150
Trencreek lakes, 113
Trenestrall Lake, 113
Trent, 19, 24, 35, 76, 77, 93, 99, 100, 101, 102, 135, 138, 141, 143, 145, 171, 172
Trent and Mersey Canal, 152, 153
Tring reservoirs, 35, 134, 171, 172
trout, 35, 43, 112, 115, 129, 132, 140, 146, 150, 151, 155, 156, 158, 159, 161, 166, 169
Tummell, 168
Turf lock, 108
Tweed, 33, 162, 164, 169, 170
Twenty Foot (Fens), 70
Twickenham, 133
Tyne, 164, 165

Ulleskelf, 97
Ullswater, 155
Union canal, 169
Upper Hobhole, 135
Upper Ouse, 172
Upper Slade reservoir, 112
Upper Tamar reservoir, 112
Upper Thames, 128, 129
Upper Thurne, 88, 138, 139
Ure, 19, 76, 97, 100, 156, 157, 158
Usk, 146, 147
Uttley, 159

vendace, 155

Wainford Mill, 139
Wakefield, 161

Wales, 33, 86, 88
Wallers Haven, 124
walleye, 71, 87
Wallingford, 129, 131
Walthamstow reservoirs, 134
Walton-le-Dale, 154
Walton-on-Thames, 173
Wandsworth, 133
Wargrave, 132
Warminster, 120
Warrington, 151, 152, 153
Warwick, 145
Wash, The, 35, 135, 136
Waveney, 19, 34, 35, 40, 77, 139, 140, 173
Waveney Valley Lakes, 139
Wear, 165
Weaver, 155
Weir Wood reservoir, 134
Welford, 145
Welland, 77, 100, 136, 138
Welling, 134
Welsh Water Authority, 146–150
Wensum, 33, 34, 35, 40, 77, 139, 171, 173
Wessex Water Authority, 109, 115–120, 121, 134
West beck (Hull), 161
West Fen, 135
West Sedgemoor, 119
West Warwick reservoir, 134
Westwood Park Lake, 65
Wetherby, 159
Wey, 117
Weymouth, 120
Whalley, 154
Wharfe, 91, 92, 95, 97, 159
Wharfe Mill, Winchester, 121
Wheal Grey, 112
Whitewater, 132
Whitley Bay, 165
Wigan, 151, 153

Willington, 143
Wilmslow, 153
Wilstone reservoir, 58, 134
Wimborne Minster, 116
Winchester, 121, 134
Windermere, 155
Windrush, 35, 129
Windsor, 132, 133
Winthorpe, 143
Winsford, 155
Wisborough Green, 121
Wissey, 77, 138
Witham, 77
Woburn, 69, 138
Wolterton Hall, 87
Wolvercote, 49
Woodbastwick Decoy, 139
Woodlands pool, 153
Woodmill, Southampton, 121
Worcester, 144
Wormingford, 140
Wormley, 133
Wraysbury, 133, 134
Wroxham, 139
Wye, 19, 77, 92, 146, 147
Wylam, 164, 165
Wylye, 85, 115
Wyndford, 169
Wyre, 154

Yare, 34, 35, 139
Yarrow, 151
Yateley, 134
Yedingham, 159
Yeo, 117
Yeo (Congresbury), 117
York, 158
Yorkshire Water Authority, 156–161

zander, 69–75, 138

Picture Credits

Vic Bellars p 42
Rodney S Coldron p 34, 36, 37, 54, 57, 58, 66, 93, 107, 119, 143, 144, 164
Adrian S Czarnecki p 60, 79, 101, 109, 110, 153, 154, 168
Colin Dyson p 16, 51, 139, 164

Neville Fickling p 73
Ray Forsberg p 94/95, 158, 160
David E Houghton p 88, 147
William J Howes p 45, 70, 92, 125, 129, 149
Mike Millman Photo Services p 110/111, 114

Arthur Oglesby p 48, 83, 84, 104
Dave Plummer p 14, 89, 106
Wessex Water Authority p 117
John Wilson p 10, Title Page, p 18, 19, 30/31, 38, 74, 77, 80, 85, 96, 98/99, 136, 170

Mike Wilson p 22, 65, 127
Chris Yates Half-Title, p 25, 26/27, 102/103, 118, 122/123, 126